ILLUSIONS OF REFORM

OS JUSTI STUDIES IN CATHOLIC TRADITION

1
*Disputed Questions
on Papal Infallibility*
John P. Joy

2
Does Traditionis Custodes
Pass the Juridical Rationality Test?
Fr. Réginald-Marie Rivoire, F. S. V. F.

3
*The Liturgy, the Family,
and the Crisis of Modernity*
Joseph Shaw

4
Illusions of Reform
edited by Peter Kwasniewski

ILLUSIONS of Reform

Responses to Cavadini, Healy, and Weinandy

IN DEFENSE OF THE TRADITIONAL MASS AND THE FAITHFUL WHO ATTEND IT

EDITED BY
PETER A. KWASNIEWSKI

with contributions by Alexander Battista,
Gregory DiPippo, Fr. Samuel Keyes,
Peter A. Kwasniewski, Roland Millare,
Fr. Peter Miller OSB, Dom Alcuin Reid OSB,
Joseph Shaw, and Janet E. Smith

OS JUSTI PRESS
LINCOLN, NE

Copyright © 2023 by Os Justi Press

All rights reserved.

No part of this book may be reproduced, stored in a retrieval system, or transmitted in any form, or by any means, electronic, mechanical, photocopying, or otherwise, without the prior written permission of the publisher, except by a reviewer, who may quote brief passages in a review.

Os Justi Press
P.O. Box 21814
Lincoln, NE 68542
https://osjustipress.com/
info@osjustipress.com

Hardback 978-1-960711-06-9
Paperback 978-1-960711-07-6
eBook 978-1-960711-08-3

Interior design: Michael Schrauzer
Cover design: Julian Kwasniewski

TABLE OF CONTENTS

Preface by *Peter Kwasniewski*   ix
Abbreviations   xii
Summary of Cavadini, Healy, and Weinandy
   by *Janet E. Smith*   xiii

Part 1. Janet Smith's Critique   1
1 Sacrificing Beauty and Other Errors   3
2 Misrepresentation of *Mediator Dei, Sacrosanctum Concilium*, and Ratzinger/Pope Benedict XVI   17
3 The Genesis of the Novus Ordo and "Theological and Spiritual Flaws" of the TLM   30
4 Unity, Charismatic Masses, and Africa   41
5 Mischaracterization of the TLM, Then and Now   46

Part 2. Peter Kwasniewski's Critique   63
6 Unconvincing Propaganda against the Latin Mass   65
7 Noble Patriarchs, Wayward Grandchildren: A More Realistic Appraisal of the Liturgical Movement   77
8 Is the Laity's Offering of the Mass a Postconciliar Rediscovery?   83
9 Offspring of Arius in the Holy of Holies   93
10 Was Liturgical Latin Introduced As—and Because It Was—the Vernacular?   114
11 The Dubious Legacy of Leonardo's Last Supper   123
12 Games People Play with the Holy Spirit   134

Part 3. Additional Commentary   151
13 *Alexander Battista*, "*Church Life Journal* Insults Eastern Liturgies with Amateur Scholarship"   153
14 *Fr. Samuel Keyes*, "The Failures of Reform"   162
15 *Roland Millare*, "Joseph Ratzinger and the New Liturgical Movement"   175

16 *Fr. Peter Miller, OSB*, "Bible by the Pound: Would the Holy Spirit Agree that More Bible is Better at Mass?" 180

17 *Dom Alcuin Reid, OSB*, "The One Thread by Which the Council Hangs" 198

18 *Joseph Shaw*, "The Art of Missing the Point" 213

Epilogue: New Liturgical Anathemas for the Post-Conciliar Rite by *Gregory DiPippo* 217

Acknowledgments 222
Select Bibliography 223
Contributors 227

PREFACE

BETWEEN SEPTEMBER AND NOVEMBER 2022, the University of Notre Dame's *Church Life Journal* published a series of articles on liturgical reform coauthored by Dr. John Cavadini, Dr. Mary Healy, and Fr. Thomas Weinandy. This series was then republished as a unit on December 1, 2022. (In the pages that follow, the trio of authors will often be referred to simply as "CHW.") Unsurprisingly, the lengthy series—with its rosy view of the Liturgical Movement, its caricature of the Catholic faithful prior to Vatican II, its virtual identification of the Novus Ordo with *Sacrosanctum Concilium* and its chrismation of both by the Holy Spirit, and its severe rejection of the "Tridentine movement"—generated much conversation, nearly all of it sharply critical of the authors' flawed scholarship, grandiose generalizations, and pastoral callousness, three qualities that run contrary to the purported aims of *Church Life Journal*.

In a spirit of fair play, it was my original plan that this book should open with the unabridged CHW series and should close with a response by CHW to their critics. This, after all, is a classic format for high-level dialogue between persons of good will, mature intelligence, and scholarly aspirations. The editors of *Church Life Journal* turned down all proposals of this kind. As a result, Janet Smith kindly offered to write a matter-of-fact summary of the series, organized according to the eight sections of the single "synoptic" version published on December 1. Dr. Smith's overview of CHW's main points enables this book to be useful even for those who are not already familiar with the series—although truly nothing can replace the experience of time-travel to the 1970s that reading it provides for readers in the 2020s.

Part 1 of the book consists of Janet Smith's five-part series, published at *Crisis Magazine* in February and March of 2023 and presented here as five chapters, with slight emendations as compared with the online version.

Part 2 gathers several refutations of my own, directed at CHW's slanted portrayal of the Liturgical Movement; the claim that the Novus Ordo is more explicitly Trinitarian in theology; the assertion that Latin was originally chosen for the Roman rite because it was the vernacular of its day; the opinion that the *versus populum* stance of the priest better reflects what the Mass is; the widespread view that only the reformed liturgy makes the baptized into (and makes them aware of being) co-offerers of the Holy Sacrifice; and, most of all, the asseveration, solemnly delivered, that "resistance to the reformed liturgy" of Paul VI is equivalent to rejecting both the Council and the Holy Spirit.

Part 3 presents the critiques of six more authors: Alexander Battista, an Eastern-rite Catholic; Fr. Samuel Keyes, a convert from Anglicanism and a priest of the Anglican Ordinariate; Roland Millare, an expert on the liturgical theology of Joseph Ratzinger; Fr. Peter Miller, a Benedictine monk who is especially well-equipped to tackle the subject of the lectionaries; Dom Alcuin Reid, one of the greatest living scholars on liturgical matters; and Dr. Joseph Shaw, President of the International *Una Voce* Federation and Chairman of the Latin Mass Society of England and Wales.

The volume is rounded out by a mordantly humorous Epilogue by Gregory DiPippo and a Select Bibliography recommending the finest resources for those who wish to equip themselves well for serious discussions of these complex issues.

Some readers might be tempted to wonder: "Why should we care about a series written by three scholars who are obviously totally out of their depth and who have done little more than make a public spectacle of themselves? Shouldn't we just let it pass and move on?" To this, I answer, we *should* care, and we should *not* let it pass. The kind of arguments given by CHW are precisely those that are still lazily regurgitated in seminaries and liturgical degree programs around the world; they are the "commonplaces" that hold on doggedly in diocesan newspapers, bulletins, homilies, blogs, and workshops. The contributors to this volume have sought to do a service to the Church by summing up major innovationist and anti-traditionalist arguments and, like a good apologetics manual, presenting Catholic counterarguments. A handy, readable, persuasive case in favor of tradition against novelty will be especially helpful for younger people today who long for the sacred and the authentic while feeling at a loss for explanations. Moreover, we are passing through a period of vengefully fierce opposition to Catholic tradition; the worst attitudes of the 1970s have reappeared in holders of the highest offices and have metastasized into a felonious campaign designed to wipe out the Latin Mass and other traditional sacramental rites and forms of prayer, not to mention the orthodox doctrine and morality of which the ancient *lex orandi* is the spotless reflection. What is almost worse than the errors in CHW is the way in which they, and the journal that published them, have allowed themselves to be co-opted by an ideology directly aimed against the immemorial *lex orandi* and therefore against the *lex credendi* and the *lex vivendi* as well—an ideology that, as a consequence, thwarts the common good of the entire Church (the nearly verbatim parallels between CHW and Cardinals Roche, Cupich, and Cantalamessa are eloquent in this regard). In other words, the CHW series is no mere ivory-tower exercise to be laughed away; it is a form of ecclesiastical-political propaganda that needs to be clearly identified and rigorously snuffed out as the distorting and perverting force it is.

I thank all of the authors for their diligent defense of the Roman Church's great liturgical heritage, now under remorseless attack but destined to survive as it has done through many evil periods in Western history—indeed, destined to thrive again. As Dom Gérard Calvet once said: "Tradition is the youth of God."

In the printed version of this book, the ugly clutter of hyperlinks and access dates has been omitted in the notes, since anyone with internet can effortlessly locate the items identified herein by author, title, website, and date.

Peter A. Kwasniewski
March 31, 2023
Seven Sorrows of Our Lady

ABBREVIATIONS

CHW = Cavadini, Healy, Weinandy
MD = Encyclical Letter *Mediator Dei* of Pius XII
NO = Novus Ordo (Missae) of Paul VI
SC = Constitution on the Sacred Liturgy
Sacrosanctum Concilium of Vatican II
TLM = Traditional Latin Mass

SUMMARY
of Cavadini, Healy, and Weinandy

JANET E. SMITH

ON DECEMBER 1, 2022, IN THE ONLINE publication *Church Life Journal*, John Cavadini, Mary Healy, and Thomas Weinandy published "A Synoptic Look at the Failures and Successes of Post-Vatican II Liturgical Reforms," a compilation of a previously published five-part series undertaken to "address the theological, liturgical, and pastoral issues that have arisen over time and that presently disrupt the unity and peace of the Church. Our hope is that, in bringing some clarity to what has developed, both positively and negatively, a constructive way forward may be found."

Permission was sought from the *Church Life Journal* to reprint the series in this volume prior to our critiques of it, and an offer was made to include a response from CHW to their critics. The request was denied, and so we offer instead the present summary of CHW's "Synoptic Look."

In their "Synoptic Look," CHW list the topics they address. 1. The rise of the liturgical renewal; 2. The state of the liturgy prior to Vatican II; 3. The Council's reforms as outlined in *Sacrosanctum Concilium*; 4. The implementation of *Sacrosanctum Concilium*; 5. The movement to return to the Tridentine liturgy; 6. The pastoral strategies of Popes John Paul II, Benedict XVI, and Francis; 7. Theological and pastoral concerns with the Traditional Latin Mass movement; 8. The way forward. Our summary follows these eight sections.

1. The Rise of the Liturgical Renewal. In the first section, CHW speak of the Liturgical Movement prior to Vatican II and review the work of monks and priests who were involved in it. Some advocated "reforms" that stressed the importance of the liturgical year, the promotion of Gregorian chant (which, it seems, all desired), and "active participation," which meant, for some, that the laity were to have a greater awareness of their participation in the priesthood of Christ, and, for others, that the laity should sing or recite the responses and join in singing the Ordinary of the Mass. Some advocated the use of the vernacular in the Mass; others opposed it. There was a general sense that the laity needed more instruction on the nature of the Mass. CHW remark especially on the founding of a center for liturgical renewal at St. John's Abbey in Collegeville, Minnesota.

CHW also review the content of Pope Pius XII's encyclical on the liturgy, *Mediator Dei* (1947), and portray it as being very favorable to the Liturgical Movement. They comment on his support for promoting a revival of Gregorian chant and especially on his advocacy of more active participation for the laity. They claim that Pius XII speaks of maintaining respect not only for the ancient liturgies but also for contemporary rites, since all were inspired by the Holy Spirit.

CHW single out two theologians who contributed to Vatican II's Constitution on the Liturgy *Sacrosanctum Concilium* (1963): Fr. Romano Guardini (1885–1968), whom they report as stressing the communal nature of the liturgy, and Fr. Louis Bouyer (1913–2004), a consultor for the Vatican II document on the liturgy and who also served on the *Consilium* that composed the *Novus Ordo* after Vatican II.

CHW portray the Liturgical Movement as a movement "from the ground up" since it was initiated primarily in monasteries. They also state that the renewal was "guided, sanctioned, and encouraged by the Church's hierarchy." They conclude that the movement was "an authentic work of the Spirit for the benefit of Christ's Church."

2. The State of the Liturgy Prior to Vatican II. In the second section, CHW portray the attendees of the Mass prior to Vatican II as mere "observers" of a great mystery and claim that only the priest and altar boys were "seen as actively engaged." They depict the laity as largely inattentive to what was going on at the altar as they "engaged in their own personal forms of prayer." CHW tell us that the laity

> had little sense of asking forgiveness of their sins during the opening penitential rite, nor did they consciously offer themselves to the Father in union with Jesus during the offertory. There was little or no engagement with the scripture readings. Likewise, unless they were following along with a bilingual missal, which must be said was fairly popular, they would not be praying along with the celebrant, for they could neither hear him nor understand what he was praying in Latin.

Further, according to CHW, the laity, while they knew they were receiving Jesus in the Eucharist,

> had little awareness that the privilege of receiving Holy Communion was founded upon their having participated in Jesus's once-for-all sacrifice of himself to the Father for the forgiveness of sins and the outpouring of the divine life of the Holy Spirit. Significantly, while the faithful knew and believed that the one God is a Trinity of persons, their liturgical and personal prayer often primarily consisted of praying to the one (generic) God.

It was not until the Mass was in the vernacular, they assert, that the faithful became "cognizant of the trinitarian nature of the liturgy and of their own ability to pray in a trinitarian manner."

CHW report that while some priests were reverent, some said the Mass in under twenty minutes, mumbling a Latin they did not understand. Moreover, there was a paucity of Scripture in the Mass, which prevented Catholics from coming to know the whole of the Bible. The sermons largely addressed the necessity of living a moral life and striving for holiness, but they did not "bring to life the mysteries of the faith" and thus most Catholics "never grew in their understanding of the doctrines of the faith beyond what they learned from catechesis as children." The priests were not much more mature in their faith.

CHW claim that few Catholics knew why the Mass was said *ad orientem* and were only aware that they could not see or hear what the priest was doing or saying.

All the above indicate that the Mass was based on an "inadequate theological understanding" which had resulted in "deficient liturgical practice."

3. The Council's Reforms. The third section discusses the reforms of the liturgy proposed by Vatican II in *SC*, which, said the Council, was undertaken to meet the needs of our time. They note that the key intent of *SC* was expressed in this passage:

> Mother Church earnestly desires that all the faithful should be led to the full, conscious, and active participation in the liturgical celebrations which is demanded by the very nature of the liturgy, and to which the Christian people, "a chosen race, a royal priesthood, a holy nation, a redeemed people" (1 Pet 2:9; cf. 2:4–5) have a right and obligation by reason of their baptism.
>
> In the restoration and promotion of the sacred liturgy the full and active participation by all the people is the aim to be considered above all else, for it is the primary and indispensable source from which the faithful are to derive the true Christian spirit. Therefore, in all their apostolic activity, pastors of souls should energetically set about achieving it through requisite pedagogy.[1]

CHW note that *SC* holds that the "promotion and restoration of the liturgy" has been prompted by the Holy Spirit. CHW claim that the Council advocates for active participation because "only through such active engagement in word and action do they [the laity] reap the graces that flow from the Eucharist."

CHW then list eight desiderata of *SC*: changes must be made if there are elements that do not harmonize with the "inner nature" of the liturgy (*SC* 21); changes may not be made to the liturgy except under the authority of the Church (*SC* 22); active participation, which involves the laity reciting prayers of the Mass and engaging in various physical movements, should be promoted (*SC* 30); liturgical rites should have a "noble simplicity" and be "short, clear, and unencumbered by useless repetitions" (*SC* 34); there should be more Scripture in the liturgy (*SC* 51); homilies should expound

---

[1] *SC* 14. See chapter 6 for a critique of the translation "above all else," which is not what the Latin of *SC* says.

"the mysteries of the faith and the guiding principles of the Christian life" (*SC* 52); Latin is to be preserved, especially in the Ordinary of the Mass, but a wider use may be made of the vernacular (*SC* 36); Gregorian chant should be given "pride of place in liturgical services" along with other forms of sacred music, "especially polyphony" (*SC* 116). In addition, respect should be given to the musical traditions of people in mission lands (*SC* 119) and the pipe organ should be held in "high esteem in the Latin Church" (*SC* 120).

CHW understand these decrees to be part of a liturgical renewal inspired by the Holy Spirit and directed towards active participation by the faithful. CHW argue that the Church intended not to *rescind* the Tridentine Mass but rather to revise it into a new version of the same Roman Rite.

4. The Implementation of *Sacrosanctum Concilium*: The Good, the Bad, and the Ugly. In the fourth section, CHW note "the achievements and disappointments" of the NO. They maintain *SC* was rightly implemented as follows:

> The active participation of the faithful was heightened in a myriad of ways: in their vocal responses in the Penitential Rite, in the restoration of the Prayer of the Faithful, in the restoration of the offertory procession in which the faithful bring forward the bread and wine, in their response to the priest's invitation to pray that his sacrifice and theirs would be acceptable to God, and in other responses and acclamations. The role of the altar servers became less prominent.

They assert that the simplification of the rubrics, accompanying a new suite of Eucharistic Prayers, allowed for greater active participation by the laity and greater understanding of the Eucharist by the priest.

It is here that CHW find "one of Vatican II's enduring and most important achievements: the recovery of the Scriptural and patristic doctrine of the priesthood of all the baptized." The NO permits the laity to realize more fully their "baptismal priesthood," for they share more in the offering of the Eucharist and are less cast in the role of "strangers and silent spectators" (*SC* 48).

A major contributor to a fuller participation of the laity in the liturgy is the use of the vernacular language, which makes possible "active, vocal, [and] intelligible participation" for both laity and priest. CHW note that the use of the vernacular was enthusiastically welcomed around the world. "The *vox populi* had spoken" in going past the limited opening to the vernacular called for in *SC*. CHW reject the claim of some opponents of the NO that in adopting the vernacular effectively to the exclusion of Latin in most places, the NO went against the intentions of *SC*, and, for support, point to the fact that Popes Paul VI and John Paul II accepted these developments.

CHW provide a fairly long list of some of the "unfortunate developments" in the English editions of the Missal: the translations were not true to the original; references to Scripture were obscure; the beautiful poetic sense of the collects and prayers was lost. They lament that the translations of the Eucharistic Prayers,[2] products of the "dubious theology" that followed Vatican II, failed to fully convey the sacrificial nature of the Mass. In their view, the several revisions of the Missal since the original edition have rectified the problem.

CHW find one of the "most pastorally advantageous changes in the reformed liturgy" to be the expanded lectionary, which has a three-year cycle of Sunday readings and a two-year cycle of weekday readings. They believe the laity have immensely benefitted from this greater exposure to Scripture which enables them to understand the Eucharist better and leads to a more intimate communion with Christ.

CHW applaud the fact that the new lectionary provides priests with more material for their homilies but maintain that priests have not taken advantage of the new riches, still giving homilies that are too moralistic. CHW deplore the fact that priests are also in the habit of "telling personal and humorous stories." The Church has responded by issuing several documents encouraging priests to speak on the mysteries of the faith as disclosed in Scripture.

---

[2] CHW call these "canons" although the liturgical reformers called them *preces*, since the term "canon" had become more or less equivalent over the centuries to the sole Western anaphora, the Roman Canon.

CHW lament the fact that, contrary to *SC*, there has not been a revival of Gregorian chant, and portions of the Mass that were to be *sung* in Latin are now simply *recited* in the vernacular. They note that "the loss of the Church's musical tradition tended to undermine the heavenly solemnity and gravitas of the Mass." They paint a mixed but largely dismal picture of modern-day Mass music:

> The use of the vernacular did give rise to the composition of vernacular hymns and new sung Masses. Some of these were of high biblical and theological quality and skillfully composed, but others were banal and sentimental, with moralistic lyrics, often focused on celebrating the congregating community rather than worshiping Christ. Many were devoid of any mention of the mysteries of the faith, the exaltation of the Holy Trinity, Jesus as the Son of God incarnate, his saving death and glorious resurrection, the new life in the Holy Spirit, or the marvel of the Eucharist. The lyrics of such hymns possessed little biblical or theological correlation to the liturgy itself and were not conducive to entering into the liturgical celebration. Likewise, some of the melodies possessed a liturgical quality, a sacred eminence that would not be found in contemporary secular music. Others, however, sounded like Broadway rejects—a poor combination of "spiritual" words with the tune of contemporary musicals.

CHW speak approvingly of the many different instruments used at Mass and portray the distress of those who complain about guitar Masses as "sometimes overwrought, fueled by an elitist mentality."

CHW are enthusiasts for the Mass said *versus populum* or with the priest facing the people. They acknowledge it was not anticipated by the Council but maintain it is in keeping with the attempt to foster the "full participation of the laity" who, because of the priest facing toward them, are better drawn into celebrating the Eucharist with the priest. Moreover, the representation of the spousal covenant is better effected because the priest, representing the bridegroom, is facing the Church, his bride (that is, the people in the nave). CHW observe that some priests used the new positioning to "assume the role of an entertainer," with the result that "instead of the liturgy being renewed and the faithful more actively engaged, it became muddled and banal."

CHW note that the Vatican has been slow to act against the transgressions that have at times characterized the NO: "Few positive measures were taken to correct the liturgical abuses and few disciplinary actions were taken against those who perpetrated them." They find signs that authentic renewal took place during the pontificates of John Paul II and Benedict XVI, but list some important steps that still needed (and need) to be made, since "not all of the changes [in the liturgical reform] have always and everywhere been accompanied by the necessary explanation and catechesis; as a result, in some cases there has been a misunderstanding of the very nature of the liturgy, leading to abuses, polarization, and sometimes even grave scandal." John Paul II observed that liturgy needed to possess a contemplative dimension to arouse "awe, reverence, and adoration," and mentioned the need for more silence in the Mass, more Latin, and more chant.

For all of its problems, however, CHW believe the Holy Spirit has been "present and active" in the implementation of the NO—a view they find echoed in John Paul's remarks on the twenty-fifth anniversary of *SC*, where he gave a long list of the good that has come from liturgical renewal, including greater knowledge of Scripture, increased participation by the laity in the Eucharist, and a greater sense on the part of the laity of their common priesthood, all of which has redounded to the vitality of Christian communities.

5. The Movement to Return to the Tridentine Liturgy. In the fifth section, CHW take up the question of the growing preference of a rather small number of priests and laity for the Tridentine Mass (TM). They list some reasons that have contributed to this preference, such as the chaotic implementation of the NO and the sense that the TM is more reverent, transcendent, and solemn. Although sympathizing with the desires of the attendees of the TM, CHW "believe that a return to the Tridentine Mass is liturgically unfortunate and doctrinally unacceptable." They cite a 1974 document that forbids the availability of the TM in areas where episcopal conferences have mandated the NO.

CHW assert that the TM was itself a reform in its day, that it is only 400 years old, that it will disappear over time, and that the NO will undergo changes as well. CHW claim that Latin was introduced because it was the vernacular of its day and that Jesus employed the vernacular of his day to enable the apostles to participate actively in the liturgy.

To the claim that the TM was not in need of reform since it had produced thousands of saints, CHW respond that many became saints *before* Trent while several have become saints who worshiped in the NO. CHW believe that a return to the TM with its "more limited and less adequate ecclesiology" would be a return to the laity being "silent spectators" sadly separated from the priest and from the offering.

6. The Pastoral Strategies of Popes John Paul II, Benedict XVI, and Francis. In the sixth section, CHW address the pastoral strategies of Popes John Paul II, Benedict XVI, and Francis. In 1984 John Paul made a concession, in the form of an indult, that permitted bishops to allow the TM under very tight restrictions, such as: that those asking for it make it publicly clear that they accept the NO; that the Mass not be held at parishes; and that the 1962 Missal be used. John Paul made further concessions after Archbishop Lefebvre's illicit ordination of four bishops and asked that ordinaries give "wide and generous" permission for the TM. In 2007 in *Summorum Pontificum*, Benedict XVI made a distinction between the NO as the "ordinary form" of the Roman Rite and the TM as the "extraordinary form" of the same Rite, and mandated that a TM should be provided for groups of the faithful who request it of their pastors. CHW question Benedict's wisdom in allowing such availability of the TM, since they find the continued presence of the TM incompatible with the movement of the Holy Spirit in respect to the liturgy and, according to them, "undercut[s] the fundamental principle of the liturgical renewal: active participation of the laity." CHW also accuse Benedict of having undermined his own principle of a hermeneutic of continuity, which CHW understand to mean that the NO must (by definition) be in continuity with the TM and not a departure from it so notable that it counts as a different form of Mass.

CHW identify a large number of problems with the TM, such as that the "silent and prayerful" participation of the laity in the Mass is not what *SC* meant by "active participation." They lament that those who attend the TM will not have the opportunity, afforded by the NO, to become more familiar with Scripture.

CHW report that Pope Francis in *Traditionis Custodes* (2021) reversed the normalization of the TM by greatly restricting its availability, since it had become a source of disunity in the Church. He mandated that parochial churches could not host the TM nor could new parishes or groups be established to provide the TM; priests and seminarians who wish to celebrate the TM must be given permission from the bishops, who must in turn consult the Holy See before the permission may be granted. Francis consulted the bishops around the world before making his decision, not only because those who attend the TM have contributed to division in the Church but also because some go so far as to reject Vatican II. In a subsequent document, Francis indicated he wanted the restrictions he mandated to be applied strictly, in order to discourage those who attend the TM from assuming they are truly a part of parish life or that they could expect the TM to be regularly available.

CHW call for a pastoral approach on the diocesan and parish levels to those who are hurt by the decisions of the Holy Father, which CHW found somewhat insensitive.

7. **Theological and Pastoral Concerns with the Tridentine Mass Movement.** In the seventh section CHW respond to those whose advocacy for the TM they find offensive and single out Peter Kwasniewski, who warns people not to participate in the NO because "it deprives the Lord of the reverence that is due to Him." They accuse him of not recognizing that the NO is often said reverently and of not recognizing that it is a source of attraction to the Church for those in Africa.

Summary

CHW believe that Vatican II is, ironically, in some way the cause of present disaffection for the NO, because Vatican II taught the importance of "an experience of active participation in something of surpassing beauty, namely, the Eucharistic sacrifice," and those who today find that surpassing beauty in the TM seek out "a self-selected group of enthusiasts who share the same ideal" and prefer not to worship with those who don't have their "level of interest, faith, or attention span." CHW believe that some romanticize the preconciliar TM, which they describe as "very routinized and in many instances almost mechanically celebrated."

CHW insist again on the importance of the laity fully experiencing their baptismal priesthood, a priority of Vatican II, and again claim that the TM risks overaccentuating the ministerial priesthood. CHW also claim that the NO better enables the laity to internalize the mystery of "Jesus' once-for-all saving sacrifice" because they can worship in their own language. They claim that the rubrics of the NO better convey mystery whereas in the TM, "it can happen that the ceremonial itself and its meticulous observance take on a life of their own, as though they were the focus and source of the feeling of transcendence."

CHW warn that "there can be a danger of loving a form of the Mass more than one loves Jesus." The unity of the Church is threatened by "a self-selected group of like-minded people within the Church" who can come to think of themselves as better Catholics. CHW reject the views of those who blame the NO for the decline in vocations, the increase of divorce, and declining numbers in the Church.

CHW point out that John Paul II, Benedict, and Francis all bemoaned the division in the Church caused by the presence of two Roman Rite liturgies and gives as evidence that they all required that attendees of the TM recognize the validity of the NO. They single out Dom Alcuin Reid's clandestine ordination to the priesthood as an indication that the TM is moving towards establishing a separate Church. They also urge devotees of the NO to grant the legitimacy of the charge that the NO is at times banal and that this problem ought to be addressed.

8. The Way Forward. In the eighth and final section, CHW "propose some positive ways forward." The first is a call to bishops and pastors to educate the laity about Vatican II, as few are familiar with it and sometimes are led astray by those who denigrate the Council. It is often the young who suffer the most from ignorance of Vatican II and thus are tempted to gravitate towards the TM.

CHW also challenge bishops and priests to "call the faithful to a deeper conversion," for which purpose a mystagogical catechesis on the Eucharistic liturgy will be necessary. This will not be effected without a "new Pentecost" wherein there will be a fresh outpouring of the Holy Spirit. CHW give a fairly extensive summary of the catechesis that they believe is necessary to lead the laity to recognize their baptismal priesthood and the truth that we are to become one with Christ; they call for parishes to provide classes on these matters and for priests to focus on these themes in their homilies.

CHW also give specific instructions on how the laity might be helped to experience liturgy as beautiful and that giving this goal due attention will be a means of fostering interior conversion. They recommend genuflecting to the tabernacle and keeping more silence before Mass and at the appropriate moments within Mass. Those who receive Communion should have a reverent posture (by this, however, they do not mean kneeling while receiving) and should be more modest and less casual in their dress. They note the need for vernacular hymns to speak of the Eucharist not only as a banquet but also as a sacrifice. They urge lectors to read with understanding. They want us to work "to recover the iconography and devotional furnishings that nourish the devotional life and help to localize it in place and time." They express their own frustration with some of the results of the new liturgy: "One can understand the impulse to leave behind the reformed liturgy if the very reasons for which it was reformed are continually subverted by bad hymnody, incomprehensible Scripture reading and psalmody, and the seeming negation of the possibility of devotion, especially to Mary, to which *Lumen Gentium* exhorted us."

Summary

CHW particularly want to find a way to link the liturgy with the New Evangelization and suggest that, during the Mass, after Communion, some of the faithful might give public testimonies about their love for the Eucharist.

Their final request is twofold. First, they "hold that it is time for those who have become part of the Tridentine movement to reconsider their position." Second, they urge "those who are responsible for overseeing the celebration of the Eucharist to get much more serious about reforming the reform, about addressing the legitimate concerns of those attracted to the Tridentine rite instead of turning a deaf ear to their complaints." Recognizing that liturgy on earth can never be perfect, CHW call upon those who worship at the TM to return to "the Church's ordinary liturgical form" and to contribute to its ongoing reform.

PART 1
Janet Smith's Critique

1
Sacrificing Beauty and Other Errors

A *RORATE CAELI* MASS EMBRACES THE attendees in an atmosphere of mystery, transcendence, and solemnity; it is very clear that something supernaturally wonderful is happening. I went to a *Rorate Caeli* Mass on a punishingly windy, cold, rainy morning—most fitting for an event marking emergence from darkness to light, from evil to goodness. The Mass began at 7 AM in a mostly dark church lit by hundreds of candles on the altar and in the church; everyone in the congregation was holding lit tapers.

The symbolism was impossible to miss. Advent is the time when we realize how dark the world is without Christ and how desperate we are for the light that He brings. The Mass is devoted to Mary who enabled that light to come into the world and enables all of us to be Christ-bearers. It was too dark for me to follow in my missal so "all" I did was meditate on those basic truths and luxuriate in the beautiful music and the dazzling candlelight. I felt completely engaged in the liturgy along with my fellow worshippers who also seemed enthralled by the occasion. (I wonder if our profoundly contemplative engagement qualifies as "active participation" or were we just passive woolgatherers?) I suspect the symbolism of the ceremony embedded itself deeply into the subconscious of the small children in attendance. It was certainly in my mind days after the event.

The Mass I attended was held in a parish church that has recently been restored to its pre-Vatican II glory. Shortly after Vatican II it was "wreckovated" into what bore some resemblance to a bordello. Pictures of the Church through several of its stages can tell us much (see Figures 1–6). The *Rorate Caeli* Mass was designed to be said in beautiful churches, with beautiful art and music; it would have been very much out of place in the bordello version of St. Thomas the Apostle, a design evidently considered fitting for the Novus Ordo—a Mass that has not spawned beautiful architecture, music, and art, but rather the opposite.

Sadly, most Catholics have never heard of a *Rorate Caeli* Mass, let alone attended one.

John Cavadini, Mary Healy, and Fr. Tom Weinandy in their five-part series [1] on the Traditional Latin Mass [2] seem determined to make the *Rorate Caeli* Mass and all forms of the Traditional Latin Mass (TLM) unavailable (though they do not state their exact intent). [3] Certainly they said nothing

---

[1] All five articles have been merged into one: John Cavadini, Mary Healy, Thomas Weinandy, "A Synoptic Look at the Failures and Successes of Post-Vatican II Liturgical Reforms" (*Church Life Journal*, December 1, 2022; hereafter, "A Synoptic Look").

[2] I prefer the term "Traditional Latin Mass" to "Tridentine Mass," since "Tridentine Mass" can be interpreted (as it often is) to suggest that a new Mass was invented at Trent, when in truth Trent codified the Order of Mass that originated around the fourth century and had developed organically since then, remaining recognizably the same rite.

[3] It seems to be a reasonable interpretation of their articles to conclude that CHW think that the Church would be better off without the general availability of the TLM and indeed, would be better off if it were more or less confined to the dustbins of history. They do not explicitly say they think that the TLM should be abrogated, but they do say: "we believe that a return to the Tridentine Mass is liturgically unfortunate and doctrinally unacceptable," and "To return to the Tridentine Mass is, then, to lose or obscure a foundational dimension of the Church and her worship." They also ask about traditionalists: "Do they [traditionalists] really expect that hundreds of years from now the Tridentine Mass will still be celebrated, even unto the coming of our Lord Jesus Christ at the end of history?" The answer to that question is that the advocates of the TLM *do* think it will be celebrated hundreds of years from now—a prospect unthinkable to CHW. Although their piece, so contemptuous of the attendees of the TLM, is not likely to persuade them of deficiencies in the TLM, they ask its attendees "for the well-being of the Body of Christ, to return to the Church's ordinary liturgical form." They certainly never address the possibility of any accommodations made to the Traditional Latin Mass community.

I sent a query to the authors for a clarification about what precisely they are proposing as to the availability of the TLM—does saying there should be no "return" to the TLM mean only that it should not *replace* the NO, or rather, that it should not be available *at all?* I heard back only from Mary Healy, who acknowledged that my questions were good ones but that she does not have the time to give them the attention they deserve. Certainly, it can be said with confidence that CHW intend to

Figure 1. Original appearance of parish church, ca. 1900.

Figure 2. Solemn Requiem Mass for Pius XI, 1939.

Figure 3. "Renovation" of the church after Vatican II, 1965.

Figure 4. Close-up of the high altar in 1965. "More renovations were made under the leadership of Msgr. G. Warren Peek, 1964–1993. Windows were covered and the apse was repainted gold. The high altar, reredos, marble angels, side altars and Communion rails were all removed. The sanctuary was extended, a simple, freestanding altar was added, and the first several rows of pews were rearranged" (*Detroit Church Blog*, September 21, 2017).

Figure 5. Restoration in 2020 by Conrad Schmitt Studios.

about retiring the architecture, art, and music together with the liturgy that inspired it, and one cannot imagine that they would want to deny the faithful that beauty.

Nevertheless, the fact is that the TLM and such beautiful architecture, art, and music are based on the same theology—one CHW deem "inadequate"—and are meant to be experienced together. CHW seem to have no sense of how devastating the loss of the TLM—and all its beautiful accouterments—would be to some very devout Catholics and how hard it will be, without it, to restore to the Church the beauty it had before the ravages of the modern age.

---

discredit the TLM and to discourage people from attending it. It is not unreasonable to think they would like to see it abrogated, so I will be using "discourage/abolish" when speaking of their intention; if they intend otherwise, I welcome a clarification from them. It is also worth noting that I submitted my essays to the *Church Life Journal* in hopes that it would be interested in hosting a thorough and fair response to CHW. I received only an automated response and withdrew the article after they had had it in their possession for several weeks.

Figure 6. Closeup of restored sanctuary.

It's a rare event when three well-respected theologians—noted for their fidelity—team up to write against a time-honored practice of the Church. CHW have put their impressive academic skills, considerable intellectual gifts, and well-deserved scholarly reputations in service of...discouraging and even perhaps abolishing the Traditional Latin Mass forever, a Mass that likely only 1–2% of Catholics currently attend.

I am sorry to say that the arguments that CHW offer are simply not up to the goal they have set themselves.[4] For the last two or three years I have immersed myself in reading about the history and meaning of the TLM and of the Novus Ordo (NO).[5] The narrative that I discovered is remarkably different from that laid out by CHW, whose reading on the

---

[4] I must thank Dr. Peter Kwasniewski for his help on my response; he provided invaluable bibliographical and editorial help, often sharpened my argument, and encouraged supplementation of my analysis in important ways. The critique remains mine but has been much improved because of his input.

[5] Here is the list of books I have purchased; many I have read in their entirety, others in part. (I am not showing off; it is just that there is such a wealth of material, I couldn't resist building at least a basic library of resources, most on the TLM but also on criticisms of Vatican II. There are also, of course, countless informative articles on the internet.) Romano Amerio, *Iota Unum: A Study of Changes in the Catholic Church in the Twentieth Century* (Kansas City: Sarto House, 1996); Louis Bouyer, *Liturgical Piety* (Providence, RI: Cluny Media, 2021); idem, *The Memoirs of Louis Bouyer: From Youth and Conversion to Vatican II, the Liturgical Reform, and After* (Brooklyn: Angelico Press, 2015); Yves Chiron, *Annibale Bugnini: Reformer of the Liturgy* (Brooklyn: Angelico Press, 2018); Michael Davies, *Liturgical Time Bombs in Vatican II: Destruction of the Faith through Changes in Catholic Worship* (Rockford, IL: TAN Books, 2003); Roberto de Mattei, *The Second Vatican Council: An Unwritten Story* (Fitzwilliam, NH: Loreto Publications, 2012); Michael Fiedrowicz, *The Traditional Mass: History, Form, and Theology of the Classical Roman Rite* (Brooklyn: Angelico Press, 2020); Klaus Gamber, *The Reform of the Roman Liturgy: Its Problems and Background* (San Juan Capistrano, CA: Una Voce Press and Harrison, NY: The Foundation for Catholic Reform, 1993); Thomas G. Guarino, *The Disputed Teachings of Vatican II: Continuity and Reversal in Catholic Doctrine* (Grand Rapids: Eerdmans, 2018); Prosper Guéranger, *The Traditional Latin Mass Explained* (Brooklyn: Angelico Press, 2017); Matthew Hazell, *Index Lectionum: A Comparative Table of Readings for the Ordinary and Extraordinary Forms of the Roman Rite* (N.p.: Lectionary Study Aids, 2016); Bryan Houghton, *Judith's Marriage* (Brooklyn: Angelico Press, 2020); idem, *Mitre and Crook* (Brooklyn: Angelico Press, 2019); idem, *Unwanted Priest: The Autobiography of a Latin Mass Exile* (Brooklyn: Angelico Press, 2022); James Jackson, *Nothing Superfluous: An Explanation of the Symbolism of the Rite of St. Gregory the Great* (Manchester, NH: Sophia Institute Press, 2021); Peter Kwasniewski, *Reclaiming Our Roman Catholic Birthright: The Genius and Timeliness of the Traditional Latin Mass* (Brooklyn: Angelico Press, 2020); idem, *Resurgent in the Midst of Crisis: Sacred Liturgy, the Traditional Latin Mass, and Renewal in the Church* (Brooklyn: Angelico Press, 2014); idem, *Tradition and Sanity: Conversations and Dialogues of a Postconciliar Exile* (Brooklyn: Angelico Press, 2018); idem, *The Holy Bread of Eternal Life: Restoring Eucharistic Reverence in an Age of Impiety* (Manchester, NH: Sophia Institute Press, 2020); idem, *Noble Beauty, Transcendent Holiness: Why the*

meaning and history of the liturgy and whose direct personal acquaintance with the current TLM and its attendees seem thin, to say the least.

Sadly, they do not worthily employ their skills of scholarship and reasoning in their critique of the TLM. The chief problems are that they omit evidence that works against their position; they draw conclusions not warranted by the evidence; they misrepresent the views of some theologians and some Church documents; they do not address the strongest arguments of the advocates for the TLM; they make arguments that are irrelevant to the question at hand; and they uncharitably depict the motivations of TLM advocates.

But before I respond to particular arguments put forward by CHW, let me explain why I find the project rather doomed

---

Modern Age Needs the Mass of Ages (Brooklyn: Angelico Press, 2017); idem, *The Once and Future Roman Rite: Returning to the Traditional Latin Liturgy after Seventy Years of Exile* (Gastonia, NC: TAN Books, 2022); Matthew L. Lamb, ed., *The Reception of Vatican II* (New York: Oxford University Press, 2017); idem, ed., *Vatican II: Renewal within Tradition* (New York: Oxford University Press, 2008); Ulrich L. Lehner, *On the Road to Vatican II: German Catholic Enlightenment and Reform of the Church* (Minneapolis: Fortress Press, 2016); Elizabeth Lev, *How Catholic Art Saved the Faith: The Triumph of Beauty and Truth in Counter-Reformation Art* (Manchester, NH: Sophia Institute Press, 2018); George J. Moorman, *The Latin Mass Explained: Everything Needed to Understand and Appreciate the Traditional Latin Mass* (Charlotte, NC: TAN Books, 2010); Aidan Nichols, *Conciliar Octet: A Concise Commentary on the Eight Key Texts of the Second Vatican Council* (San Francisco: Ignatius Press, 2019); John W. O'Malley, *What Happened at Vatican II* (Cambridge, MA: Belknap Press, 2010); Aurelio Porfiri, *Uprooted: Dialogues on the Liquid Church* (Hong Kong: Chora Books, 2019); Lauren Pristas, *The Collects of the Roman Missals: A Comparative Study of the Sundays in Proper Seasons Before and After the Second Vatican Council* (London/New York: Bloomsbury T&T Clark, 2013); Joseph Ratzinger, *Theological Highlights of Vatican II* (Mahwah, NJ: Paulist Press, 2009); Athanasius Schneider, *The Catholic Mass: Steps to Restore the Centrality of God in the Liturgy* (Manchester, NH: Sophia Institute Press, 2022); idem, *The Springtime That Never Came: In Conversation with Paweł Lisicki* (Manchester, NH: Sophia Institute Press, 2022); H. J. A. Sire, *Phoenix from the Ashes: The Making, Unmaking, and Restoration of Catholic Tradition* (Brooklyn: Angelico Press, 2015); Bernard Tissier De Mallerais, *Marcel Lefebvre* (Kansas City, MO: Angelus Press, 2004); George Weigel, *To Sanctify the World: The Vital Legacy of Vatican II* (New York: Basic Books, 2022); Brian Williams, *Why Tradition? Why Now?* (Clackamas, OR: Regina Magazine, 2018); Ralph Wiltgen, *The Rhine Flows into the Tiber: A History of Vatican II* (Charlotte, NC: TAN Books, 2014).

from the start, if it is designed to convince any of us who now attend the TLM and have studied its history and that of the NO to eschew the TLM in favor of the NO.

A POOR DEAL

What we are to get in return for giving up the TLM is a "reformed" NO of some as-yet-unknown description. Reformed, because, as CHW readily and even frequently acknowledge, all too often the NO has proven to be a very inadequate form of worship. Indeed, never in the history of mankind have congregations been subjected to such faith-destroying, banal, silly, and even blasphemous versions of the liturgy. Those are not everyday occurrences to be sure, and yes, there are "reverent NOs" (I have attended many and still do), but few adult Catholics have not encountered or heard about a NO that has shocked and offended their Catholic sensibilities, and in some parishes and some parts of the world offensive NOs are the rule rather than the exception.

CHW say we are to overlook these abuses as glitches in the performance of the NO since it is still "young" and trust that the abuses will eventually be a thing of the past and that it is possible that some future form of the NO will have all the virtues of the TLM—without its flaws—and more. Of course, I pray that happens, but I am not foolish enough to be willing to give up a liturgy organically one with the most beautiful architecture, art, and music the world has ever known for a liturgy that is perfectly at home in some of the ugliest churches ever built, with sing-song tunes offered as hymns, and abstract art without aesthetic or religious value. Case closed for some of us.

In short, the kind of art, architecture, hymns, and poetry that the TLM has inspired compared with that which the NO has inspired is pretty much in itself a sufficient "argument" that we cannot and must not let the TLM be taken from us again.

But when respected Catholic scholars spend their valuable time trying to convince others that the Mass used by the Church for at least a millennium and a half is a danger to the faith, a response is in order. Indeed, some will be persuaded simply because it is CHW who are critiquing the TLM, and their witness will be trusted. I believe my analysis of their position will show that trust to be misplaced.

There are many who are much more capable than I of responding to the arguments of CHW—some have already done so[6]—but I want to add my voice to the cry of those who find antipathy to the TLM among faithful Catholics, and learned ones at that, to be perplexing in the extreme.

After all, those who attend the TLM to a person have a profound devotion to the Eucharist; they study the Mass inside and out; they withdraw their children from pernicious public and Catholic schools; indeed, they make great sacrifices to drive a long way with their many children who are evidently quite content to attend a liturgy long and peculiar—though fascinating—to them. These families and other attendees at the TLM produce a greatly disproportionate number of vocations to the priesthood and life-affirming marriage. But none of that seems to matter to CHW.

It would require a book to respond to the series in detail; what I have written is a partial response that gives representative samples of what seem to me to be patently unfair and weak scholarly and argumentative approaches to the question of the value of the TLM.

AGE OF THE TLM

Factual errors in the articles undermine confidence in how much CHW know about the TLM. For instance, they claim that the TLM is just "400 years old" and that the Tridentine Mass was a "reform" of the liturgy. All sound scholarship indicates, however, that the TLM goes back to

---

6   Among others, see Peter Kwasniewski, "A More Realistic Appraisal of the Liturgical Movement and Its Destructive Descent," *One Peter Five*, September 21, 2022 (see chapter 7 below); Joseph Shaw, "A Reply to Cavadini, Healy & Weinandy," *Rorate Caeli*, November 25, 2022 (see chapter 18); Sam Keyes, "The Failures of Reform: A Response to Cavadini, Healy, and Weinandy," *Covenant*, December 13, 2022 (see chapter 14); Dom Alcuin Reid, "The One Thread by Which the Council Hangs: A Response to Cavadini, Healy, and Weinandy," *One Peter Five*, January 19, 2023 (see chapter 17).

the early stages of the Western Church and was found in its essential Latin form 1,500 years ago (if not before)—not four hundred years ago. Joseph Cardinal Ratzinger made this point emphatically:

> There is no such thing as a Tridentine liturgy, and until 1965 the phrase would have meant nothing to anyone. The Council of Trent did not "make" a liturgy. Strictly speaking, there is no such thing, either, as the Missal of Pius V. The Missal which appeared in 1570 by order of Pius V differed only in tiny details from the first printed edition of the Roman Missal of about a hundred years earlier. Basically the reform of Pius V was only concerned with eliminating certain late medieval accretions and the various mistakes and misprints which had crept in. Thus, again, it prescribed the Missal of the City of Rome, which had remained largely free of these blemishes, for the whole Church.[7]

The Mass of the sixth century resembled the TLM much more than the NO resembles the TLM—just as the other ancient liturgies of the Church, such as the Byzantine liturgy, resemble the TLM more than they do the NO in regard to a host of characteristics.[8]

Again, Pope Pius V in 1570 did not introduce a "new" or "reformed" liturgy but codified a form of the liturgy that was already in place, his missal being nearly identical to the one published a century earlier in 1474, and this, in turn, very like the missal of Innocent III from the early thirteenth century. Changes made were largely in accord with the wishes of those in remoter areas of the Church who wanted to have their liturgies be in conformity with prestigious ancient Rome.

There is absolutely no similarity between the codification of what was already in place well before 1570 and the introduction of a "new rite" in 1969. Moreover, Pius V permitted

---

[7] Joseph Cardinal Ratzinger, *The Feast of Faith: Approaches to a Theology of the Liturgy* (San Francisco: Ignatius Press, 1986), 85.

[8] See "Byzantine, Tridentine, Montinian: Two Brothers and a Stranger," in Peter Kwasniewski, *The Once and Future Roman Rite: Returning to the Traditional Latin Liturgy after Seventy Years of Exile* (Gastonia, NC: TAN Books, 2022), 279–311.

the continued saying of any rite or use of Mass that had been said for at least 200 years, whereas Pope Paul VI wanted the TLM completely suppressed (although he made a few exceptions for elderly priests and for Agatha Christie and friends in England!).[9]

LATIN AS VERNACULAR

Another factual misconception that CHW perpetuate is the oft-refuted claim about the reason that the traditional liturgy of the Church was conducted in Latin; they say:

> Earlier, the Mass came to be celebrated in Latin in the western Church not because it was a sacred language but because it was the vernacular of its day; likewise, earlier still, with Greek. Jesus himself employed Aramaic, the vernacular of his time and place. If he had not, the apostles would have had no clue as to what he was doing at the Last Supper, nor could they then have actively participated in that first Eucharistic liturgy. The same holds true for the faithful today.

But Latin was not "the vernacular" in all places when it was chosen. It was the official, bureaucratic language of the Roman empire, an empire that included many peoples whose native language was not Latin; it was not the "vernacular" for them. Moreover, scholarship has shown that the Latin of the liturgy was a highly refined or "cultic" version of language, not the language "of the people"; it was, in fact, chosen because it already had features of a sacral or hieratic language and was utilized in part for that reason.[10]

The reference to the Last Supper is a red herring, for two reasons: first, Jesus would have celebrated much of the Passover in the (by then sacral) language of Hebrew, which was *not* the common language of his day and place;

---

9 K. V. Turley, "The Mystery of the 'Agatha Christie Indult,'" *National Catholic Register*, November 5, 2021.
10 For an explanation of Latin as a sacred language, see Christine Mohrmann, *Liturgical Latin: Its Origins and Character* (Washington, DC: Catholic University of America Press, 1957); Peter Kwasniewski, "Why Latin Is the Right Language for Roman Catholic Worship," *Rorate Caeli*, June 4, 2022. See also chapter 10 below.

and second, we still have a "clue" what is going on at the liturgy even when we don't understand the language. I have been to Melkite liturgies and others where I understand nothing of what is being sung, but I know precisely the kind of event in which I am participating—and participating actively because I am conscious of what the event is and the response it demands of me in faith, adoration, and love.

THE LITURGICAL MOVEMENT AND BOUYER

CHW attempt to tie the NO to the Liturgical Movement that preceded it, as though the NO were the logical and perhaps inevitable development of that movement and were embraced by Vatican II. What CHW fail to mention is how unwelcome some of the proposals of the Liturgical Movement were to the authorities in the Church. Indeed, the primary aspects of the Liturgical Movement that made their way into *Sacrosanctum Concilium*, the constitution on which the Fathers of Vatican II voted, were the call for some use of the vernacular in the Mass and a call for more active participation on the part of the laity.

CHW quite selectively report on the Liturgical Movement and particularly on some of the views of the individuals cited. For example, they cite the work of Fr. Louis Bouyer, who wrote on the history of liturgical movements and reported that at different periods in Church history, reform of the liturgy was needed, but a reform that generally involved removing inappropriate accretions.[11]

While CHW acknowledge that Bouyer "was not entirely happy, during and especially after the Council, for he anticipated and after observed the subsequent liturgical aberrations, both theological and pastoral," that demurral is a serious misrepresentation of Bouyer's sharply expressed disgust with how the NO was *composed* and with the NO itself. There are few individuals who have written more acerbically about Vatican II and the NO, both ventures in which he was closely involved. He is famous for this claim:

---

[11] Louis Bouyer, *Liturgical Piety* (Providence, RI: Cluny Media, 2021).

You'll have some idea of the deplorable conditions in which this hasty reform was expedited when I recount how the second Eucharistic prayer was cobbled together. Between the indiscriminately archeologizing fanatics who wanted to banish the *Sanctus* and the intercessions from the Eucharistic prayer by taking Hippolytus's Eucharist as is, and those others who couldn't have cared less about his alleged *Apostolic Tradition* and wanted a slapdash Mass, Dom Botte and I were commissioned to patch up its text with a view to inserting these elements, which are certainly quite ancient—by the next morning!.... I cannot read that improbable composition without recalling the Trastevere café terrace where we had to put the finishing touches to our assignment in order to show up with it at the Bronze Gate by the time our masters had set.

I prefer to say nothing, or little, about the new calendar, the handiwork of a trio of maniacs who suppressed, with no good reason, Septuagesima and the Octave of Pentecost and who scattered three quarters of the Saints higgledy-piggledy, all based on notions of their own devising! Because these three hotheads obstinately refused to change anything in their work and because the pope wanted to finish up quickly to avoid letting the chaos get out of hand, their project, however insane, was accepted.[12]

A theologian who writes such words in his memoirs can hardly be included in a list of enthusiasts for the NO! The sort of criticisms we have quoted from Bouyer can easily be found in other theologians and bishops who were closely involved in the liturgical reform.[13] Expression of regrets about what happened and even of support for the return of the former rites are by no means rare in the literature, but no one would know that from CHW's series.

---

[12] Louis Bouyer, *The Memoirs of Louis Bouyer: From Youth and Conversion to Vatican II, the Liturgical Reform, and After*, trans. John Pepino (Brooklyn: Angelico Press, 2015), 221–23.

[13] See also chapters 6 and 7.

2

Misrepresentation of Mediator Dei, Sacrosanctum Concilium, *and Ratzinger/Pope Benedict XVI*

VERY MISLEADING IS CHW'S CLAIM THAT Pius XII's encyclical *Mediator Dei* (1947, *MD*) is "the highest magisterial endorsement of the liturgical renewal as found at that time." The fact is, it can hardly qualify as any kind of endorsement of the whole of the Liturgical Movement; rather, it approves only a few recommendations of the Liturgical Movement (basically, a greater participation in the responses, prayers, and hymns) but overall is a vibrant endorsement of the *existing* TLM, which had regularly incorporated organic and appropriate changes. There is certainly no call in *MD* for a *new rite* of Mass. Indeed, for the most part, *MD rejects* the very changes the NO makes.

Consider this early passage in *MD*:

> We observe with considerable anxiety and some misgiving, that elsewhere certain enthusiasts, over-eager in their search for novelty, are straying beyond the path of sound doctrine and prudence. Not seldom, in fact, they interlard their plans and hopes for a revival of the sacred liturgy with principles which compromise this holiest of causes in theory or practice, and sometimes even taint it with errors touching Catholic faith and ascetical doctrine.[1]

Indeed, CHW seriously misinterpret *MD* in respect to the meaning of the following passage:

> Ancient usage must not be esteemed more suitable and proper, either in its own right or in its significance for later times and new situations, on the simple ground that it carries the savor or aroma of antiquity. The more recent

---

1   *MD* 8.

liturgical rites likewise deserve reverence and respect. They too owe their inspiration to the Holy Spirit, who assists the Church in every age even to the consummation of the world. They are equally resources used by the majestic Spouse of Jesus Christ to promote and procure the sanctity of men.[2]

On this, CHW comment: "Pius XII thus acknowledges the need to venerate the ancient liturgies. Yet he insists that contemporary rites likewise deserve respect and reverence, for they too are inspired by the Holy Spirit and so freshly foster the sanctity of the faithful."

Pius XII's reference to "ancient liturgies," however, is *not* to the TLM, which had developed much in the Middle Ages and into the Baroque period, but rather to those who think we need to go back to the earliest days of the Church to discover true liturgy (a notable tendency of some in the Liturgical Movement). His reference to "more recent liturgical rites" is to the so-called "Tridentine" form of the TLM, against which some antiquarians objected. Contra CHW, he is not (prospectively) endorsing the novelties of the NO. As mentioned, he wrote against many of the key elements of the NO (see below). While *MD* is open to modifications in the liturgy, there is no hint that there is some "desperate" need for change. Rather it states:

> From time immemorial the ecclesiastical hierarchy has exercised this right in matters liturgical. It has organized and regulated divine worship, *enriching it constantly with new splendor and beauty*, to the glory of God and the spiritual profit of Christians. What is more, it has not been slow—keeping the substance of the Mass and sacraments carefully intact—to modify what it deemed not altogether fitting, and to add what appeared more likely to *increase the honor paid to Jesus Christ and the august Trinity*, and to instruct and stimulate the Christian people to greater advantage.[3]

Strikingly, several passages of *MD* speak *disapprovingly* of a whole host of practices, most of which are now a part of the NO:

---

2   *MD* 61.
3   *MD* 49, emphasis added.

Misrepresentation of Mediator Dei...

> *It has pained Us grievously to note, Venerable Brethren, that such innovations are actually being introduced,* not merely in minor details but in matters of *major importance* as well. We instance, in point of fact, those who *make use of the vernacular in the celebration of the august eucharistic sacrifice*; those who *transfer certain feast-days*—which have been appointed and established after mature deliberation—to other dates; those, finally, who *delete from the prayerbooks approved for public use the sacred texts of the Old Testament*, deeming them little suited and inopportune for modern times.⁴

And further:

> Thus, to cite some instances, one would be straying from the straight path *were he to wish the altar restored to its primitive table form*; were he to want *black excluded as a color* for the liturgical vestments; were he to forbid the use of sacred images and statues in churches; were he to order the crucifix so designed that the divine Redeemer's body shows no trace of His cruel sufferings; and lastly *were he to disdain and reject polyphonic music or singing in parts*, even where it conforms to regulations issued by the Holy See.⁵

A complaint CHW make against the TLM is that they think it does not sufficiently reflect the participation of the laity in the priesthood of Christ. Pius XII in *MD* makes it very clear that he thinks the TLM very adequately gives full recognition to this truth. While the priest, as an ordained minister, is the principal celebrant of the Eucharistic sacrifice, he does so in communion with and on behalf of the faithful, for "they participate, according to their condition, in the priesthood of Christ."⁶

Pius is "very pleased to learn that this teaching, thanks to a more intense study of the liturgy on the part of many, especially in recent years, *has been given full recognition*."⁷ This passage is cited by CHW in service of stating that Pius XII found a need for serious changes in the liturgy.

---

4   *MD* 59, emphasis added.
5   *MD* 62, emphasis added.
6   *MD* 88; see also 92.
7   *MD* 94.

On the contrary, *MD* praises the existing liturgical rites of the Church, lists positive developments that had already occurred, and speaks *against* changes that eventually do appear in the NO.

These remarks, taken together with many other statements of Pius XII on behalf of liturgical tradition (such as *Musicam Sacram*'s lavish praise of Gregorian chant), do not at all amount to a ringing endorsement of the "reform" of the Mass that CHW imagine they find in *MD*.

PIUS XII AND JOHN PAUL II ON ACTIVE PARTICIPATION

A major point raised in defense of the NO is that it requires more "active participation" on the part of the laity. The meaning of "active participation" has always been a matter of considerable controversy—there is a very respected line of interpretation that does not put the emphasis on exterior action or movement but which emphasizes complete internal concentration on the part of the worshippers whereby they internally unite themselves with Christ in His mysteries, above all in His redemptive sacrifice. *MD* describes active participation in this way:

> It is therefore desirable, Venerable Brethren, that all the faithful should be aware that to participate in the eucharistic sacrifice is their chief duty and supreme dignity, and that not in an inert and negligent fashion, giving way to distractions and daydreaming, but with such earnestness and concentration that they may be united as closely as possible with the High Priest, according to the Apostle, "Let this mind be in you which was also in Christ Jesus." And together with Him and through Him let them make their oblation, and in union with Him let them offer up themselves.[8]

As is clear from the adjacent paragraphs of *MD*, Pius XII finds nothing in the TLM that prohibits or discourages such active participation; rather, he is simply identifying the usual human frailties that impede active participation: a propensity to scattered thoughts, a sad lack of understanding about what is really happening on the altar, and an unworthiness to

---

8   MD 80.

receive. It is by no means clear that these frailties will be or could be absent from any liturgy, no matter how "reformed"; how many of us have experienced the "in one ear, out the other" effect of the bland NO liturgies we attend?

There is no doubt that *MD* promotes a liturgy that involves a greater active participation of the congregation, but no indication is given that anything *in the inherited liturgy* needs to be significantly modified to bring that about. Rather, it asks priests to instruct the laity in the deeper meaning of the Mass and to invite them to give the responses to prayers and to sing the chants and hymns.

Of considerable interest is an *ad limina* address Pope John Paul II gave in 1998 on the meaning of "active participation," which is cited selectively by CHW:

> Active participation certainly means that, in gesture, word, song and service, all the members of the community take part in an act of worship, which is anything but inert or passive. Yet active participation does not preclude the active passivity of silence, stillness and listening: indeed, it demands it. Worshippers are not passive, for instance, when listening to the readings or the homily, or following the prayers of the celebrant, and the chants and music of the liturgy. These are experiences of silence and stillness, but they are in their own way profoundly active. In a culture which neither favors nor fosters meditative quiet, the art of interior listening is learned only with difficulty. Here we see how the liturgy, though it must always be properly inculturated, must also be countercultural.[9]

Pope John Paul II clearly states that being silent and still, receptive to what the liturgy itself is presenting to us, is conducive to "active participation," since those being silent can more easily have a *consciousness* of the meaning of what is happening in the Mass—which is at the heart of "active participation." Testimonials published not only online but in major newspaper stories that followed *Traditionis*

---

9 Interestingly, among other omissions, CHW fail to mention the pope's assertion that the faithful attentively listening "are in their own way profoundly active." The full text may be found at www.vatican.va/content/john-paul-ii/en/speeches/1998/october/documents/hf_jp-ii_spe_19981009_ad-limina-usa-2.html.

Custodes verify that this is in fact the lived experience of TLM attendees.¹⁰

MISREPRESENTATION OF *SACROSANCTUM CONCILIUM*

We saw previously that CHW make use of Pius XII's *Mediator Dei* in a selective and misleading manner. Their treatment of Vatican II's *Sacrosanctum Concilium* likewise involves numerous misrepresentations. Insistence that the NO is what was called for by Vatican II has repeatedly been shown to be false.¹¹

Many Catholics are stunned to learn that *Sacrosanctum Concilium* (*SC*) did not call for a "new rite" and that much of what makes the NO distinctive was *not* called for by *SC*—elements that, as we saw above, were roundly rejected by Pius XII. Indeed, *SC* itself speaks of "preserving and fostering" all lawfully acknowledged rites:

> In faithful obedience to tradition, the sacred Council declares that holy Mother Church holds all lawfully acknowledged rites to be of equal right and dignity; that

---

10   For examples of testimonials, see "Teenager's TLM Testimony (Part 1)," *Unam Sanctam Catholicam*, November 23, 2022; "'O Beauty Ever Ancient Ever New!' Teenager's TLM Testimony (Part 2)," *Unam Sanctam Catholicam*, December 3, 2022; David Mills, "What I Saw When I Went to a Traditional Latin Mass," *National Catholic Register*, September 22, 2021; Jeremiah Bannister, "Atheists Find God at the Latin Mass: A Review of *Mass of the Ages*," *OnePeterFive*, August 19, 2021; "An Ex-Muslim's Impressions of the Traditional Mass," *Rorate Caeli*, September 2, 2022; Jim Graves, "Finding What Should Never Have Been Lost: Priests and the Extraordinary Form," *Catholic World Report*, August 19, 2014; *Ever Ancient, Ever New: Why Younger Generations Are Embracing Traditional Catholicism*, ed. David Dashiell (Gastonia, NC: TAN Books, 2022). Similar articles have appeared in the *Wall Street Journal*, the *New York Times*, and the *Washington Times*, among other major papers.

11   There is copious literature on this subject. See, for some examples, Robert W. Shaffern, "The Mass According to Vatican II," *The Catholic Thing*, July 10, 2022; Joseph Shaw, "Vatican II on Liturgical Preservation," *LMS Chairman*, January 17, 2017; Cardinal Alfons Maria Stickler, "Recollections of a Vatican II Peritus," *New Liturgical Movement*, June 29, 2022; Peter Kwasniewski, "Is Your Liturgy Like What Vatican II Intended?," *New Liturgical Movement*, December 4, 2013; Alcuin Reid, "The Liturgy, Fifty Years after Sacrosanctum Concilium," *Catholic World Report*, December 4, 2013; Alcuin Reid, "Does *Traditionis Custodes* Pass Liturgical History 101?," *Catholic World Report*, December 18, 2021; Peter Kwasniewski, "*Sacrosanctum Concilium*: The Ultimate Trojan Horse," *Crisis Magazine*, June 21, 2021.

she wishes to preserve them in the future and to foster them in every way. The Council also desires that, where necessary, the rites be revised carefully in the light of sound tradition, and that they be given new vigor to meet the circumstances and needs of modern times.¹²

SC does not call for a new liturgy; it speaks of reform (five times), but reform in the sense of "restoration" (seven times):

In order that the Christian people may more certainly derive an abundance of graces from the sacred liturgy, holy Mother Church desires to undertake with great care a general *restoration* of the liturgy itself. *For the liturgy is made up of immutable elements divinely instituted, and of elements subject to change*. These not only may but ought to be changed with the passage of time if they have suffered from the *intrusion of anything out of harmony* with the inner nature of the liturgy or have become unsuited to it. In this *restoration*, both texts and rites should be drawn up so that they express more clearly the holy things which they signify; the Christian people, so far as possible, should be enabled to understand them with ease and to take part in them fully, actively, and as befits a community.¹³

Astonishingly, CHW acknowledge that the Council Fathers *had no anticipation* that the TLM would be replaced—on this point they are very right. Yet this acknowledgment seems to undercut badly the claim that the NO is what *SC* wanted.

It is crucial to recognize that the Council Fathers *never thought in terms of rescinding the Tridentine Mass*, precisely because *it was that rite that they were revising and rejuvenating*. If they had suppressed the old rite, it would mean that they were creating an entirely new rite. They would then be employing *a hermeneutic of discontinuity*. Rather, they were engaging in a strong hermeneutic of continuity: *the old rite was to continue in a revised form*. Because of this hermeneutic of continuity, *they never considered the possibility of the unrevised rite continuing to be celebrated. Such an option would have never entered their minds*. For the Council, the revised Eucharistic liturgy would simply be the Roman rite of the Catholic Church.¹⁴

---

12   *SC* 4, emphasis added.
13   *SC* 21, emphasis added.
14   Emphasis added.

The claim of CHW here that "it never entered the minds" of Council Fathers that the unrevised rite would be used alongside the revised rite contradicts a mandate in *SC* that states explicitly that competent territorial authorities may decide "*whether and to what extent the vernacular liturgy is to be used.*"[15]

It is hard to maintain that the NO is what Vatican II called for when it never called for a new rite. Changes were to be made to the TLM, but the changes were to be relatively minor. Those familiar with the development of the TLM know that many changes have occurred through the ages, but the changes were organic and never radically altered the liturgy; for instance, prayers were added and removed (the number of prefaces has varied considerably). The NO, on the other hand, can hardly be described as a revision of the TLM; rather, it is manifestly discontinuous with the previous liturgy, as numerous studies have shown.[16]

No one denies that there are aspects characteristic of the NO that were called for by SC—most importantly, the call for increased participation of the faithful: "... the people should be encouraged to take part by means of acclamations, responses, psalmody, antiphons, and songs, as well as by actions, gestures, and bodily attitudes. And at the proper times all should observe a reverent silence."[17] But the fathers at Vatican II thought those changes could be accommodated in the TLM, with its existing content.

---

15   Emphasis added.
16   See, *inter alia*, Aidan Nichols, *Looking at the Liturgy: A Critical View of Its Contemporary Form* (San Francisco: Ignatius Press, 1996); László Dobszay, *The Restoration and Organic Development of the Roman Rite* (London/New York: T&T Clark, 2010); Anthony Cekada, *Work of Human Hands: A Theological Critique of the Mass of Paul VI* (West Chester, OH: Philothea Press, 2010); Lauren Pristas, *The Collects of the Roman Missals: A Comparative Study of the Sundays in Proper Seasons Before and After the Second Vatican Council* (London/New York: Bloomsbury T&T Clark, 2013); Matthew Hazell, *Index Lectionum: A Comparative Table of Readings for the Ordinary and Extraordinary Forms of the Roman Rite* (N.p.: Lectionary Study Aids, 2016); Michael Fiedrowicz, *The Traditional Mass: History, Form, and Theology of the Classical Roman Rite* (Brooklyn: Angelico Press, 2020); Peter Kwasniewski, *The Once and Future Roman Rite: Returning to the Traditional Latin Liturgy after Seventy Years of Exile* (Gastonia, NC: TAN Books, 2022). This partial list covers a period of twenty-eight years; CHW seem to be unaware of any of this relevant literature.
17   *SC* 30.

In fact, while an official "reform" of the TLM never happened, some of the reforms that were requested have spontaneously happened and others could be easily enough incorporated into the TLM. At most of the TLMs I attend, the congregation joins in many of the responses, sings the hymns, and usually the Gloria, the Creed, the Sanctus, the Agnus Dei, and the Asperges as well. Additional readings could be added to the missal for the unimpeded weekdays of Advent and Paschaltide.

(Oddly, in some of the NO Masses I attend, there is very little participation on the part of the congregation in the singing of the hymns, which I suspect is a product of the quality of the hymns and of the musicianship.)

The claim that the NO is a legitimate instantiation of the reforms called for by Vatican II in *SC* will not fool those who have compared the list of changes made in the NO with the TLM: the NO fails to include elements called for in *SC*, and has many elements never dreamed of by the fathers of Vatican II. For example, *SC* required that when Mass was partly offered in the vernacular, Latin would still be retained, and that Gregorian chant would be the norm as well as polyphony.

Elements that appear in the NO that were *not* called for in *SC*:

1. Communion received while standing and in the hand
2. Mass offered *versus populum*
3. No communion rail
4. Lay readers (including children) and lay ministers of Holy Communion
5. Secularization of vessels, vestments, architecture, and music
6. Disappearance of Latin
7. Disappearance of Gregorian chant and polyphony
8. Significantly changed Mass Propers
9. New calendar
10. The omission of biblical texts believed to be offensive to moderns

Not only were many of these changes not called for by *SC*, many do not even appear in the sacramentary for the NO. For instance, no official mandate was given for the priest to say the Mass *versus populum*, for the removal of the communion rail, or for reception of the Eucharist in the hand. It seems the NO brings with it a spirit of novelty that invites even unmandated changes.

The fact is that a "reform" of the TLM never happened. Instead, there was a chaotic period of time in the mid-sixties when a vernacular version of the old missal, essentially the word-by-word translation that was in the bilingual missals, appeared virtually overnight. Other changes were made in the years to follow, such as eliminating the prayers at the altar and the final gospel. And in 1969, with little to no warning, a new rite was imposed upon the faithful and the TLM was nearly completely suppressed.

I occasionally ask attendees of the NO what they would do if the NO were suppressed overnight and the only liturgy made available to them were a radically different replacement, such as the TLM; would they readily accept that? The response I get is usually a stunned silence: they tend to think it is not possible.

But a brutal change like that happened in 1969. Millions left the Church since they believed not just a new rite but a new religion (in a way) had been imposed upon them. Paul VI's description of what happened as representing a "new epoch" in the Church (address of November 19, 1969) as well as calls by theologians for changes in doctrine suggests their impressions were not completely unfounded.

We know that laity, priests, and religious were already leaving the Church or their states in life before 1969, but the instability the Church was experiencing was not in any way steadied or reversed and, in fact, seems to have been exacerbated by major liturgical changes. Those who left often remarked poignantly that "The Church left me; I didn't leave the Church."

RATZINGER/POPE BENEDICT XVI ON THE LITURGY

CHW also attempt to enlist Joseph Ratzinger/Pope Benedict XVI as an ally in their attempt to promote the NO. But the evidence is overwhelming that he favored the TLM. He certainly

Misrepresentation of Mediator Dei...

did not believe that the guidance of the Holy Spirit was lacking in the composition of the TLM, and he never indicates that the TLM is theologically flawed; in fact, there is considerable evidence that he considered the TLM to be a superior liturgy.

He was greatly disturbed by the "man-made" origin of the NO and repeatedly over time expressed that it was wrong to suppress the TLM.[18] Indeed, he expressed the desire that the TLM be offered wherever laity expressed a desire for it. He spoke of the TLM as a "juridical right," not a privilege.[19]

It is shocking that CHW never mention the extraordinary book *The Spirit of the Liturgy*, written in 1999 when he was Cardinal Joseph Ratzinger, let alone use the principles he identifies there as those that should guide our worship.[20] Their series would be very different had the authors employed the principles of that text. For instance, he speaks very strongly against the priest praying *versus populum*:

> After the Council (which says nothing about "turning toward the people") new altars were set up everywhere, and today celebration *versus populum* really does look like the characteristic fruit of Vatican II's liturgical renewal. In fact it is the most conspicuous consequence of a reordering that not only signifies a new external arrangement of the places dedicated to the liturgy, but also brings with it a new idea of the *essence* of the liturgy—the liturgy as a communal meal.[21]

Ratzinger laments the results of this change:

> In reality what happened was that an unprecedented clericalization came on the scene. Now the priest—the "presider," as they now prefer to call him—becomes the real point of reference for the whole liturgy. Everything depends on him. We have to see him, to respond to him, to be involved in what he is doing. His creativity sustains

---

18   For an extensive collection of statements by Ratzinger on the TLM and the NO, see Peter Kwasniewski, "Best Quotes on the Liturgy by Joseph Ratzinger/Benedict XVI," *New Liturgical Movement*, Tuesday, January 2, 2023.
19   Shawn Tribe, "Full text of Cardinal Castrillon Hoyos address to the Latin Mass Society," *New Liturgical Movement*, June 16, 2008.
20   Cardinal Joseph Ratzinger, *The Spirit of the Liturgy*, trans. John Saward (San Francisco: Ignatius Press, 2014).
21   Ratzinger, *Spirit of the Liturgy*, 77, emphasis added.

the whole thing. Not surprisingly, people try to reduce this newly created role by assigning all kinds of liturgical functions to different individuals and entrusting the "creative" planning of the liturgy to groups of people who like to, and are supposed to, "make their own contribution." Less and less is God in the picture. More and more important is what is done by the human beings who meet here and do not like to subject themselves to a "predetermined pattern." The turning of the priest toward the people has turned the community into a self-enclosed circle. In its outward form, it no longer opens out on what lies ahead and above, but is closed in on itself.[22]

This is what Ratzinger says about having the altar, priest, and congregation oriented toward the east:

> A common turning to the east during the Eucharistic Prayer remains essential. This is not a case of something accidental, but of what is essential. Looking at the priest has no importance. What matters is looking together at the Lord. It is not now a question of dialogue but of common worship, of setting off toward the One who is to come. What corresponds with the reality of what is happening is not the closed circle but the common movement forward, expressed in a common direction for prayer.[23]

Although CHW mention the permissibility of the priest facing eastward in the NO, they fail to take seriously arguments in its favor, such as Ratzinger's. This is a serious omission since the orientation of the priest is one of the most distinctive differences between the TLM and the NO (indeed, the latter's own rubrics, almost universally ignored, are favorable to the *ad orientem* orientation).[24] Clearly Ratzinger thought it an issue of the greatest importance—indeed he spoke of it as affecting the "essence" of the Mass.

CHW speak of Benedict as "generously accommodat[ing]" the TLM and characterize the movement that welcomed the

---

22 Ratzinger, *Spirit of the Liturgy*, 79–80. It should be noted that Ratzinger quotes Bouyer at this point as one who adamantly supports *ad orientem* on the basis of all known records and for theological reasons.
23 Ratzinger, *Spirit of the Liturgy*, 81, emphasis added.
24 See Peter Kwasniewski, "The Normativity of *Ad Orientem* Worship According to the Ordinary Form's Rubrics," *New Liturgical Movement*, November 23, 2015.

renewed availability of the TLM as "exploiting Pope Benedict's benevolence for its own agenda of proselytizing others to their liturgical cause," claiming that "the more radical elements in the movement have, unfortunately, undercut Benedict's wish that there be no division in the Church."

It is a serious distortion of the text and tone of *Summorum Pontificum* to speak of it as an "accommodation." Rather, Benedict is clearly restoring a liturgy that he maintains should never have been denied the faithful who find in it—as he says "young persons" do—"an encounter with the Mystery of the Most Holy Eucharist particularly suited to them."[25]

Indeed, he says that "what earlier generations held as sacred, remains sacred and great for us too, and it cannot be all of a sudden entirely forbidden or even considered harmful."[26] Certainly he hoped there would be no division between devotees of the two forms of worship, but it is not at all clear he would hold the devotees of the TLM as responsible for whatever divisions have come to exist. Language used by CHW such as "exploiting Pope Benedict's benevolence for its own agenda of proselytizing others to their liturgical cause" certainly does more to foment division than to overcome tensions, and, additionally, misrepresents Benedict's negative assessment of the NO.

Anyone familiar with *The Spirit of the Liturgy* would never characterize Benedict as an opponent of the TLM or an enthusiast for the NO as it was developed and implemented. What he said about the TLM and the NO made it likely that he would have been very unhappy with *Traditionis Custodes*, and we have some strong evidence that he was: after Pope Benedict's death, Archbishop Gänswein, the pope's assistant for decades, stated, "I believe it broke Pope Benedict's heart to read [*Traditionis Custodes*]..."[27]

---

25 Benedict XVI, *Con Grande Fiducia* (letter to the bishops of the world, accompanying *Summorum Pontificum*).
26 Ibid.
27 See the relevant passage from Archbishop Gänswein's book, translated and posted at *Rorate Caeli* on January 10, 2023. For the video clip see "Document restricting the Latin Mass 'broke Pope Benedict's heart' says Archbishop Gänswein," *Corpus Christi Watershed*, January 3, 2023.

3

The Genesis of the Novus Ordo and "Theological and Spiritual Flaws" of the TLM

CHW FAIL ALTOGETHER TO ADDRESS THE circumstances in which the NO was composed, who composed it, and how it was promulgated. It is a very disturbing story. I wonder if they have read Yves Chiron's meticulous biography *Annibale Bugnini: Reformer of the Liturgy*,[1] which well documents Bugnini's deviousness as secretary of the reforming body called the *Consilium*. Chiron is cautious about accepting the claim that Bugnini was a Freemason, but for CHW not to acknowledge or address that elephant in the room as well as the substantiated claims that Bugnini operated by lying both to Paul VI and to the authors of the NO, and that there was an explicit intent to downplay Catholic elements in the liturgy for the sake of ecumenism with Protestants,[2] is to sidestep grave concerns about the actual origins of the NO.

A shortened version of Chiron's reporting on Bugnini's role has been published in the Notre Dame *Church Life Journal*.[3] Chiron shows that many members of the Commission were opposed to or very reluctant to accept the changes made. Chiron demonstrates that Bugnini manipulated Paul VI, a pope known for his habit of ambivalence, which likely made it easy for him to be manipulated.

This habit was amply shown in speeches Paul VI made in the years and months previous to the imposition of the

---

[1] Yves Chiron, *Annibale Bugnini: Reformer of the Liturgy*, trans. John Pepino (Brooklyn: Angelico Press, 2018).
[2] See Kwasniewski, *Once and Future Roman Rite*, 208–15.
[3] See Chiron, *Bugnini*, 127–51, the better part of which was published online as "How the Novus Ordo Mass Was Made," *Church Life Journal*, July 22, 2021.

The Genesis of the NO and the "Flaws" of the TLM

NO. Writing in 1966 (after *SC* had been approved and before the NO was finalized) in a letter to religious orders that were being pressured to pray in the vernacular, Paul VI makes a strong case for the importance of Latin; what he says about Latin could be easily applied to the liturgy as a whole:

> What is in question here is not only the retention within the choral office of the Latin language, though it is of course right that this should be eagerly guarded and should certainly not be lightly esteemed. For this language is, within the Latin Church, an abundant wellspring of Christian civilization and a very rich treasure-trove of devotion. But it is also the seemliness, the beauty and the native strength of these prayers and canticles which is at stake: the choral office itself, "the lovely voice of the Church in song" (Cf. St Augustine's *Confessions*, Bk 9, 6). Your founders and teachers, the holy ones who are as it were so many lights within your religious families, have transmitted this to you. The traditions of the elders, your glory throughout long ages, must not be belittled. Indeed, your manner of celebrating the choral office has been one of the chief reasons why these families of yours have lasted so long, and happily increased. It is thus most surprising that under the influence of a sudden agitation, some now think that it should be given up.
>
> In present conditions, what words or melodies could replace the forms of Catholic devotion which you have used until now? You should reflect and carefully consider whether things would not be worse, should this fine inheritance be discarded. It is to be feared that the choral office would turn into a mere bland recitation, suffering from poverty and begetting weariness, as you yourselves would perhaps be the first to experience. One can also wonder whether men would come in such numbers to your churches in quest of the sacred prayer, if its ancient and native tongue, joined to a chant full of grave beauty, resounded no more within your walls. We therefore ask all those to whom it pertains, to ponder what they wish to give up, and not to let that spring run dry from which, until the present, they have themselves drunk deep.[4]

Indeed, Paul VI *forbids* use of the vernacular by the religious:

---

4 Apostolic Letter *Sacrificium Laudis*, August 15, 1966; text at www.ccwatershed.org/2013/08/05/paul-vi-disturbed-and-saddened-purge-latin/.

> In any case, beloved Sons, the requests mentioned above concern such grave matters that We are unable to grant them, or to derogate now from the norms of the Council and of the Instructions noted above. Therefore we earnestly beseech you that you would consider this complex question under all its aspects. From the good will which we have toward you, and from the good opinion which we have of you, We are unwilling to allow that which could make your situation worse, and which could well bring you no slight loss, and which would certainly bring a sickness and sadness upon the whole Church of God. Allow Us to protect your interests, even against your own will. It is the same Church which has introduced the vernacular into the sacred liturgy for pastoral reasons, that is, for the sake of people who do not know Latin, which gives you the mandate of preserving the age-old solemnity, beauty, and dignity of the choral office, in regard both to language and to the chant.[5]

Tragically, this letter, *Sacrificium Laudis*, was scuttled by the direct intervention of Rembert Weakland in Rome, as the latter details in his memoirs.[6]

In several talks and audiences delivered upon the implementation of the NO, Paul VI is emphatic about the need to accept the NO but speaks of the TLM with extremely strong affection. In a general audience on November 26, 1969, he stated:

> A new rite of the Mass: a change in a venerable tradition that has gone on for centuries. This is something that affects our hereditary religious patrimony, which seemed to enjoy the privilege of being untouchable and settled. It seemed to bring the prayer of our forefathers and our saints to our lips and to give us the comfort of feeling faithful to our spiritual past, which we kept alive to pass it on to the generations ahead.
>   It is at such a moment as this that we get a better understanding of the value of historical tradition and the communion of the saints. This change will affect the

---

5 Ibid.
6 See Rembert Weakland, *A Pilgrim in a Pilgrim Church: Memoirs of a Catholic Archbishop* (Grand Rapids, MI: William B. Eerdmans, 2009), 121–23, 130–31. See John Byron Kuhner, "Rembert Weakland, Proud Vandal," *First Things* online, August 26, 2022.

ceremonies of the Mass. We shall become aware, perhaps with some feeling of annoyance, that the ceremonies at the altar are no longer being carried out with the same words and gestures to which we were accustomed—perhaps so much accustomed that we no longer took any notice of them. This change also touches the faithful. It is intended to interest each one of those present, to draw them out of their customary personal devotions or their usual torpor.

We must prepare for this many-sided inconvenience. It is the kind of upset caused by every novelty that breaks in on our habits. We shall notice that pious persons are disturbed most, because they have their own respectable way of hearing Mass, and they will feel shaken out of their usual thoughts and obliged to follow those of others. Even priests may feel some annoyance in this respect.[7]

He speaks almost with a broken heart of the loss of Latin as the principal language of the Mass:

It is here that the greatest newness is going to be noticed, the newness of language. No longer Latin, but the spoken language will be the principal language of the Mass. The introduction of the vernacular will certainly be a great sacrifice for those who know the beauty, the power and the expressive sacrality of Latin. We are parting with the speech of the Christian centuries; we are becoming like profane intruders in the literary preserve of sacred utterance. We will lose a great part of that stupendous and incomparable artistic and spiritual thing, the Gregorian chant.

We have reason indeed for regret, reason almost for bewilderment. What can we put in the place of that language of the angels? We are giving up something of priceless worth. But why? What is more precious than these loftiest of our Church's values?

The answer will seem banal, prosaic. Yet it is a good answer, because it is human, because it is apostolic.[8]

Paul VI seems to be trying to persuade himself even more than others that Latin can be dispensed with, and that the

---

7 Pope Paul VI, *Changes in Mass for Greater Apostolate*, November 26, 1969; full text published in Kwasniewski, *Once and Future Roman Rite*, 387–91; commentary in ibid., 128–38.
8 Ibid.

NO is truly a good thing. He chose the drastic measure of abandoning Latin, the beautiful prayers of the TLM, and Gregorian chant as a means to awaken the congregation out of their "usual torpor." The not at all drastic solution of *Mediator Dei* to the problem of daydreaming and distraction should have been promoted instead: the solution of ensuring that the priests and faithful had a deep understanding of the Mass.

Some take the overwhelming positive vote for *SC* (2,147 in favor, 4 against) to have been a vote for the NO. What few know is that an introduction of the NO (in the form of a so-called *Missa Normativa*) to cardinals and bishops at a Synod in Rome in 1967 did *not* get the votes needed for approval. As Chiron reports:

> There were 187 voters; the two-thirds majority was therefore 124. For some of the votes, the tally was far from it, with the *non placet* (nays) and *placet juxta modum* (approval on condition of modifications) having a broad margin.... More spectacular yet was the refusal to give unreserved approval to the general structure of the normative Mass: 71 *placet*; 43 *non placet*; 62 *placet juxta modum*; 4 abstentions.[9]

That is not surprising, of course, given that those who voted for *SC* had no reason to believe that radical changes, such as those in the NO, would be made.[10] It is also not surprising that that was the last vote ever taken in regard to the NO.

It should be noted that not only did Paul VI introduce a new Eucharistic liturgy for the Roman rite, he changed the rites for all of the other sacraments as well. As a reviewer of Yves Chiron's biography of Pope Paul VI observes:

> Paul changed the formula of consecration during the Mass, as well as the rites of baptism, marriage, confession, extreme unction (anointing of the sick), and burial. He entirely restructured ordination, banishing the seven-step structure Holy Orders had once known. To the governing apparatus of the Church, Paul gave the definitive power

---

9 Chiron, *Bugnini*, 131.
10 See, for one example of many, the recollections of a Vatican II peritus, Cardinal Alfons Maria Stickler, who was a member of the conciliar liturgy committee: "Recollections of a Vatican II Peritus," *New Liturgical Movement*, June 29, 2022.

structure it enjoys today. Very nearly every religious community in the Church altered its formation, daily life, habit, governance, bylaws, and prayer life in response to Paul's demands for change. Church thinking changed as well, with wave after wave of innovative theological ideas ushered in by Paul. In almost every respect, Church life can be described dualistically: either Prepaulian or Postpaulian.[11]

Let us note again, the post-Vatical II reform ushered in not a "tweaked" or "reformed" liturgy but a wholesale rewriting of the sacramental rites of the Church.

THEOLOGICAL FLAWS

CHW make several very dubious claims about the differences between the TLM and the NO. One is the claim—asserted but not substantiated—that the personal and liturgical prayer of those who attended the TLM before the Council "primarily consisted of praying to the one (generic) God" whereas only with the NO did the faithful become "more cognizant" of the possibility of personal and liturgical trinitarian prayer. It seems impossible for anyone to make that claim who has done even a superficial comparison between the TLM and the NO. Dr. Peter Kwasniewski, who has a most impressive intimate knowledge of the TLM and the NO both from his study and from decades of experience of each, has shown (not just asserted) that the NO systematically *removed* Trinitarian and Christological confessions.[12] This, for example, is his list of the diminution of reference to the Blessed Trinity in the NO:

1. *Both* the prayer of offering to the Trinity ("*Suscipe, Sancta Trinitas*") *and* the prayer of homage to the Trinity ("*Placeat tibi, Sancta Trinitas*") were abolished.
2. The Preface of the Most Holy Trinity, required to be said or sung between 24 and 32 Sundays a year

---

[11] John Byron Kuhner, "Paul VI: Refounder of Catholicism," *One Peter Five*, January 26, 2023, a review of Yves Chiron, *Paul VI: The Divided Pope*, trans. James Walther (Brooklyn: Angelico Press, 2022).
[12] See chapter 9.

in the TLM, is heard extremely rarely in Novus Ordo liturgies; according to the rubrics it is required only for Trinity Sunday itself.[13] As a result, most Catholics will not be formed in any sustained way by the rich dogmatic teaching of this Preface, which demands to be heard many times before one can begin to grasp what it is saying.

3. The recitation of the *Gloria*, a Trinitarian hymn, has been severely curtailed to Sundays and major feast days.
4. All iterations of the *"Gloria Patri"* have been abolished from the Mass.
5. The use of the sign of the cross, very frequent in the TLM, has been reduced to the start of the liturgy and its conclusion.
6. In like manner, the use of the sign of the cross in priestly blessings of objects involved in the liturgy has dwindled to almost nothing.

MOVEMENT OF THE HOLY SPIRIT

There are several places in the series where CHW do not merely imply, but state outright, that the way the Catholic Church worshiped for many centuries, even millennia, was somehow theologically or spiritually flawed. They assert, for example, that the faithful were less adequately able to "enact...their indelible baptismal character"; that, in the absence of the vernacular language, the "participation of the faithful...would have been impossible"; that a "rich banquet of God's word" was unavailable and that, implicitly, the old liturgy made it "incidental"; that celebration *ad orientem* was less "congruent with the reality of the liturgy as an action of Christ and of his Body"; that a return to the traditional form of the liturgy would be *"doctrinally* unacceptable," which on the face of it asserts a doctrinal rupture or contradiction between the old and new *leges orandi;* that

---

13   This Preface must be used on all Sundays after Pentecost, which vary in number from 24 to 28. It is also assigned for the four Sundays of Advent, but the proper Preface of Advent may be used instead.

the old rite "*systematically* positioned the faithful as silent spectators" and therefore disengaged from the act of worship; that the old rite possesses a "more limited and less adequate ecclesiology" and "*undermines* the doctrine that the ordained priesthood is ordered to the service of the baptismal priesthood of the faithful"; indeed, they maintain that "to return to the Tridentine Mass is...to lose or obscure a *foundational dimension* of the Church and her worship" (emphases added).

These are very grave charges to make against the Holy Church of God and against the Holy Spirit that guides her.[14] It is one thing to argue that perhaps there may be several good ways to conduct divine worship, e.g., in various Eastern and Western rites, and that they may differ from one another in legitimate points of emphasis. It is even possible to argue that some things need to be emphasized more in this or that period of time, or among this or that group of the faithful.

By no means, however, can it be maintained that there is something *wrong* with the Church's long-approved traditional manner of worship. To assert this is to fall into a serious ecclesiological error. Is it really possible that so many popes received and handed down a form of worship that was objectively misleading or malforming? It is far more likely that a wholesale departure from constant tradition would be damaging to the Church.

Whatever happened to "the Spirit's enduring infallible guidance" (to use CHW's own phrase) in respect to the TLM? Did not the Holy Spirit accompany the Church in its composition of the TLM over the centuries? Was the TLM so flawed that it needed to be jettisoned altogether? Certainly, the Church has needed reform in many of its elements over

---

14 In fact, Pius VI's *Auctorem Fidei*, to which proponents of the Novus Ordo sometimes appeal as evidence that the Church can never promulgate a defective ritual, establishes a truth quite different than such proponents themselves hold—namely, the rightness of the Church's traditional way of doing things, to which the Synod of Pistoia, and later the twentieth-century liturgical reformers, were opposed. See "Does Pius VI's *Auctorem Fidei* Support Paul VI's Novus Ordo?," in Peter Kwasniewski, *The Road from Hyperpapalism to Catholicism*, vol. 1: *Theological Reflections on the Rock of the Church* (Waterloo, ON: Arouca Press, 2022), 84–90.

the ages, but clearly Vatican II did not intend a replacement of the TLM with the NO. So, did the Holy Spirit misguide the authors of *Sacrosanctum Concilium*? Is it not possible that the authors of the NO imposed their own views on the liturgy and were not faithful to the guidance of the Holy Spirit? Why did the Holy Spirit permit such a mess in respect to liturgy and doctrine after Vatican II?

Alexander Battista's thoughtful response to the CHW series[15] does not deny that the NO is the work of the Holy Spirit, but he expresses disbelief that CHW can suggest that the Holy Spirit could allow a "less adequate ecclesiology," as they put it, and "a rite [which] undermines the doctrine that the ordained priesthood is ordered to the service of the baptismal priesthood of the faithful," to develop and be utilized *for over a millennium*. To hold such an opinion of the supposed deleterious effects of the TLM upon the faithful is in direct contradiction of the orthodox teaching of Pope Pius XII. As we have seen before, in his 1947 encyclical *Mediator Dei*, the Holy Father states the following:

> The more recent liturgical rites [e.g., the Tridentine Rite as compared with the ancient rites prized by the antiquarians about whom Pius XII is speaking here] likewise deserve reverence and respect. *They, too, owe their inspiration to the Holy Spirit, who assists the Church in every age* even to the consummation of the world. They are equally the resources used by the majestic Spouse of Jesus Christ to promote and procure the sanctity of man.[16]

Battista also finds the position of CHW to be an insult to Eastern Catholic liturgies, which share so many fundamental features of the TLM—the very features CHW disparage—such as use of a sacred language, a one-year cycle of biblical readings, worship *ad orientem*, and the prominence of the priest in the liturgy, to the exclusion of lay ministries. Moreover, the confection of the Eucharist in some rites takes

---

15 Alexander Battista, *"Church Life Journal* Insults Eastern Liturgies with Amateur Scholarship," *OnePeterFive*, November 19, 2022 (see chapter 13 below).
16 *MD* 61, emphasis added.

place in a sanctuary altogether closed off from the laity's view (and, *a fortiori*, from their entrance into it). Again, do CHW want these liturgies abolished also? If not, why not?

Although CHW readily and rightfully acknowledge that the experience of the NO has been chaotic and, in fact, full of abuses, there is the sense throughout the articles that the NO is a product of the movement of the Holy Spirit and that the demise of the TLM is something that the Holy Spirit desires. Indeed, CHW makes this claim:

> The liturgical movement thus needs to be acknowledged as an authentic work of the Spirit for the benefit of Christ's Church. It was not free from weaknesses and errors, as Pius XII acknowledged, yet it cannot be denied that the Holy Spirit was guiding sinful and fallible people—the only kind he had to work with—to undertake this renewal that was desperately needed for the good of the Catholic faithful.

I find nothing in the article that warrants such a high estimation of the Liturgical Movement or that demonstrates that the renewal was "desperately needed for the good of the Catholic faithful."

When CHW state: "The Church's tradition, of which the liturgy is a constitutive element, is not frozen in time but is a living tradition that develops with the help of the Holy Spirit, in fidelity to the deposit of faith," they imply that the TLM has been frozen in time. That is a completely insupportable claim. As we saw above, *Mediator Dei* presents a long list of changes that have been made to the TLM over the ages, and it is still undergoing changes; after all, very recently, new prefaces have been added as well as rules governing the honoring of saints more recently canonized.[17]

Indeed, the resurgence of interest in the TLM might rightly be seen as a movement of the Spirit and a kind of "new Pentecost." The grassroots enthusiastic explosion of the TLM is a sign that both the *sensus fidelium* and the Holy Spirit want this liturgy to continue. Many of us do expect that the TLM will still be celebrated to the end of history (which

---

17 See Peter Kwasniewski, "Vatican Issues Two Decrees: More Prefaces and Recent Saints in the TLM," *OnePeterFive*, March 25, 2020.

CHW believe is absurd)—just as we expect Catholics forever to love the beautiful music, art, and architecture that grew up alongside it, all of which were and are and will always be an irreplaceable expression of the timeless Catholic Faith.

As a matter of fact, in recent years some of the features that had been most associated with the NO are disappearing from that Mass and are being replaced by practices inherited from the TLM, such as the priest praying *ad orientem*, the use of incense and chant, communion rails, and the reception of communion on the tongue. The reappearance of these elements has begun to restore a sense of reverence for the Mass and the Eucharist.[18]

Whereas CHW do not mention this phenomenon, some clergy have discovered that parishioners who have never experienced the reverence of the TLM welcome the incorporation of elements from the TLM into the NO. Indeed, they sometimes discover that parishioners, when exposed to the TLM, come to prefer it. I know one priest who during Covid celebrated the TLM as his private Mass. He left the church open and parishioners started coming—at first just a few and then dozens who, after the Covid restrictions were lifted, asked that the parish provide the TLM.

---

[18] See Peter Kwasniewski, "Why Restricting the TLM Harms Every Parish Mass," *Crisis Magazine*, August 13, 2021.

4

Unity, Charismatic Masses, and Africa

THE VIEW THAT ABROGATION OF THE TLM and exclusive adoption of the NO is the path to unity is prima facie a claim hard to defend. The fact is that the NO by its very nature works against unity in that all language groups have their own vernacular liturgy—whereas having Latin be the universal language of the Church is a powerful unifying feature of the Mass.

The fact that the NO has many approved Eucharistic prayers, a variety of options, and even opportunities in the rubrics for extemporized comments makes the content of Masses different from Mass to Mass. And, of course, the "styles" of the priests who say the NO can be radically different, from devout adherence to the rubrics and a dignified and reverent demeanor, to the master of ceremony of an event, who ad libs as he considers suitable. Yes, the second is a regrettable deviation from what the NO should be, but it is not an uncommon reality, and one wonders if such deviations can ever be eliminated.

The Church, in fact, tolerates and even welcomes different liturgies. The Latin rite in the Western Church has seen multiple liturgical rites (such as Roman, Ambrosian, Mozarabic) and "uses" (such as Dominican, Carthusian, Premonstratensian, Cistercian) and has had them for centuries; for some reason it is only the TLM—the most ancient and most distinguished of all Western rites—that CHW deem divisive.

The Church permits diversity of many kinds—there are many "spiritualities" and communities: Dominican, Franciscan, Carmelite, etc.—and such diversity is celebrated as meeting the various needs of Catholics. And many of those, "arrogantly" but "humanly," think their spirituality is the best. Should they be suppressed for that reason? Do CHW not want diversity? Or is it only the diversity provided by the TLM that they find unacceptable? It shares many features with other liturgies; consistency would require that they be discarded, too. Have CHW really thought through the full implications of their position?

IDIOSYNCRATIC: MORE SO THAN CHARISMATICS?

CHW repeatedly express a dislike of the attitude of some of those who attend the TLM, and believe it to be a major source of disunity in the Church. Undoubtedly some few are arrogant, but newcomers rarely find such individuals to be representative of the congregation. Even if that were the case, however, it is hard to believe that the authors would deny everyone the TLM, both now and in the future, because of the faults of some of the current attendees, who are a small percentage of the small percentage that attend the TLM. It has often been said that Vatican II's *Nostra Aetate* once and for all eliminated the concept of "collective guilt" from the Church's mentality, but sadly it seems to have reappeared in the treatment of TLM-loving Catholics, who are to be held collectively responsible for their weaker brethren.

One of the several uncharitable characterizations of the TLM attendees is that they have chosen the TLM because this allows them to worship with a "self-selected group of enthusiasts who share the same ideal." CHW observe: "No matter what 'camp' one might be in, there can be a danger of loving a form of the Mass more than one loves Jesus, whose saving sacrifice is made present and whose risen body and blood we receive."

These are painfully judgmental statements. Most people have strong preferences in liturgy and want to worship with like-minded individuals in a church which has the pastor, music, and fellowship they prefer—few like to attend even neighboring parishes. A Charismatic parish in Ann Arbor has tremendous allegiance among its attendees. Charismatics are definitely a "self-selected group of like-minded" individuals in the Church. The members have often moved their families from distant places to be close to the Mass and community. But to other devout Catholics, the Charismatic liturgies are often off-putting. For instance, Charismatics break out into "tongues" during the liturgy and wave their arms in the air. Are not those practices divisive?

Let's apply CHW's questions about the TLM and their charges against TLM enthusiasts to Charismatics: Do Charismatics love the Charismatic Mass more than they love Jesus? More than the Church? Some Charismatics take as their a priori that whatever advances the Charismatic movement is good and whatever impedes it is bad. They are confident that the Holy Spirit is behind all things Charismatic—so confident that they feel no need to acquaint themselves with the meaning of the TLM through reading qualified scholars or by attending the TLM over a period of time with an open mind to experiencing what it has to offer!

CHW observe: "Some Catholics have come to identify themselves by rite preference, as 'Latin Mass goers' in opposition to 'Novus Ordo Catholics,' often with the implication that the latter are lesser Catholics than those who identify with the traditionalist movement." Yet, can't the same be said of some Charismatics who often identify as just that— "Charismatics," some of whom even feel a greater affinity for Pentecostalism than for Catholicism?

Some Charismatics give the impression that those who have been "baptized" in the Spirit are more fully Christian than those who have not—indeed, that they have special access to the Holy Spirit. CHW state that "[Latin Mass goers] become an idiosyncratic liturgical camp within the Church." Some would certainly characterize Charismatics in those terms, as well as other groups such as the Neocatechumenal Way.

CHW suggest that the TLM community does not sufficiently submit to "duly constituted authority," which has been a problem of other groups in the Church; indeed, several Charismatic communities have had to be reined in by local authorities.

Not all Charismatics are hostile to the TLM: many, who found a safe haven in the Charismatic movement from the doctrinal madness that the Catholic Church has experienced for decades, have discovered the TLM. They continue to find orthodoxy, but now in worship as well as in doctrine.[1]

As the old saying has it, what's sauce for the goose is sauce for the gander. Either the Holy Spirit desires a diversity of charisms in the Church to the enrichment of all—in which case there is plenty of room for both Charismatics and traditionalists—or we all need to adopt one monolithically uniform program of life and worship.

AFRICAN EXCEPTIONALISM?

CHW also draw dubious conclusions from their observations: "Across the continent of Africa, for example, celebrations of the Mass that are both vibrant and reverent attract thousands of people to the Church." The assessment of Mass in Africa as "vibrant and reverent" matches my very limited experience of worship in Africa, but I am not at all certain that it is these celebrations rather than Christ Himself who draws people to the Church or that their claim is true "across the continent of Africa."[2]

We must note that before the imposition of the NO, it was the TLM that served marvelously to convert Africans to Catholicism in the first place. I suspect anyone visiting their Masses then would have found them full of reverence and joy.[3] It seems fair to note that Archbishop Marcel Lefebvre was a missionary in Africa from 1932–1959 and oversaw an

---

[1] On why some Charismatics now attend the TLM and see its benefits, see Clement J. Harrold, "Tradismatic Trentecostalism," *First Things*, March 2022, and Peter Kwasniewski's lecture at Steubenville, "Why Charismatic Catholics Should Love the Traditional Latin Mass," *Rorate Caeli*, October 7, 2020.

[2] The following report shows that although the number of Catholics is growing across Africa (very unevenly), it is not doing so at the same rate as the population as a whole; it also shows that the reception of the sacraments is falling off: Cathy Lynn Grossman, "More Catholics, Fewer Receiving Sacraments, a New Report Maps a Changing Church," *Religion News Service*, June 1, 2015.

[3] For a fuller response to the claim that Vatican II has been the cause of the vibrancy of Catholic worship in some places in Africa, see Peter Kwasniewski, "Mythbusting: 'African Catholicism is a Vatican II Success Story,'" *New Liturgical Movement*, January 23, 2023.

astonishing spread of Catholicism in the regions of Africa for which he was responsible, which came to include twelve archdioceses, thirty-six dioceses, and thirteen Italian Apostolic Prefectures. In having the TLM taken away from them, Africans, too, just like everyone else on the globe, have been denied something that had already been an appreciated part of their Catholic heritage. The several flourishing TLM parishes currently in Africa, especially in Nigeria and Gabon, suggest that African Catholics, like so many in the West, might flock to the TLM were it made more available to them.

Here it is not inopportune to mention that the notion of an "inculturated" African-style liturgy was not the work of Africans themselves but of European experts who imagined in their classrooms how their southern brethren might best be served.[4]

Lastly, any honest examination of the state of Catholicism in the "global south" must include reference to the fact that, while Catholicism is growing in absolute numbers due to population growth, Protestant and Pentecostal sects are experiencing much higher *rates* of growth — and tragically, attracting fallen-away Catholics into their numbers. This does not sound like an unmitigated "success story."[5]

---

4 See the exhaustive research presented in the article "Inculturation: A Wrong Turn," *New Liturgical Movement*, published in five parts, August–September 2022 and available in a single PDF at http://bit.ly/4ozNgmG.
5 Interestingly, the growth rate of Catholicism in Africa was *proportionately* much higher prior to 1970 — that is, at the tail end of the much-maligned "Tridentine" period: see the Pew Research Center, "Overview: Pentecostalism in Africa" (www.pewresearch.org/religion/2006/10/05/overview-pentecostalism-in-africa/).

5

Mischaracterization of the TLM, Then and Now

IT MUST BE ACKNOWLEDGED THAT EVEN those who love the TLM recognized deficiencies in how the Mass was said in the middle of the twentieth century. Fr. Bryan Houghton, a diocesan priest who retired early from parish ministry so that he could continue to say the TLM, puzzled over the ready acceptance of the NO by priests. He mused:

> But there was a problem to which I found an answer difficult. All priests had said the old Mass daily and with due decorum and even with apparent devotion. How came it that ninety-eight percent were perfectly willing to change it — and this not at the behest of the Council or of the Pope? A pure permission was given, and they all jumped to it like the Gadarene swine. Besides, I had been dean for a number of years and knew the priests of my deanery very well. Only two of them were sufficiently stupid to think themselves brilliant — and consequently welcomed the opportunity to express their personality. The rest, in private, were against the changes. However, only one, a Dominican, stuck to the old Mass. What made the others change? Obedience, apathy, fear of reprisals, anything for a quiet life — all those sort of motives undoubtedly played their part, but the fact remains that they cannot have *loved* the old Mass. It was just a ritual which could be changed like a pair of pants. But if they did not love the Mass it must be that they were incapable of adoration. They must consider Mass as something they do, not as something God does.
>
> "Lex credendi, lex orandi" — faith rules prayer and prayer faith. I had no doubt about the faith of my fellow priests — except one, perhaps — so the trouble must lie with prayer. Here, indeed, I found us priests singularly lacking. We were much too busy saying Mass, saying our breviary or doing something, to spend a moment in

prayer in front of the Blessed Sacrament. We encouraged the laity to do so, but rarely did it ourselves. Now I come to think of it, during my seminary course at the Beda I received plenty of instruction on ascetics, on how to perfect myself; but none on prayer, how to adore God. What little I know about the adoration of God I had picked up by reading the mystics—such as Gertrude of Helfta and Teresa of Avila—or spiritual writers such as Augustine Baker, Surin and Grou.[1]

It would seem the solution to the problem of priests not saying the Mass with a full consciousness of its meaning would be that recommended by Houghton—and by several popes: teach them *how to pray* and the importance of Eucharistic adoration. These are virtues that must be learned and practiced in spiritual reading, meditation, and personal prayer. Imposing a new rite of Mass and a new breviary is not at all the obvious solution to the problem.

Although many priests may not have been especially attached to the TLM as such (I suspect, as Houghton intimates, that it was because they did not have a good understanding of or preparation for it), there is an abundance of evidence that the TLM captured the attention and devotion of its attendees and powerfully nurtured their faith. Indeed, the same Fr. Houghton who describes what he regarded as the sad state of priests' spiritual life and the effect of that on the TLM says this about how his parishioners, by contrast, responded to it in 1969:

> I wonder how many Catholics attend Mass on any given Sunday in England and Wales? Not far short of three million, as far as I can make out. Even in Norfolk and Suffolk, where we are notoriously thin on the ground, the figures soon mount up: over three thousand at Norwich and Ipswich, over a thousand at Bury and Yarmouth, and in numerous parishes around the five hundred. Obviously—the figures themselves prove it—we love our Mass: that incomprehensible ceremony in which the only thing we understand is the utter mystery of the True Presence of Jesus Christ under the appearance of bread and wine.

---

1 Bryan Houghton, *Unwanted Priest: The Autobiography of a Latin Mass Exile*, ed. Gerard Deighan (Brooklyn: Angelico Press, 2022), 68–69.

> We love our Mass as it is, with its Latin mumbling, strange silences, sudden bells. Well, it is all going to be changed for us before this month is out—on November 29th....
>
> Humans are not prone to change, and least of all in the ritual of their religion. In fact, in many religions the ritual long outlives the belief; men continue to perform the traditional acts of worship when they have long since lost any positive faith in why or what they are worshipping. So, of course, the overwhelming majority of practising Catholics in this country will be desperately sorry to see their Latin Mass go. The traditions of a thousand years and habits of a lifetime cannot be chucked overboard without the passing tear. For my own part, I rather think that the last time I cried was in 1936; I shall probably do it again on November 29th.
>
> Of the priests I have talked to, slightly over half are in favour of the change, especially among the younger clergy who are not yet sick of the sound of their own voices. Of the many, many hundreds of laity, I have only found four individuals in favour, and they highly educated and thoroughly unrepresentative.
>
> This is, I think, a point of some importance. The English Mass has not come about in response to any popular demand; it has been imposed by the hierarchy. It is an act of pure clericalism if ever there was one.[2]

Houghton expresses great sympathy for the laity, who were not consulted about making the changes and who were not consulted about how the changes affected them:

> The new reforms in general and of the liturgy in particular were based on the assumption that the Catholic laity were a set of ignorant fools. They practised out of tribal custom; their veneration of the Cross and the Mass was totem-worship; they were motivated by nothing more than the fear of hell; their piety was superstition and their loyalty, habit. But the most gratuitous insult of all was that most Catholics had a Sunday religion which in no way affected their weekly behaviour. This monstrous falsehood was—and still is—maintained by bishops and priests who, for the most part, have never been adult laymen. Every day the Catholic workman had to put up

---

[2] Houghton, *Unwanted Priest*, 93–94.

with the jeers of his colleagues, as the more educated with their sneers. Every night they took their religion to bed with them.

I am not in a position to judge other priests' parishioners. I am, however, in a position to judge what were my own. No words are adequate for me to express my admiration for the conscious faith and piety of my flock, both in Slough and in Bury. This is where the trouble lay. The reforms were based on criticism; I was unwilling to take any action which might make me appear to criticise the wonderful people whom I was ordained to serve. I was perfectly conscious that I learned more about God from them than they were likely to learn from me.[3]

Peggy Noonan writes of her experience of the TLM in the fifties with her aunt, an immigrant from Ireland:

> If we were together on a Sunday, she took me to Mass. I loved it. They had bells and candles and smoke and shadows and they sang. The church changed that a bit over the years, but we lost a lot when we lost the showbiz. Because, of course, it wasn't only showbiz. To a child's eyes, my eyes, it looked as if either you go to church because you're nice or you go and it makes you nice but either way it's good.
>
> Jane Jane [as they called her] carried Mass cards and rosary beads—the Sacred Heart of Jesus, the Blessed Mother, the saints. She'd put the cards on a mirror, hang the rosary beads on a bedstead. I look back and think, wherever she went she was creating an altar. To this day when I am in the home of newcomers to America, when I see cards, statues and Jesus candles, I think: I'm home.
>
> She didn't think life was plain and flat and material, she thought it had dimensions we don't see, that there were souls and spirits and mysteries.[4]

Children loved the TLM then and children love it now. Whereas my parish is having difficulty finding altar servers for the NO, it regularly has fifteen or more altar boys (out of a

---

3 Houghton, *Unwanted Priest*, 81. Two other books by the same author, who was right in the thick of things, give a good picture of how the TLM was received in some places: *Mitre and Crook* (Brooklyn: Angelico Press, 2019) and *Judith's Marriage* (Brooklyn: Angelico Press, 2019).
4 Peggy Noonan, "Home Again, and Home Again, America for Me," *Wall Street Journal*, November 23, 2022.

much larger pool of trained servers) each Sunday for the TLM; at least two-thirds are under twelve years of age. They come from large families who arrive half an hour before Mass and stay half an hour afterwards (some of that spent in prayers of thanksgiving and others in playful fellowship with their peers), with the Mass being at least an hour and a half long.

THE TLM OF TODAY

I am sorry to say that the criticisms of CHW do not seem to stem from any prolonged personal experience of the TLM as offered today. I truly wonder how many traditional Masses the authors have attended or how many devotees of the TLM they have spoken with — who are mostly young people who have spent their whole lives worshiping at NO liturgies and who have found something in the TLM that they did not find in the NO.

We have been told endlessly that many of the elements of the NO are there because they "appeal to the young," but the exodus of young people from the Church indicates the NO has been a failure in that regard. The Catholics most resistant to any change in the NO are those over 65, not the young. Most Catholics under 60 or so have never attended a TLM; one wonders how many would switch over were they to experience it. In a way, the TLM is exotic and requires an openness to the unfamiliar and even the arcane; nearly everyone who attends, even those who do not adopt the TLM as their mode of worship, speak of its being dramatically more reverent and transcendent than even the best of the NO liturgies they have attended. Those won over by it find themselves doing a deep dive into why the TLM "does what it does" and into why it was replaced by the NO. They find their faith deepening in that process.

CHW choose to focus on what was (purportedly) once the case rather than on what we have *now* in the TLM. What seems of greater importance to reading the "signs of the times" is not what the TLM once was or might have been, but what it is today in our midst, as a living force that speaks to people in a powerful way, including not only lifelong

Catholics but converts and religious seekers. Its attendees are not "desperate" for an alternative. Again, much of the "restoration" that *SC* called for has happened in the TLM.

I have attended a wide variety of NO Masses over the last 55+ years, here and abroad, and believe I have more than a decent data base on which to compare the two experientially. I grew up with the TLM until I was fifteen. Many times, the liturgy was not at all inspiring; sometimes it took only nineteen minutes for a Mass to be said. But I have to say, when the NO was introduced, it did not strike me as an improvement. It, too, was largely uninspiring. In spite of the desiccated form of the TLM I attended (and my experience was perhaps not typical), I had a sense that the TLM had hidden treasures; to be sure, I found even the desiccated form more transcendent than the NO. When I was on the faculty at the University of Notre Dame in the 1980s, I consciously decided to learn nothing about the rules and rubrics governing the Mass since I was already tremendously disturbed by such practices as the presence of women at the altar during the consecration, the coercive "invitation" to the small congregation at daily Mass to "gather round the altar," and by the displacement of the tabernacle in the crypt to the space occupied by extra chairs.

At any rate, CHW seem to have read only about the kind of TLM I experienced and not the grand version available to many throughout the centuries and which is certainly the norm today. If the TLM once was what CHW say it was, it is no longer that in our times—now it is beautiful and riveting, hardly boring, and the attendees are fully engaged. Some follow in the missalettes or their own missals, others seem to be in a serene contemplative state. Most come early and stay late and yearn for the day when they can find a TLM wherever they find themselves. After all, the TLM is basically the same wherever we go (a wonderful unifying feature!), whereas one never knows what one will find in churches that offer the NO—travelers often vet possibilities before they get on the road since they don't want to subject themselves to some quirky liturgy or even one with an invalid Eucharist.

Why should the faithful be denied access to a mode of worship that is, with some regularity, indescribably beautiful, simply because some people think it was once boring? And why must they be compelled to embrace a liturgy that nearly everyone agrees has not had a good track record for reverence? Indeed, the authors recommend a large number of changes to the NO in order to improve it. Why are they so surprised that so many seek a better liturgy when the one they have been offered needs so much improvement?

CHW's portrayal of how the TLM was used or experienced prior to Vatican II is tendentious. They acknowledge that many were fed spiritually by it but in general characterize the laity who attended it as the proverbial lumps on a log who were mere spectators, who "had little sense of asking forgiveness of their sins during the opening penitential rite, nor did they consciously offer themselves to the Father in union with Jesus during the offertory."

How can they possibly know that? They make claims about what those who attended the TLM knew or didn't know about the Mass: for instance, they claim that "hardly anyone, even priests, were cognizant of...[the] theological significance [of the *ad orientem* posture of the priest]." This kind of remark seems a gratuitous and condescending characterization of the attendees, and hardly worthy of mention in a serious critique of the TLM; surely people's engagement in the Mass varies from time to time and from place to place. At various times, concern about the level of understanding of the Mass has been remarked upon by popes who have urged greater instruction of both priests and laity, but they did not call for a new rite in order to make it happen.

Moreover, do CHW think attendees at the NO have any idea of what might be the theological significance of the *versus populum* posture? Sadly, until very recently, most have not known that there was ever an alternative. And let me note, nearly every attendee at today's TLM could tell you why the altar is *"ad orientem."* But not knowing the reason for the postures does not negate the impact they have; at the TLM it is very clear that the Mass is being offered to God; at the NO it can appear that the congregation is the audience and the priest the performer, without much notion of a holy offering to God at all. At the TLM the personality of the priest is very muted by the fact that his back is to the congregation, while in the NO, as Ratzinger noted, the priest himself can sometimes become the focus of the attention of the congregation.[5]

REJECTION OF VATICAN II?

CHW claim that along with a devotion to the TLM often comes a rejection of Vatican II, and that that is a reason for ending the availability of the TLM. Do we have any studies that indicate such an alliance? Even so, is that a good reason for abolishing the TLM? On the other hand, we *do* have evidence that the majority of the attendees of the NO do not believe in the Real Presence[6] and that they contracept and think homosexual acts are not immoral. Should we therefore abolish the NO because of what its attendees do or do not believe?

CHW make claims that seem completely impressionistic. They bemoan the fact that many of the faithful have little knowledge of Vatican II and state: "This ignorance is especially found among those of the younger generation who are tempted to join the Tridentine movement." Is that group really more ignorant of Vatican II than other young people? My guess is that in fact the young people who attend the

---

5 CHW claim that Mass *versus populum* resembles more closely the Last Supper. The Church, however, regards the Mass not as a reenactment of the Last Supper but as the living commemoration of the Sacrifice of Calvary, which was anticipated the night before in the institution of the Holy Eucharist and of a priesthood distinct from the laity. Thus, the Mass looks back primarily to *Good Friday*, not to Holy Thursday; it was Martin Luther who first called the worship service a "supper." It seems CHW are not aware of scholarship that discusses how the Last Supper was not conducted as a tête-à-tête between Christ and the Apostles and cannot serve as a template for the modern *versus populum* arrangement. See Peter Kwasniewski, "The Possibly Dubious Liturgical Legacy of Leonardo's Last Supper," *New Liturgical Movement*, December 16, 2019 (chapter 11 below).

6 See Gregory A. Smith, "Just one-third of U. S. Catholics agree with their church that Eucharist is body, blood of Christ," *Pew Research Center*, August 5, 2019.

TLM have much greater knowledge of the content of Vatican II than the young people who attend the NO, for they read books by such astute churchmen as Bishop Athanasius Schneider, whose critique of Vatican II is founded on a deep and penetrating knowledge of theology and of Vatican II.[7]

Bishop Schneider is not being irresponsible in raising questions about some of the positions taken in Vatican II. Concerns like his and those of Fr. Thomas Guarino[8] need to be addressed, not dismissed. Why do CHW want to send the message to a very select group of those who dare question the Council that what is most valuable to them will be taken away from them, especially at a time when pro-abortion atheists are welcome to serve on the Pontifical Academy for Life?[9]

CHW suggest that there are those who "promote the Tridentine liturgy as a way of disparaging the Council." I think the more frequent occurrence is that those who discover the TLM wonder why it seems to be a *hidden* treasure and strive to learn about it. They have been told that the NO is what the Council wanted, and when they discover that that is false, they begin to question other things they have been told. From their own experience of the NO they begin to question whether Vatican II was such a good thing if it or its "interpreters" produced the NO.

They also discern a connection between innovations of the NO and theological dissent and, again, begin to wonder about Vatican II. For many, it is their discovery of the TLM that has strengthened their belief in a large number of teachings of Vatican II that many Catholics doubt, such as the definitive revelation of God in Jesus Christ, the unicity of the Church and its necessity for salvation, the reality of Hell, the privileges of the Virgin Mary, and so forth.

---

7   Bishop Athanasius Schneider, *The Springtime That Never Came: In Conversation with Paweł Lisicki* (Manchester, NH: Sophia Institute Press, 2022).
8   Rev. Thomas G. Guarino, *The Disputed Teachings of Vatican II: Continuity and Reversal in Catholic Doctrine* (Grand Rapids, MI: Eerdmans, 2018).
9   See Edward Pentin, "Pontifical Academy for Life Appoints Pro-Abortion Atheist Member," *National Catholic Register*, October 18, 2022.

REVERENCE FOR THE EUCHARIST AND ACCEPTANCE OF DOCTRINE

CHW somewhat ironically but most revealingly comment not only on the abuses of the NO that many have experienced over the years, but also on the call of the U. S. bishops to restore understanding of the Eucharist. Neither at that point nor later in the series do they consider the possibility that (at the very least) irregular offerings of the NO, if not the NO itself, might have contributed to the diminution of the understanding of the Eucharist and respect for it.

Few comparing the two liturgies would not readily observe the much greater reverence displayed in prayers, movements, and gestures toward the Eucharist in the TLM, where the Eucharist is received by people kneeling and on the tongue and where the priest, accompanied by an altar boy with a paten, distributes the Eucharist; these are all visible signs of something phenomenally supernatural happening. In the NO, on the other hand, the use of lay readers (sometimes children), the presence of lay ministers of Communion often in quite casual garb (crocks and frocks), and the reception of the Eucharist on the hand and through an assembly line process, all diminish the grandeur of what is happening.

I haven't seen studies on the matter, but I am confident that a survey of the beliefs of those who worship at the TLM would discover a nearly universal belief in the Real Presence, compared to the 30% belief among attendees at the NO. The failure to note a likely causal effect of the NO on Eucharistic belief suggests at the outset a regrettable unawareness of the relation between liturgy and belief—a relation that has long been recognized, all the way back to the adage, adapted from Prosper of Aquitaine, that the *lex orandi* is the *lex credendi*.

There are, however, studies that compare the beliefs and practices of those who attend the TLM with those who attend the NO (see Figures 7 and 8).

Those numbers should give pause to anyone who argues that the TLM should not be available to all.[10]

---

10 See Fr. Donald Kloster, "National Survey Results: What We Learned About Latin Mass Attendees," *Liturgy Guy*, February 24, 2019; see also

Figure 7. Results of Fr. Kloster's First Survey.

SURVEY QUESTION	TLM	TLM samples	NOM	NO Data Source
1. Approve contraception	2%	1773	89%	Pew Research 2016 (Sept 28)
2. Approve abortion	1%	1769	51%	Pew Research 2018 (Oct 15)
3. Weekly Mass attendance	99%	1763	22%	CARA 2017 (Apr 11, 2018)
4. Approve gay marriage	2%	1759	67%	Daily Wire (July 2, 2017)
5. Income % donated	6%	1702	1.2%	Catholicphilly.com (May 17, 2013)
		Protestants	2.5%	Relevant Magazine (March 8, 2016)
	All Christians during the Great Depression		3.3%	
6. Annual Confession and Weekly Mass	98%	1753	25%	CARA 2014 (Feb 16)
7. Fertility Rate (number of children)*	3.6	1085	2.3	Pew Research 2015 (May 12)

*This question was directed to women only.
Traditional Latin Mass national survey conducted by Fr. Donald Kloster (March 2018 through November 2018).

Figure 8. Results of Fr. Kloster's Second Survey.

Norwalk National 2019–20 Traditional Latin Mass Adult Study

What is your state in life?	Married	Single	Priest	Religious	In Formation
	40%	53%	1%	2%	4%
Have you thought about a Priestly or Religious vocation?	Yes	No			
	80%	20%			
What is your age?	18–19	20–29	30–39		
	187	921	671		
What is your sex?	Male	Female			
	57%	43%			
What is your dominant race/ethnicity?	Caucasian	Black	Asian	Mixed	
	84%	1%	5%	10%	
Number of years of education after high school?	0	1 to 2	3 to 4	5 to 7	8 to 12
	9%	19%	39%	24%	9%
Do you go to Mass every Sunday?	Yes	No			
	98%	2%			
Were you raised in the TLM (at least from the age of 7)?	Yes	No			
	10%	90%			

(continued overleaf)

Number of siblings including yourself (not including step and half)?	1	2	3	4	5 to 9	10 or more
	23%	20%	19%	13%	21%	4%
Are you a convert or a revert*?	Convert	Revert	Neither			
	20%	25%	55%			
In what family structure were you raised?	Married	Remarried	Not Married	Single	Grandparent	Other
	84%	4%	3%	6%	1%	2%
What lead you to the TLM?	Parents	Friends	Solemnity	Curiosity	Reverence	Music	Spouse	Other
	16%	13%	8%	12%	35%	3%	5%	8%
Did your father regularly attend Church?	Yes	No				
	65%	35%				
Did your mother regularly attend Church?	Yes	No				
	75%	25%				

*"Revert": baptized Catholic, stopped practicing, and then returned to practicing.
Study conducted from October 22, 2019 to March 1, 2020. Findings based on 1,779 responses received.

Moreover, there is data that show that the TLM is a marvelous tool for evangelization—for drawing in converts and reverts and retaining the faith of young people: the TLM is made up of around 20% converts. The Novus Ordo has a much more modest number of 2% converts. The reverts in the TLM were also an elevated number of 25%. There is evidence that the number of reverts who attend the Novus Ordo is about 10%.[11] Only 16% of the respondents attributed their preferred TLM attendance to their parents.[12]

A REFORM OF THE REFORM?

One has to admire the honesty of the authors in their acknowledgment that not infrequently the NO has been a disaster; it has featured priests dressed in "rainbow" robes and women in diaphanous costumes dancing around the altar—charges that never could be made against the TLM. These and other not uncommon "abuses" of the NO do not deter the authors from intimating that the NO should now be the only available liturgy for most (all?) in the West.

They recommend changes, but essentially, we are being asked to surrender a mountain of gold for a handful of dust that they promise us can be shaped into a worthy liturgy. Indeed, it would take a vastly more concerted global effort, with total buy-in from the clergy at all levels and also from the laity, to bring about the kind of consistently high-level NO that CHW are looking for. In short, the probability of the NO being "done well" is distressingly low.

"2019–20 TLM Survey: What We Learned About Latin Mass Attending Young Adults," *Liturgy Guy*, May 26, 2020.

11 See "Who Are U. S. Catholics? Numbers Show a Surprising Shift," *National Geographic*, September 17, 2015, quoting Dr. Mark Gray, head of CARA: "Gray points out that historically, it's not unusual for young people who leave the faith to come back later in life. Of those who abandon Catholicism in their teens and 20s, a handful return in their 30s and 40s, when they will register with their local parish and baptize their children. Gray estimates that these 'reverts' comprise about 10 percent of the Catholic population in the U. S."

12 Fr. Donald Kloster, "Latest data show Latin Mass continues to flourish in the US despite Vatican suppression," *LifeSiteNews*, February 20, 2023.

CHW believe that the NO can be so reformed as to avoid the problems they have noticed. A full paragraph is given to the need for the congregation to dress more modestly and fittingly and to be attentive to small "rubrical" actions which help orient all that is being done to the "heavenly" realm. Those who want to see fitting, modest dress and attention to small rubrical actions need not look to some future Church but need only come to any TLM where such behavior is routine. Indeed, much of what CHW call for to improve the NO is *already present* in the TLM, which leads some to conclude that the NO becomes better to the extent that it becomes more like the TLM, or, in other words, the more like the liturgy envisioned in *Sacrosanctum Concilium*.

If we have any hopes that the proposals made by CHW will result in an improved NO, our hopes are dashed when we read that: "One way to foster this understanding would be by providing an opportunity for the faithful to bear public witness to their love for the Eucharist, perhaps in one or two brief testimonies after communion. While such testimonies may need to be monitored and even rehearsed, they would not only benefit the congregation but would also confirm more strongly in the speakers their own love for the Eucharist."

SC tells us that all changes to the liturgy must be organic (no. 23): to what element of any liturgy that has ever existed would such a practice correspond? Every Catholic loves a good evangelization, conversion, or miracle story and would also love a "What the Eucharist Means to Me" story, but there are abundant opportunities that exist and more could be created for sharing those in the parish hall or at a conference. Behind this proposal is a concept of the liturgy as man-made and malleable to any discerned momentary need.

What CHW don't consider is the possibility that the NO should be reformed not in accord with the perceived needs of the moment but in accord with the vision of *SC* for the liturgy. It is surprising that strong advocates for Vatican II are not insisting on such a reform. As noted earlier, CHW acknowledge that the Fathers at Vatican II did not at all

Mischaracterization of the TLM, Then and Now

have in mind the NO that was composed under the guidance of Bugnini. Indeed, the crafters of the NO were clearly motivated more by the "spirit" of Vatican II than the letter.

Reformers of the NO should be more motivated by the letter of Vatican II than the spirit. The NO reformed in accord with the vision of Vatican II would have the priest praying *ad orientem*; there would be a communion rail where the congregation would kneel for communion; there would be no extraordinary ministers of Holy Communion; there would be only one Eucharistic Prayer; Latin would still have a primacy of place and the music of the Mass would be the Latin chant or something similar. Most of the changes made in the NO do not correspond with the principle articulated in *SC* that all changes must be "organic," a principle that disallows novelty. There would be much more unity between the Roman liturgies had the principles of *SC* been honored.

My intent in this series of essays has not been to demonstrate that the TLM is superior to the NO or to point out all the excellent features of the TLM or to critique the NO: it has been to show that the critique of the TLM by CHW fails miserably. My hope is that those who read the CHW series do not take the claims made there at face value and deny themselves and their families the extraordinarily spiritually satisfying experience of attending a TLM.

Most people are hesitant to attend because they don't know Latin and "won't be able to follow." The fact is that most of those who attend the TLM don't know Latin and even if they did, it helps them follow only some parts of the Mass. Much of the Mass is said silently and often the music continues while the priest is saying his prayers. They will need to learn a very different way of attending Mass; one that resembles time spent in Adoration more than time spent at a NO. The experience is much more contemplative: the atmosphere, the silence, and the beautiful music invite the congregation to enter into a state of receptivity to God's voice.

Individuals do not need to slavishly try to "keep up" with the prayers of the Mass; they may linger on the beauty and content of a prayer and be led by the prayers to become truly contrite and truly full of gratitude for God's mercy on us, our loved ones, and all human beings. I pray that Catholics everywhere have easy access to the TLM so that they can experience the beauty of our tradition, one that has the power to reinvigorate our faith.

Vatican II was a council that wanted the Church to return to its sources; making the TLM widely available fits much more with that vision of *ressourcement* than the abolition of it. Vatican II was not meant to be a "great reset," an opportunity to remake the Church in accord with whatever are the trends and tastes of the time. Those who ratified the documents of Vatican II, looking to find ways to advance the Gospel, to promote the love of Jesus in the modern world, did not mean to force Catholics to abandon their heritage—especially when it turns out that this heritage speaks powerfully to modern man.

PART 2
Peter Kwasniewski's Critique

Unconvincing Propaganda against the Latin Mass

THERE IS MUCH ONE COULD SAY IN response to the five-part *Church Life Journal* series concerning the liturgical reform. For simplicity's sake, one might sum it up as an embarrassing exposé of intellectual ignorance on the part of its authors Cavadini, Healy, and Weinandy (CHW), who should be ashamed of themselves—as also should the editors of the *Journal* in which it appeared, whose reputation has been thereby tarnished.

Not to put too fine a point on it, they haven't got a clue what they are talking about, either academically or experientially. The scholarship is slipshod, superficial, and selective. They appear to have no sustained experience with traditional liturgical rites of either East or West (as evidenced by certain remarks about, e.g., *ad orientem* and "repetition"). It's like the blind talking about colors, or the deaf talking about music. They appear to have read no good books on the history, form, and theology of the traditional Roman Rite such as Michael Fiedrowicz's or Fr. Uwe Michael Lang's, or even any of the standard older writers like Dom Prosper Guéranger and Adrian Fortescue, as out-of-date as they are in some respects.

They seem to have no notion of how constant is the presence of certain traditional liturgical practices and elements across the entire history of Western worship, not to say Eastern Christian worship too.[1] They appear to be unaware that Pius XII's *Mediator Dei* was describing the virtues of the Tridentine rite and cautioning the Liturgical Movement against exactly those excesses that were soon to be embraced by the *Consilium* and pushed even further, to the dismay of

---

1   See chapter 13 below.

==many faithful who wanted none of this experimentation.²==
They do not mention Bugnini even once (!), in spite of the fact that, whether he's a Freemason or not,³ he was involved in liturgical reform from 1948 to 1975, and obviously the key mover and shaker under Paul VI, as Yves Chiron meticulously documents.⁴ Imagine, for the sake of comparison, a five-part series on the Protestant Reformation that never mentioned Luther. Nor do they acknowledge the hesitations and regrets later expressed by major figures involved in the reform (e.g., Guardini,⁵ Antonelli,⁶ Martimort,⁷ Bouyer,⁸ et al.) or the plentiful evidence that it went far beyond what the Council Fathers had asked for.⁹

Did CHW ever notice the sizable body of literature written about how the liturgical reform as it transpired deviated from some of the manifest indications of *Sacrosanctum Concilium* of the Second Vatican Council? Here are seven articles that

---

2   See the account I shared at *New Liturgical Movement* on October 25, 2021, under the title "An American Layman Reminisces about Liturgical Upheaval," as well as *A Bitter Trial: Evelyn Waugh and John Carmel Cardinal Heenan on the Liturgical Changes*, ed. Alcuin Reid (San Francisco: Ignatius Press, 2011).
3   See my article "Does It Really Matter If Bugnini Was a You-Know-What?," *OnePeterFive*, August 11, 2021.
4   See Yves Chiron, *Annibale Bugnini: Reformer of the Liturgy*, trans. John Pepino (Brooklyn: Angelico Press, 2018).
5   See my article "'Plumber's Work!': Romano Guardini and Petrus Tschinkel on the Liturgical Reform," *New Liturgical Movement*, August 10, 2020.
6   See Jeff Ostrowski, "'Father Bugnini has only one interest: press ahead and finish'—Cardinal Antonelli, 1967," *Corpus Christi Watershed*, March 10, 2014, discussing the content of Nicola Giampietro's *The Development of the Liturgical Reform: As Seen by Cardinal Ferdinando Antonelli from 1948 to 1970* (Fort Collins, CO: Roman Catholic Books, 2009).
7   See Gregory DiPippo, "The 'Consilium ad Exsequendam' at 50—An Interview with Dom Alcuin Reid (Part 2)," *New Liturgical Movement*, February 12, 2014.
8   See Gregory DiPippo, "Fr Louis Bouyer on the Liturgical Reform and Its Architects," *New Liturgical Movement*, September 17, 2014; naturally, an essential source is *The Memoirs of Louis Bouyer: From Youth and Conversion to Vatican II, the Liturgical Reform, and After*, trans. John Pepino (Kettering, OH: Angelico Press, 2015).
9   See my articles "What They Requested, What They Expected, and What Happened: Council Fathers on the Latin Roman Canon," *New Liturgical Movement*, August 8, 2022, and "The Council Fathers in Support of Latin: Correcting a Narrative Bias," *New Liturgical Movement*, September 13, 2017.

Unconvincing Propaganda against the Latin Mass

may easily be found by anyone who has learned how to use a search engine and key terms:
- Alfons Maria Stickler, "Recollections of a Vatican II Peritus"[10]
- Robert W. Shaffern, "The Mass According to Vatican II"[11]
- Joseph Shaw, "What Sort of Mass Did 'Vatican II' Want?"[12]
- Joseph Shaw, "Vatican II on Liturgical Preservation"[13]
- Alcuin Reid, "The Liturgy, Fifty Years after *Sacrosanctum Concilium*"[14]
- Alcuin Reid, "Does *Traditionis Custodes* Pass Liturgical History 101?"[15]
- Peter Kwasniewski, "Is Your Liturgy Like What Vatican II Intended?"[16]

CHW can't get right even a basic fact like how old the content of the 1962 Missal actually is. They say "400 years," when it is easily 800, 1200, or 1600, depending on which layer you are speaking of. And again, this is readily available information.

Three more examples should suffice.

First, the way the Lord's Prayer is recited or sung in the Roman Mass. In a footnote, CHW claim: "The faithful of course prayed the Our Father on their own [e.g., for the Rosary]. However, in the Tridentine Liturgy, only the priest recited the Our Father, with the server reciting the final petition, 'sed libera nos a malo,' followed by the priest's 'Amen.'" They offer this as one of many examples that they seem to think show how the old Mass excludes the people from their proper role.

But it was none other than Pope St Gregory the Great who wrote in an epistle to John of Syracuse: "The Lord's Prayer, among the Greeks, is said by all the people; among us, *by the priest alone.*"[17] (Let's not forget he spent eight years as

---

10   *New Liturgical Movement*, June 29, 2022.
11   *The Catholic Thing*, July 10, 2022.
12   *LMS Chairman*, May 24, 2016.
13   *LMS Chairman*, January 17, 2017.
14   *Catholic World Report*, December 4, 2013.
15   *Catholic World Report*, December 18, 2021; also published in *From Benedict's Peace to Francis's War: Catholics Respond to the Motu Proprio Traditionis Custodes on the Latin Mass*, ed. Peter Kwasniewski (Brooklyn: Angelico Press, 2021), 252–59.
16   *New Liturgical Movement*, December 4, 2013.
17   Bk. 9, Ep. 26, PL 77:964–65.

ambassador to the imperial court in Constantinople, so he was quite familiar with how the Greeks did things.) And he speaks of this Latin priestly recitation of the Lord's Prayer as already customary in his day: this was the authentic Roman practice. As Abbé Claude Barthe points out: "St Gregory seems to confirm a tendency (guaranteed by St Augustine and observable in Milan and Spain) to make the prayer a priestly prayer, a tendency that he heightens by noting that the prayer concludes the Eucharistic prayer: the priest then moves away from the altar, and the Fraction follows."[18] St Augustine preached to his people: "In the church, this prayer of our Lord, *to which the faithful listen*, is recited every day at the altar of God."[19]

Now, St Gregory reigned from 590 to 604. St Augustine lived earlier still: 354–430.

Drs. Cavadini, Healy, and Weinandy: Is this what you are calling "the Tridentine Liturgy"? Are St Augustine and St Gregory the Great part of the problem, too—part of that grand conspiracy to exclude the laity from the exercise of their Christian duties? How far back do we need to go to find something you'd accept as correctly "involving the laity" in the offering? The year 223? 104? 33? It's curious, come to think of it, how few laity seemed to be involved in the Last Supper, an occasion when Our Lord made all of His apostles the first priests. It was a highly clerical affair!

Second, CHW make a rather big deal out of the Spirit-invoking *epiklesis*:

> Only the Holy Spirit can awaken in the faithful the "Eucharistic amazement" that will enable them to enter fully into the liturgy and be transformed by it. The Eucharistic prayers themselves express this renewed descent of the Spirit in the *epiclesis*, by which the Holy Spirit is invoked not only on the elements of bread and wine but on the whole assembly, so that they may be transformed into Christ.

Apparently, they are unaware that the "Eucharistic prayers" of the Western Church never had such an *epiklesis* until the 1960s, when it was invented out of whole cloth. The Roman

---

18 Claude Barthe, *A Forest of Symbols: The Traditional Mass and Its Meaning*, trans. David J. Critchley (Brooklyn: Angelico Press, 2023), 123–24.
19 *Sermon* 68, ch. xiii, 12 (PL 38:399), emphasis added.

Canon, one of the most ancient anaphoras in the Church, predates the Macedonian or Pneumatomachian heresy of the East to which Catholics *in the East* responded by emphasizing the role of the divine Spirit in the transformation of the offerings. In the Roman Canon, on the other hand, a different kind of *epiklesis* occurs in the *Supplices te rogamus*: "Command that these things be borne by the hands of thy holy angel to thine altar on high." As Abbé Barthe points out: "The liturgists speak of a 'communion *epiklesis*,' that is an invocation aimed at uniting the earthly altar and the heavenly altar, distinct from the 'consecration *epiklesis*' of the Eastern liturgies, where God is asked to descend on the sacred elements by the power of his Spirit."[20] As I pointed out elsewhere:

> The antiquity and *Romanitas* of the Roman Canon can be seen in many features, of which the *Hanc igitur* is a vivid example. Here, God is the *Paterfamilias*, the one on whose Word hangs the life and death of all members of the family. If the Father speaks the word of command, the sacrifice will occur; if He deigns to receive it, it will be efficacious. This is why the Roman Canon has no *epiclesis*. Predating the Macedonian controversy over the divinity of the Holy Spirit, it reflects a Patricentric theology in which the Father's good pleasure with the Son, together with His omnipotence, furnishes a sufficient explanation of why the prayer of the Church prevails and the Body and Blood of Christ come to be present on the altar.[21]

Fr. John Hunwicke explains:

> For the Roman Canon, Consecration means that we offer bread and wine to the Omnipotent Father so that he, by accepting them, makes them the Body and Blood of His Son in accordance with the words uttered by the Incarnate Word. In Byzantium, the Priest, bidden by the Deacon, invokes the Holy Ghost to descend upon the elements so that by His Transformation, they may be the Lord's Body and Blood. Each tradition is entitled to its own integrity.[22]

---

20 Barthe, *Forest of Symbols*, 117.
21 *The Once and Future Roman Rite: Returning to the Traditional Latin Liturgy after Seventy Years of Exile* (Gastonia, NC: TAN Books, 2022), 230–31.
22 "The Worst Evil of Uniatism?," *Fr Hunwicke's Mutual Enrichment*, June 30, 2019.

If CHW's view commits them, on the other hand, to a "consecration *epiklesis*" as the optimal or necessary expression of the sole agent of "Eucharistic amazement" and "transformation into Christ," once again they would be forced to consider the Western liturgy to have been defective for the better part of two millennia. One senses a pattern here.

A third example. "In the restoration and promotion of the sacred liturgy the full and active participation by all the people is the aim to be considered before all else..." I quote this famous passage of Vatican II's *Sacrosanctum Concilium* from the official English translation, which is quoted by nearly everyone—including CHW, who conclude, on the basis of it, that the Council Fathers' "primary concern is that the faithful actively participate, for only through such active engagement in word and action do they reap the graces that flow from the Eucharist."

Do CHW really believe that it is *only* through "active engagement" in *speaking* and *doing things* that the faithful obtain Eucharistic grace? What about listening, meditating, watching, hearing music, praying interiorly, being moved to the depths by something one has beheld? What about learning by what one sees and hears others doing? What of quiet Eucharistic adoration, or spiritual communions? Surely, a combination of all of these things, with appropriate adjustments for different roles and temperaments, is what will open a way to reaping graces from the Holy Eucharist.

In any case, it turns out this passage from *SC* 14 has been mistranslated, as is true of many other passages in the available translations of Vatican II documents. Rather ironic, isn't it, in a constitution that proposes an increase in the use of the vernacular? I, too, was thrown off in the past by this mistranslation.

Here's what the Latin says: "Quae totius populi plena et actuosa participatio, in instauranda et fovenda sacra Liturgia, summopere est attendenda..." The word *summopere* means "very much, highly, exceedingly, extremely." The sense here is: "In the restoring and fostering of the sacred liturgy, very great attention is to be given to the full and actual participation of the whole people..." If we look at three other translations, we see that they more accurately render the phraseology.

Italian: "A tale piena e attiva partecipazione di tutto il popolo va dedicata una *specialissima cura* nel quadro della riforma e della promozione della liturgia." French: "Cette participation pleine et active de tout le peuple est ce qu'on doit viser *de toutes ses forces* dans la restauration et la mise en valeur de la liturgie." The Spanish is downright unenthusiastic: "Al reformar y fomentar la sagrada Liturgia hay que *tener muy en cuenta* esta plena y activa participación de todo el pueblo." That gives quite a different sense, doesn't it? No doubt SC emphasizes participation (rightly understood); but then again, so did Pius X, Pius XI, and Pius XII, all of whom were cited in footnotes in an earlier draft of SC—footnotes that were removed at the last moment, ostensibly to prioritize Scripture citations but, in reality, to cut SC free of its magisterial encumbrances—and all of whom loved and praised the traditional Roman rite, seeing it as fully capable of calling forth and rewarding the people's full participation in it. Be that as it may, an accurate translation of SC 14 simply won't get you the "active participation at all costs!" view that CHW, in lockstep with six decades of liturgical martinets, wish to enforce.

In a surprising plot twist, the place where you will see the most abundant *participatio actuosa*—the full, conscious, actual involvement of the faithful in the liturgy—is at the traditional Latin Mass, where the people in the pews unite themselves intensely to the sacred action; meditate on the prayers, readings, chants, and ceremonies, which prompt or provide occasions for those interior acts of faith, hope, charity, contrition, adoration, supplication, that are obviously at the very heart of any meaningfully Christian worship; sing the responses and the Ordinary of the Mass in Latin chant, as Vatican II demanded (SC 54); and very obviously put their bodies to work for their souls as they stand, sit, and especially kneel for long stretches, beating their breasts, making signs of the cross, bowing their heads, and in many other ways showing far more *active* involvement than one ever sees at the Novus Ordo.[23] Martin Mosebach describes it well:

---

23 For a detailed treatment of *participatio actuosa* and errors concerning it, see Peter Kwasniewski, *Noble Beauty, Transcendent Holiness: Why the Modern Age Needs the Mass of Ages* (Kettering, OH: Angelico Press, 2017),

The believer can "participate actively" in a variety of ways. He can follow the priest step by step along the high road of the mysteries, subordinating his prayers, as the priest does, to the traditional gestures—standing, bowing, moving to one side or the other, and so on. But he can also simply contemplate the work of Christ that is carried out in Holy Mass; in doing this he does not necessarily have to join in every one of the liturgy's prayers, but may silently and in solitude adore the miracle that is taking place before his eyes. It is one of the greatest paradoxes of [the traditional] Holy Mass that, with all its liturgical strictness, it particularly facilitates prayer that is radically personal and contemplative.[24]

Another commentator, J. Nebel, observes:

Especially by the silent performance of many rites and prayers, one avoids a situation in which the faithful in their participation are, so to speak, "served," and run the risk of no longer sufficiently feeling the need to engage themselves in a personal prayer. With the silent performance of the rites, the participation of the faithful in the liturgical acts depends much more strongly on their personal spiritual engagement, thus uniting themselves spiritually with the sacred action. It is precisely in this way that the faithful, in their dignity and maturity, are taken seriously as baptized Christians.[25]

These two quotations resonate powerfully with those who assist at the TLM. Before our encounter with it, we barely knew how to pray the Mass, or even that you *could* pray deeply at Mass (as opposed to going through a lot of external motions and words), until the old liturgy taught us how to do it, compelled us to do it. I was a willing pupil, but I was clueless and needed guidance. The prayers and ceremonies gave me that guidance—but they also said: "We're throwing you into the deep end: one, two, three, *swim!*" Funnily enough,

---

191–213; idem, *Reclaiming Our Roman Catholic Birthright: The Genius and Timeliness of the Traditional Latin Mass* (Brooklyn, NY: Angelico Press, 2020), 55–75; idem, *Ministers of Christ: Recovering the Roles of Clergy and Laity in an Age of Confusion* (Manchester, NH: Crisis Publications, 2021), 131–51.
24 Martin Mosebach, *The Heresy of Formlessness: The Roman Liturgy and Its Enemy*, rev. ed., trans. Graham Harrison (Brooklyn, NY: Angelico Press, 2018), 93–94.
25 Quoted by Michael Fiedrowicz, *The Traditional Mass: History, Form, and Theology of the Classical Roman Rite* (Brooklyn: Angelico Press, 2020), 228n109.

it seems to work for someone who is already a believer and who is ready to learn. The Mass was never intended as a kindergarten for unbelievers; it was seen by the ancient Church as the summit of the Christian life, the final threshold for the formed believer. It should therefore honor and respect the dignity of the believer and his or her own prayer, inserted into the Great Prayer of Christ the Eternal High Priest.

The topic of participation—where the experience on the ground turns out to be nearly the opposite of what the "experts" tell us it is or should be—furnishes one more illustration of a rule I learned from decades of observation and study: Of anything the liturgical reform's proponents say, we can know with a high degree of probability that the opposite is true. At many NO Masses the participation of the people is atrociously passive and minimal, while at many TLMs the involvement is intensely palpable, even electrifying. CHW think they have an explanation: this, they tell us, is due to TLM participants being "primed" for better participation thanks to decades of habits built up from the NO. They don't seem to realize what a double-edged sword that argument is. If it's quite possible for the faithful to be deeply engaged with and nourished by the TLM today, that only goes to show that a massive reform of the TLM itself was by no means necessary to achieve the goals of the Council. Rather, *as always*, it is education and development of better habits that count. Moreover, CHW's supposition backfires when it becomes clear that the NO, in spite of its purported advantages, has not led to the paradise of participation that was promised as its primary (or sole?) justification.[26]

Rather than dismissing a millennium and a half of tradition (St. Gregory the Great, the Roman Canon...) and the actual desiderata of Vatican II, in reality CHW need to go humbly back to the drawing board and rethink the

---

26 In this connection it is worth noting that the Vatican's strategy for winning over the faithful to a new liturgy hasn't changed in over half a century. First, insult Catholics who are quietly praying at Mass, caricaturing them as lazy and passive. Second, use papal authority to force them to pray out loud in the vernacular. Third, proclaim victory no matter how few people show up to church to participate "actively." Rinse and repeat.

entire question from the ground up—as many of us have already done for ourselves over the past several decades. For most of Church history, outward activity and ease of access have never been conflated with fervent inward participation. Indeed, the earliest records indicate that the offering of the Eucharist in both East and West was always veiled from the people, first by curtains and later by icons. The Eastern Christians whose tradition was so highly praised by the Second Vatican Council have retained such a practice to this day.

CHW do not seem to recognize that their entire argumentative approach aligns with that of the Protestants and Modernists who maintained that the worship (and, indeed, the doctrine of the Catholic Church: *lex orandi, lex credendi*) had become corrupted over time, and that only a "return to antiquity" could correct it—the error, in other words, that Pius XII castigated as "antiquarianism."[27]

Most strikingly, they barely mention the name or work of Joseph Ratzinger, in spite of his unparalleled contribution to liturgical theology both as a scholar and as Pope.[28] In a *damnatio memoriae*, even as they denigrate most of what came before Vatican II, so too they denigrate what came before Pope Francis, and take only enough time to chide Benedict XVI for his naiveté. Again, this would be like doing a five-part series on the Counter-Reformation without giving a prominent place to Trent or Pius V.

Speaking of Pius V... it would also appear that CHW are unaware of (or deliberately chose not to mention?) the commission of nine cardinals summoned by John Paul II in 1986 to investigate the question of whether Paul VI ever legally abrogated the old missal; eight out of nine concluded that he had not, which served as the basis for the clarification

---

27 See "Growth or Corruption? Catholic versus Protestant-Modernist Models" in Kwasniewski, *The Once and Future Roman Rite*, 197–215; "The Problem of False Antiquarianism" in idem, *Reclaiming Our Roman Catholic Birthright*, 149–60.

28 See Joseph Ratzinger, *Collected Works*, vol. XI: *Theology of the Liturgy* (San Francisco: Ignatius Press, 2016); cf. the florilegium I published under the title "Best Quotes on the Liturgy by Joseph Ratzinger/Benedict XVI," *New Liturgical Movement*, January 2, 2023.

of *Summorum Pontificum* on this matter.[29] John Salza and Robert Siscoe[30] also demonstrate that the new missal was never promulgated in such a way that its use was canonically obligatory, although anyone who dared to exercise his freedom in this regard was punished until Benedict XVI took steps to remedy this injustice. Readers may also wish to consult Fr. Réginald-Marie Rivoire's careful canonical study, *Does "Traditionis Custodes" Pass the Juridical Rationality Test?* (Lincoln, NE: Os Justi Press, 2022).

CHW's basic premise seems to be a variation on Chesterton's old quip about Christianity. Here's how the new version runs: "The liturgical reform has not been tried and found wanting; it has been found difficult and left untried."

The trouble is, there's only so much "benefit of the doubt" that one can extend to a certain idea or ideology before its fraudulence becomes undeniably apparent. The apt parallel here is Communism. For a long while, the mentality not only behind the Iron Curtain but even among Western academics was: "Communism has not been tried and found wanting; it has been found difficult and left untried."

Yet Communism helped itself to the blood of millions of victims in order to establish its new paradise on earth—a paradise that never came to be. It was discredited by its own internal contradictions, its absolute impracticability, its failure to deliver even basic goods like bread and clothes.

CHW tell us that all we need to do is give the liturgical reform another chance, more time, *more effort!* They admit that for fifty years things have not gone well; abuses, irreverence, lack of mystery, secularization… But the trouble isn't—*couldn't* be!—the reform. (Remember, the Holy Spirit, who according to their position must have been curiously absent for so many centuries of unfolding liturgical life,

---

29 See, among other sources, Peter Kwasniewski, "Minutes from the Commission of Cardinals That Advised John Paul II to Lift Restrictions on the Old Missal," *New Liturgical Movement*, January 9, 2023.
30 I refer to chapter 16 of their helpful book *True or False Pope: Refuting Sedevacantism and Other Modern Errors* (Winona, MN: STAS Editions, 2015).

roused Himself from inactivity and made up admirably for lost time.) Rather, it must be our *lack of enthusiasm* for it, our unwillingness to implement—THE PROGRAM!

Meanwhile, the reform helped itself to the souls of millions of victims in order to establish its new paradise of active participation. Millions left the Church, confused, bewildered, scandalized, bored. Millions more who stayed have lost their faith in the Real Presence, in the Sacrifice of Calvary, in the unique dignity of the priest. Many of *these* warm bodies fell away in recent years when Mass was treated as an inessential service. The demographic sinkhole widens and deepens. In their vast enthusiasm for increased "active participation," CHW need to be reminded that the most basic form of participation is to show up for Mass—something fewer and fewer in the modern West choose to do, except at flourishing Latin Mass parishes... at least until they are shut down by bishops who seem to hate tradition more than they dread apostasy.

Nor is the evidence from the Third World as hopeful as CHW seem to think it is. The growth of the Catholic Church in Africa, for example, was *proportionately* much higher prior to 1970, that is, at the tail end of the "Tridentine" period.[31] Since then, the Church has grown roughly in proportion to natural population growth, whereas Protestant and Pentecostal sects have exploded in numbers, including the many fallen-away Catholics who have gone over to their ranks.

The liturgical reform has been discredited by its own internal contradictions, its absolute impracticability, its failure to deliver even basic goods like sound faith and reverence. We may still be waiting for our "Berlin Wall" moment, but it will come. Indeed, it has already come in the vitality of the traditionalist movement and the impossibility of writing convincing propaganda against it.

---

31 See the evidence gathered in my article "Mythbusting: 'African Catholicism is a Vatican II Success Story,'" *New Liturgical Movement*, January 23, 2023. It almost seems as if CHW are not aware that the entire globe was evangelized by priests who brought into every culture the admirable beauty, impressive discipline, and sublime spirituality of the Tridentine Mass. Its replacement has not brought about missionary gains that are even remotely comparable.

7

Noble Patriarchs, Wayward Grandchildren:
A MORE REALISTIC APPRAISAL OF THE LITURGICAL MOVEMENT

CENTURY AFTER CENTURY, HOLY MOTHER Church employed all her care in worshiping the Lord—from hidden gatherings of persecuted Christians to the grand basilicas of Constantine, within the great cathedrals of the Middle Ages and the ornate edifices of the Counter-Reformation, through the upheavals of modern Revolutions down to the eve of the Second Vatican Council. Always and everywhere, the holy mysteries were performed, venerated, and received in a continuum of Catholic faith accompanied by growing theological insight and spiritual devotion that matured into well-established rituals perfectly suited to their content and purpose.

The Fathers of the Second Vatican Council celebrated the Tridentine Mass in all four sessions.[1] They did not vote to retire or abolish this form of Mass, or even to alter its most striking features: Latin as the primary language, Gregorian chant as the primary music, ample silence, the east as a common direction for all worshipers, overlapping hierarchical activity entrusted to male ministers, the temporal cycle in the calendar, Communion received kneeling and on the tongue, and so forth.

How, then, did we end up getting, in the late 1960s, a new Mass so different from the Mass prayed by the Church for so many centuries? The answer to that question is closely

---

[1] The public meetings of the Council began with solemn liturgies, most often in the venerable Roman rite but also on occasion in various Eastern and non-Roman Western rites as well.

bound up with the influential "Liturgical Movement" of the nineteenth and twentieth centuries. This movement to rediscover the central place of the Church's public worship in the Christian life can be described in terms of three distinct phases, although the boundaries from one to the next were somewhat fluid.

The first phase, exemplified by the pioneering figure Dom Prosper Guéranger (1805–1875) and his great work *The Liturgical Year*,[2] aimed at a better understanding and celebration of the inherited Roman liturgy through popular explanations and clerical-religious education. The leading idea was to take the treasures we already had and get to know and love them intimately. Guéranger often cited ancient sources to flesh out his commentaries, but without implying that the Church had erred in the medieval and post-medieval development of her liturgy, or that she should revert to these primitive models. This phase coincided with a blossoming of renewed monastic life.

The second phase—of which Dom Lambert Beauduin (1873–1960), Ildefonso Cardinal Schuster (1880–1954), Fr. Pius Parsch (1884–1954), and Fr. Romano Guardini (1885–1968) may be taken as representatives—was characterized by outstanding progress in historical, archaeological, linguistic, and theological research. It retained a profound respect for the wealth of tradition but sometimes spoke of medieval and Baroque "deviations" and showed a decided preference for what was (or, at times, was imagined by scholars to be) the most ancient—and therefore, presumably, most "authentic"—practice. This led certain individuals to dabble in experiments that conflicted with ecclesiastical legislation, e.g., celebrating Mass facing the people out of a conviction that this was how the Eucharist was originally celebrated by Christians.[3] The dangerous tendencies of this

---

[2] Different publishers have kept this masterpiece in print over the years. The most recent edition: Dom Prosper Guéranger, OSB, *The Liturgical Year*, trans. by Dom Laurence Shepherd, OSB (Fitzwilliam, NH: Loreto Publications, 2017), 15 vols. Some sections may be found online.

[3] We now know that this is not true and that the history is more complicated. For a good overview, see Michael Fiedrowicz, *The Traditional*

phase were called out by Pope Pius XII in his 1947 encyclical letter *Mediator Dei*.

Despite the encyclical that was meant to put the brakes on, the Liturgical Movement entered a more radical third phase in the fifties and sixties, as more of its members indulged in pastoral experiments and crafted paraliturgies intended to "reach people where they're at" and "get them involved." Heavy liturgical reform of the general calendar, the rubrics, and the rites of Holy Week prior to the Second Vatican Council already announced that the attitude of respect for longstanding practice had lost its self-evident force. This third phase combined selective antiquarianism with a utilitarianism that sought above all "the people's benefit," understood in activist terms.

All three phases of the Liturgical Movement, be it noted, emphasized lay involvement. The first phase saw it primarily in terms of acquiring education: being initiated into a great tradition that one could explore for a lifetime yet never exhaust, and participating in the liturgy through prayerful engagement with the rites. The second phase strongly promoted the use of hand missals, devotional aids for living the Church year, and popular singing of plainchant. The third phase took an ideological turn, as prominent liturgists embraced the conviction that liturgy ought to be clear, comprehensible, accessible, verbal, linear, and group-oriented: modernized for Modern Man.

Paul VI lent his full papal support to the ideals and plans of this radical phase of the Liturgical Movement. When the ink was barely dry on the Council's first approved document, the Constitution on the Sacred Liturgy *Sacrosanctum Concilium* (1963), the pope set up a body called the Consilium. The pope and the Consilium took Vatican II's call for moderate reform as *carte blanche* for an unprecedented wholesale reconstruction of the Roman rite in every area—Mass, lectionary, calendar, Divine Office, sacraments, sacramentals, pontifical and papal ceremonies, and so forth. The controversial Vincentian priest and later archbishop Annibale Bugnini

---

Mass: History, Form, and Theology of the Classical Roman Rite (Brooklyn: Angelico Press, 2020), ch. 7, "Direction of Prayer," 141–52.

(1912–1982), who worked on a succession of schemes of liturgical reform at the Vatican from 1948 to 1975, could be described as the general contractor of this massive project of demolition and reconstruction.[4]

While we can admit that the reformers were responding to certain problems of their time, we see looking back from our present vantage that they were often mistaken in their theories, naïve in their assumptions, and callous in their pastoral approach. The qualities of easy rational accessibility, immediate verbal comprehension, and community-centeredness are surely desirable in some social situations, but there is ample reason to question whether they suit well the religious ceremonies by which man comes before the God who wrapped Himself on Mount Sinai with voices, flames, the sound of the trumpet, and a dark cloud, wrought wind, rent rocks, shook stone, and whispered words, who names Himself "I AM" and "dwells in light inaccessible";[5] the worship that leads to communion with the God-Man Christ Who baffled His own mother and foster father, who unwithered a man's hand and withered a fig tree, Who blessed little children, raised the dead, drove out merchants with a whip, and sweated blood;[6] the operation of the Spirit who moved upon the face of the waters, descended as a dove from opened heavens, and entered as a violent rushing wind, to rest on the apostles as tongues of fire.[7]

Indeed, prominent voices in favor of liturgical reform, such as Fr. Louis Bouyer (1913–2004), subsequently expressed their regrets and dismay at much of what was done to and with the liturgy.[8] A close associate and disciple of Pius

---

[4] For an even-handed biography that also summarizes the liturgical fermentation and change from 1945–1975, see Yves Chiron, *Annibale Bugnini: Reformer of the Liturgy*, trans. John Pepino (Brooklyn: Angelico Press, 2018). There was a short period during the Second Vatican Council when Bugnini was not working for the Vatican in an official capacity. He nevertheless remained in Rome, in close contact with all the major players, until he was reappointed as secretary of the Consilium.

[5] Cf. Ex 20:18–21; 1 Kg 19:11–12; 1 Tim 6:16.

[6] Lk 2:43; Mt 12:13, Mt 21:19; Mk 10:16, Jn 11:43, Jn 2:15, Lk 22:44.

[7] Gen 1:2; Mt 3:16; Acts 2:2–3.

[8] See *The Memoirs of Louis Bouyer: From Youth and Conversion to Vatican

Parsch, Fr. Petrus Tschinkel of Klosterneuburg, admitted in an interview:

> Now I can tell you that Pius Parsch would not at all have agreed with the changes of the post-conciliar era. That's not what he wanted. Yes—(the liturgy) in the mother tongue. That is all, however. But also, the Mass as mystery, as a reality *hic et nunc*, here and now.... After the Second Vatican Council these liturgical forms are nothing but idling: only text after text. Not a trace of internal disposition nor of mystery.[9]

Fr. Tschinkel relates that Guardini, when he received the texts of the new liturgy, looked at them for a long time and then said: "Plumbers' work!" (*Klempnerarbeit*).[10] Joseph Ratzinger renders a similarly negative judgment, though in more elegiac language:

> The Liturgical Movement had in fact been attempting to... teach us to understand the Liturgy as a living network of Tradition that had taken concrete form, that cannot be torn apart into little pieces but has to be seen and experienced as a living whole. Anyone who, like me, was moved by this perception at the time of the Liturgical Movement on the eve of the Second Vatican Council can only stand, deeply sorrowing, before the ruins of the very things they were concerned for.[11]

II, the Liturgical Reform, and After, trans. John Pepino (Kettering, OH: Angelico Press, 2015), 218–25.

9 See Wolfram Schrems, "The Council's Constitution on the Liturgy: Reform or revolution?," *Rorate Caeli*, May 3, 2018; cf. Peter Kwasniewski, "'Plumber's Work!': Romano Guardini and Petrus Tschinkel on the Liturgical Reform," *New Liturgical Movement*, August 10, 2020.

10 Ibid. The German colloquialism means work done in a hasty, slipshod way, with inadequate care and botched results. The reference to a hack plumber doing a mechanical job carries the implication that the reform of the liturgy was approached like the fixing, cutting, adapting, or welding of pieces of metal pipe, rather than as a subtle work of skill on a delicate living reality that would require holiness, discretion, and learning. *Klempnerarbeit* might also convey in this case a lack of aesthetic value in the misnamed "reforms."

11 Preface to Alcuin Reid, *The Organic Development of the Liturgy: The Principles of Liturgical Reform and Their Relation to the Twentieth-Century Liturgical Movement Prior to the Second Vatican Council*, 2nd ed. (San Francisco: Ignatius Press, 2005), 11.

In any case, we can say that history has moved on and the Church is now in a much different place than it was fifty years ago. If anything, the passage of decades has shown how urgently our traditional Roman liturgy responds to essential and universal human needs as well as needs peculiar to the postmodern era. Although a stubborn Old Guard of Bugninians remains ensconced in many a university chair and chancery office,[12] the energy is with the Ratzingerians, whose banner is *Summorum Pontificum* and whose motto is "what earlier generations held as sacred, remains sacred and great for us too." As Dom Alcuin Reid observes:

> the reality in the life of the Church at the beginning of the twenty-first century [is] that the *usus antiquior* is a living liturgical rite in which people—indeed significant and growing numbers of young people—participate fully, actually, consciously and fruitfully in a manner that would have brought great satisfaction to the Fathers of the Second Vatican Council and to the pioneers of the twentieth-century liturgical movement which preceded it.[13]

When Joseph Ratzinger called for a "new liturgical movement,"[14] he seems to have had in mind a new beginning, a movement characterized by the features of the first and healthiest phase, in which filial piety, grateful receptivity, and warm devotion are directed toward a rich heritage developed over twenty centuries of continuous worship—a tradition that should never have been rejected, and, happily, was never entirely forgotten or lost.[15]

---

12 Notable figures who staunchly support the liturgical reform of Paul VI include Bugnini's quondam secretary Archbishop Piero Marini (b. 1942), Msgr. Kevin Irwin (b. 1946), Fr. John Baldovin, SJ (b. 1947), Cardinal Arthur Roche (b. 1950), Andrea Grillo (b. 1961), Fr. Anthony Ruff, OSB (b. 1963), and Massimo Faggioli (b. 1970).
13 "The older form of the Roman rite is alive and well," *The Catholic World Report*, April 3, 2020.
14 Joseph Ratzinger, *Milestones: Memoirs 1927–1977*, trans. Erasmo Leiva-Merikakis (San Francisco: Ignatius Press, 1998), 149.
15 See Fr. Thomas M. Kocik, *Singing His Song: A Short Introduction to the Liturgical Movement*, rev. and expanded ed. (Hong Kong: Chorabooks, 2019); cf. "The New Liturgical Movement: Urgent Care for a Sick Church," in Kwasniewski, *Noble Beauty*, 89–112.

8

Is the Laity's Offering of the Mass a Postconciliar Rediscovery?

ARCHBISHOP ROCHE—LIKE EVERYONE trained by modern liturgists—keeps saying that the new rite *finally* recognizes that the faithful are also part of the offering of the Mass, instead of it just being the priest's work:

> In the former [rite], he says, it was the priest who "represented the intentions of the people" and took that to God in the liturgy. Vatican II changed that. "With the understanding of the priesthood of all the baptised it's not simply the priest alone who celebrates the Eucharist, but all the baptised who celebrate with him. That surely has to be the most profound understanding of what 'participation' means."[1]

He doubled down on this claim in a BBC radio interview on March 19, 2023:

> You know, the theology of the Church has changed. Whereas before the priest represented, at a distance, all the people. They were channelled, as it were, through this person who alone was celebrating the Mass. It is not only the priest who celebrates the liturgy, but also those who are baptised with him. And that is an enormous statement to make.[2]

This view is so common that one can stumble upon it as upon a cat or a pair of shoes in whatever direction one walks. Let me give some examples "in the wild." From the Swinging Sixties:

> To understand this religious program and to enjoy its hoped-for results we must all change our settled way of thinking

---

1 Interview with Christopher Lamb in *The Tablet*, February 24, 2022.
2 See, for the quotation and further commentary, Joseph Shaw, "Cardinal Roche on the Vatican II Rupture," *OnePeterFive*, March 24, 2023.

regarding sacred ceremonies and religious practices as calling for no more than a passive, distracted assistance.³

The Council has taken the fundamental position that the faithful have to understand what the priest is saying and to share in the liturgy; to be not just passive spectators at Mass but souls alive.⁴

And a more recent sighting:

Without going into much detail here, suffice it to say that one of the great scandals of the Roman Rite over the centuries has been its progressive disconnect from the people. Slowly over time, partly from a desire to preserve Latin as the language of worship, partly due to increased complexity and dramatic elements introduced by Frankish liturgists, and partly due to historical factors I will not rehearse here, the Mass became a purely clerical affair. The priests and other ministers would be gathered around the altar saying the Mass, and the people would be observing, almost like they were attending a play.... Why do you think the last 57 years have been liturgically so chaotic? Because the Church is suddenly trying to focus on something that she has not deeply considered for more than a millennium. The Church is trying to answer the question of how to include the people in the liturgical action of the Mass.⁵

Coming closer to the focus of this book, CHW go to great lengths to argue that, before the Council, the laity had very little to do with the offering of Mass:

The vast majority of Catholic faithful recognized that they were attending the all-holy sacrifice of the Mass, and that they were receiving the body and blood of Christ in Holy Communion. The Mass did create an awe and reverence among the faithful. However, for the most part, they had the mindset of being observers of a great mystery. Only the priest (along with the altar boys) was seen as actively engaged in the Eucharist rite. Except at the consecration of bread and wine, when the faithful adored the elevated sacred species, accompanied by the ringing of bells, many of the faithful engaged in their own personal forms of

---

3 Paul VI, General Audience, January 13, 1965.
4 Paul VI, Homily, March 27, 1966.
5 Fr. Jeffrey Moore, "Liturgical Participation," https://frmoore.com/2020/02/01/february-02-2020-liturgical-participation/.

prayer.... Likewise, unless they were following along with a bilingual missal, which must be said was fairly popular, they would not be praying along with the celebrant, for they could neither hear him nor understand what he was praying in Latin. The spiritual high point for the faithful was reverently receiving on their tongue Holy Communion, which they rightly believed was the body, blood, soul, and divinity of the incarnate and risen Son of God. However, they had little awareness that the privilege of receiving Holy Communion was founded upon their having participated in Jesus's once-for-all sacrifice of himself to the Father for the forgiveness of sins and the outpouring of the divine life of the Holy Spirit.

Opinions of this kind lead CHW to the conclusion that, "prior to Vatican Council II," the Catholic Church displayed "inadequate theological understanding and deficient liturgical practice." After the Council, however, the lay faithful's rightful place has been restored to them:

> These changes [to the Mass in the 1960s] embody one of Vatican II's enduring and most important achievements: the recovery of the Scriptural and patristic doctrine of the priesthood of all the baptized.... The renewed liturgy empowers the baptized to enact more fully their indelible baptismal character.... The Council's promotion of the faithful's "full, conscious, and active participation" in the liturgy means that "Christ's faithful, when present at the mystery of faith, should not be there as strangers and silent spectators. On the contrary, through a good understanding of the rites and prayers they should take part in the sacred action, conscious of what they are doing, with devotion and full collaboration.... Offering the immaculate victim, not only through the hands of the priest but also together with him, they should learn to offer themselves" (SC §48).

In other words: they quote Vatican II's constitution on the sacred liturgy as if it were saying something not only true, but forgotten, neglected, and therefore poorly lived. In this connection, CHW also make the astonishing claim: "Without the vernacular, the active, vocal, intelligible participation of the faithful would have been impossible—at least for the vast majority." How superficial a notion of participation is at work in such comments has been well explained elsewhere.⁶

The trouble is, the view recycled by Archbishop Roche, Fr. Moore, CHW, and so many others, like its analogues in Pope Paul VI, corresponds to nothing that was ever taught to Catholics in their catechisms and prayerbooks or from the pulpit, nor does it correspond in the main to the experience of the laity who assist at the Latin Mass. Let's have a look at two splendid and typical examples from the tradition.

The first is from Fr. Martin von Cochem (1630–1712), who wrote the following in his extremely popular book *Die Heilige Messe für die Weltleute* [Holy Mass for the Laity], published in 1704:

> Ponder well, O Christian, what the holy Catholic Church, infallible in matters of faith, declares to us.... She expressly states, and imposes on our belief, that no other work can be performed by the faithful so holy and divine as the tremendous mystery of the Mass. This does not only refer to priests, but to the faithful in general.
>
> Priests can indeed do nothing more holy and divine than celebrate Mass; the laity can do nothing more holy and divine than hear Mass, serve Mass, *join in offering Mass*, have Mass said for their intentions, follow the prayers and unite in spirit with the celebrant. Since to do this is of all works the most holy and divine, it stands to reason that it should also be the most profitable and meritorious....⁷

And again:

> One of the greatest graces which are granted to the children of the Church is that the privilege of *offering* to the Divine

---

6   See, for example, "Understanding Liturgical Participation" in Joseph Shaw, *The Liturgy, the Family, and the Crisis of Modernity* (Lincoln, NE: Os Justi Press, 2023), 57–85. It is arrogant and condescending for CHW to speak as if the laity were incapable of vocal participation prior to the Council. In point of fact, small children were learning Gregorian chant in their hundreds of thousands—to take one example, a children's choir of 62,000 sang the Latin chants of the Mass at the Eucharistic Congress in Chicago in 1926, a fact that can be easily verified—and poor people in Africa were singing the Ordinary of the Mass in Latin by heart. It is usually academics who underestimate the ability of normal people to engage liturgically with tradition.
7   *Cochem's Explanation of the Holy Sacrifice of the Mass: With an Appendix, Containing Devotions for Mass, for Confession, and for Communion* (New York: Benziger Brothers, 1896), 238, emphasis added. TAN Books has published a new edition, with different pagination.

Majesty the sacred and sublime sacrifice of the Mass is not the prerogative of priests alone, but *belongs to the laity as well,* to men, women, and children. This favor was not shown to the Jews; no one but the priest was permitted to offer the holocaust, or to kindle the incense in the temple....

In the New Testament the case is very different; under this dispensation it is graciously permitted to ordinary people to offer, not incense only, but the precious blood of Christ in the holy Mass.... *The faithful of either sex are members of a spiritual priesthood, and have received from God the power to offer spiritual sacrifices.* But when they offer the Mass by the hands of the priest they do more, they offer what is better than a spiritual oblation, namely, a visible one, even the self-same victim Whom the priest holds in his hands.

Happy indeed are the laity in being thus privileged, through the divine bounty, to purchase the inestimable treasure of the body and blood of Christ, and with a few words to offer it to God for their own immeasurable profit! Make frequent use, O pious Christian, of this thy glorious prerogative; it is the easiest way of acquiring eternal riches. This sacrificial act is the chief, the most important, part of hearing Mass, for without it thou wilt neither gain much profit to thyself nor give pleasure to God. "Hearing Mass," says a spiritual writer, "does not merely consist in being present in person when it is celebrated, but *in offering it to God conjointly with the priest.*"

All this is undeniably true. *It is not enough to be present at Mass in order to share in the fruits of the Mass: we must make a definite offering of it to God in union with the officiating priest.* The Mass is a sacrifice, and it appertains to the nature of a sacrifice that it should be offered to the Deity. Therefore those persons who fail to do this, either with their lips or in their heart, do not derive half the benefit from the Mass that others do, although they fulfil the precept of the Church, whilst piously reciting other prayers that have nothing of the character of an offering.[8]

And yet again:

Ponder well the immense favor Christ bestows on thee in making thee a mystical priest, and *empowering thee to offer the holy sacrifice of the Mass,* not for thyself alone, but also for others. Bishop Fornerus tells us: "It is not

---

8   *Cochem's Explanation,* 298ff., emphasis added.

the priest alone who offers the Mass for himself and for others: *every Christian who is present* may do the same, for his own needs and those of his friends." This is expressed in the prayer following after the Sanctus: "Be mindful, O Lord, of thy servants N. and N.; and of all present, whose faith and devotion are known, for whom we offer, or who offer, up to Thee this sacrifice for themselves, their families and friends..." The meaning of these words is too obvious to be mistaken.

Moreover, when the priest says the *Orate fratres*, he turns towards the people and invites them to help him in offering the holy sacrifice: "Brethren, pray that my sacrifice and yours may be acceptable to God the Father Almighty." As if he would say: I am about to perform a work of great importance, to offer an oblation which in my own strength I cannot do; I ask you to pray for me and assist me with your cooperation, for it concerns you nearly, *the sacrifice is yours as well as mine*, and for this reason you are bound to help me.⁹

A near-contemporary, Saint Leonard of Port Maurice (1676–1751), another popular preacher of his day, addressed the same topic in his book *The Hidden Treasure* (also still in print from TAN Books). First, he establishes that it is Our Lord Jesus Christ who is the principal celebrant, which I assume no one would criticize as clericalism:

> At every hour, then, in various parts of the world, this most perfectly holy Priest offers to the Father His Blood, His Soul, and His whole self for us: and all this He does as many times as there are Masses celebrated in the whole world. O boundless treasure! O mine of inestimable stores thus possessed by us in the Church of God! O happy we if we could but assist at all these Masses! What a store of reward would be thus acquired! What a heaping up of graces in this life, what a fund of glory in the other, would be the fruit of so loving an attendance!

Then he talks about how the faithful *also* offer the holy sacrifice:

> But what is implied in this word "attendance"? *Those who hear Mass not only perform the office of attendants, but likewise*

---

9   *Cochem's Explanation*, 301–2, emphasis added.

Is the Laity's Offering of the Mass a Postconciliar Rediscovery?

of offerers, having themselves a right to the title of priests. "Fecisti nos Deo nostro regnum et sacerdotes" (Apoc. v. 10). The celebrating priest is, as it were, the public minister of the Church in general; he is the intermediary between all the faithful, particularly those who assist at Mass, and the invisible Priest, Who is Christ; and, together with Christ, he offers to the Eternal Father, both in behalf of all the rest and of himself, the great price of human redemption. But *he is not alone* in this so holy function, since *all* those who assist at Mass *concur with him in offering the sacrifice*; and, therefore, the priest turns round to the people and says, "Orate fratres ut meum ac vestrum sacrificium acceptabile fiat...—Pray, brethren, that mine and your sacrifice may be acceptable to God," in order that the faithful may understand that, *while he indeed acts the part of principal minister, all those who are present make the great offering together with him.* So that when you assist at Holy Mass, you perform, after a certain manner, the office of priest.

What say you, then? Will you ever dare, from this time forward, to be at Mass sitting, prating, looking here and there, perhaps even sleeping, or content yourselves with reciting some vocal prayers, without at all taking to heart the tremendous office of priest which you are exercising? Ah me! I cannot restrain myself from exclaiming, O dull and incapable world, that understandest nothing of mysteries so sublime! How is it possible that anyone should remain before the altar with a mind distracted and a heart dissipated at a time when the holy Angels stand there trembling and astonished at the contemplation of a work so stupendous?

Now, these two authors, Martin von Cochem and St. Leonard of Port-Maurice, were not obscure figures writing esoteric tomes for religious scholasticates. They were, as already mentioned, popular preachers and writers and highly typical figures of Counter-Reformation Catholicism. The traditional doctrine they preached was being spread all over the place as part of the Church's response to Protestant errors and as a means for encouraging the laity to live a devout liturgical life.

One might object: Would they need to have insisted so much on these truths if the laity had not forgotten them and if the liturgy they were accustomed to did not foster the contrary attitude?

My response: the truth about the identity of the baptized as co-offerers of the Sacrifice of Christ is always in danger of being forgotten because it is a matter of *faith*, not something patently obvious to the senses. It will *always* need to be taught, *regardless* of the form the liturgy takes. But we can go a step further and say that the form the Mass takes will have a lot to do with how much the laity can perceive it to be the mystical offering of the sublime sacrifice of Christ on the Cross, and how much opportunity and incentive it gives them for entering profoundly into that sacrifice.

Ultimately, the problem is *not* that the old Mass encourages passivity or laziness. Laity can be uninvolved in *any* liturgy. (I don't know when's the last time Arthur Roche has observed teenagers at the Novus Ordo, texting and surfing on their phones—and not just teenagers, I'm afraid.) The real problem is that the modern liturgists tend to have a Protestant understanding of what active participation means: they think it must look *just like* what the priest is doing, so if the priest is speaking, the laity must speak; if he sings, the laity must sing; if he stands at the altar, at least some of the laity have to go stand at the altar with him; if he is distributing communion, some of the laity should as well. It is only a barely lingering sense of decency that has prevented (in most cases) laity from lifting up the consecrated host and chalice along with the priest at the elevations.

In short: the Novus Ordo theoreticians tiptoe as close as they possibly can to the heresy that the laity are priests *in the same way as* the priest is a priest, and so it bothers them a great deal if there is a liturgical rite in which there is a clear and sharp distinction *externally* between how the priest offers Mass and how the laity offer it with him and by his hands. Their complaint, in other words, appears to be directed at the "sacerdotalism" of the Catholic Mass. They would like to overcome it as much as possible, while (at least sometimes) not technically running afoul of the canons and decrees of Trent.

The great irony, then, becomes this: for over half a century, Catholics have been habituated by the Novus Ordo into thinking that if they show up for Mass, sing, speak, sit, and stand, and *especially* if they "volunteer to minister," they have actively participated: they can, as it were, punch the ticket. What it all means for my inner prayer life is, sadly, quite untouched; people are too busy and too distracted to get to that level. Yet the Magisterium of the Church, together with the *pars sanior* of the Liturgical Movement, have *always* said that the interior spiritual dimension is the more fundamental and the more important dimension of *participatio actuosa*, and that the external activity is worthwhile inasmuch as it supports the internal engagement in the Mystery of Faith.

With the emphasis on doing and the paucity of intense personal prayer, the current regime strikingly calls to mind the warning of Our Lord: "Woe to you scribes and Pharisees, hypocrites; because you tithe mint, and anise, and cumin, and have left the weightier things of the law; judgment, and mercy, and faith. These things you ought to have done, and not to leave those undone" (Matt. 23:23). That is, translated into this conversation, you should do the little active things with your body when and as appropriate, but don't forget the weightier things of the spiritual order.

Fr. Hunwicke recently cited a most relevant passage from Dom Gregory Dix:

> If the word had not come to have as offensive a sound for many as "clericalism" itself, the old term "sacerdotalism" might well be used to describe the reconciling principle of the primitive church, so dear to S Paul, "that there are diversities of ministries, many members, yet but one Body," in which they find their hierarchic unity; and that all are necessary to the perfection of the Church, the Body of Christ. Clericalism, I take it, means in itself simply undue exaltation of the person and importance of the minister, whether he claims priestly character and special sacramental power, or not. "Sacerdotalism," on the other hand, means simply the belief that certain men are given by God certain priestly powers on behalf of their fellows, which their fellows have not got. These are not the same thing ... the pre-Nicene Church was certainly not "clericalist," but it was profoundly "sacerdotalist."

The "sacerdotalism" of the old rites, in which the clergy — bishops, priests, deacons, subdeacons, those in minor orders or their substitutes—are manifestly the primary agents executing the services, and the congregation attends, or to use an old-fashioned term, "assists" in a mostly quiet and apparently passive way, is uniformly deplored by modern liturgists as a form of clericalism and a separation or exclusion of the people from the liturgical action. Yet they fail to grasp the paradox of the spiritual involvement, attraction, and even fascination provoked by the hieratic "distance" of the clergy in the sanctuary, the architectural boundaries and barriers that turn spaces into symbols, and the entrustment of rites to men who exemplify the worship of God in their ceremonial vesture, scripted words, and carefully-controlled motions.[10]

In other words, something that is routinely assumed to be anti-participational and anti-corporate is nothing of the kind. The development that took place in history accentuated features already clearly present in the old covenant and continued in the new covenant in the Cross of Christ—a covenant pre-interpreted in an Upper Room cut off from the marketplace, consummated on a mount cut off from the city, achieved in the torturous separation of Body and Blood, echoed in the *Nolite me tangere* ("Do not touch me," John 20:17) of the risen Lord who must ascend beyond us that we may follow him: *Trahe me, post te curremus* ("Draw me, we will run after thee," Song 1:3). A certain kind of hierarchic and bodily differentiation and separation is part of the essence of the Christian religion as lived in this in-between time, between the Fall and the Second Coming; when lived rightly, it serves charity and spiritual union.

As our two Counter-Reformation preachers remind us, the message of the laity's real participation in offering the Mass has always been a part of Catholic catechesis. We should not be too quick to credit claims of corruption advanced by the class of professional liturgists as pretexts for their radical makeover of the Roman Rite.

---

10 For a robust defense of the sacerdotalism of the traditional Mass, see my lecture "The Relationship between Priest and People in the Latin Mass: Space and Time for Divine Intimacy," *Rorate Caeli*, August 23, 2022.

9
Offspring of Arius in the Holy of Holies

IMAGINE MY SURPRISE WHEN I READ, IN the second installment of the five-part series at *Church Life Journal* by Drs. Cavadini, Healy, and Weinandy, the following claim:

> Significantly, while the faithful [before The Council] knew and believed that the one God is a Trinity of persons, their liturgical and personal prayer often primarily consisted of praying to the one (generic) God. Only after Vatican II, with the revision of the rite and the use of the vernacular, did the faithful become more cognizant of the trinitarian nature of the liturgy and of their own ability to pray in a trinitarian manner.

Apart from the authors' preternatural ability to know intimately how millions of Catholics prayed and engaged with the liturgy prior to the 1960s—and in particular, their ability to know that widely-available and popular devotional materials, explicitly Trinitarian in content, in fact must *not* have been used by anyone who bought them—together with their crystal-ball glimpse into the Trinitarian literacy of modern Catholics (which I am sure a Pew Research survey could quickly establish, together with their literacy in Eucharistic doctrine) and *their* intimate Trinitarian prayer lives, we should, with discipline, zero in on the central claim: that it was specifically "the revision of the rite and the use of the vernacular" that brought about this renaissance in Trinitarian knowledge and prayer.

In my book *Resurgent in the Midst of Crisis*, published in 2014—a book frequently reviewed and easily available to those who have a taste for liturgical studies—I devote one of the chapters to documenting the systematic *removal* of Trinitarian and Christological confessions from the reformed liturgy, demonstrating that the vernacular rite Catholics were given after 1969 was far *less* centered on the mystery of the Trinity than the Tridentine liturgy to which the faithful were accustomed (especially from the unofficial vernacular versions they would have encountered in widely-used hand missals—unless CHW somehow know, once again, that the millions of copies of such missals that were sold over many decades were never actually used by anyone).

Figure 9. Archbishop Lefebvre in one of many flourishing preconciliar missions run by the Holy Ghost Fathers in Africa; sadly, their liturgy did not help them much in their conquest of the continent for Christ.

Given the magnitude of this claim—that, essentially, God had allowed the Church to leave her faithful deficient *for centuries* in their knowledge of and devotion to the Holy Trinity, the core dogma of our religion—it seems opportune to give this 2014 chapter a new home in the present collection, in the interests of making the truth better known.

In the New Testament two basic "orientations" of prayer are displayed and inculcated: first and foremost, in keeping with Jewish tradition, prayer addressed to "God" or "Lord" (into this category may also be placed the altogether novel

Offspring of Arius in the Holy of Holies

way in which our blessed Savior intimately addresses his "Father," as we see, for example, in the farewell discourses in the Gospel of John,[1] and occupying a secondary but still important place, prayer addressed to Jesus Christ himself.

To the former and more familiar Jewish practice, Jesus adds a new and crucial element that concerns the very essence of the revelation he embodies: God is to be invoked *in Jesus's name*, for the Son of God is now the Son of Man, the one and only Mediator between God and man, through whom all our prayers ascend to the Father and all his graces are given to us in the Mystical Body. Hence the Lord teaches his disciples: "You did not choose me, but I chose you and appointed you that you should go and bear fruit and that your fruit should abide; so that whatever you ask the Father *in my name*, he may give it to you" (Jn 15:16), and again: "Truly, truly, I say to you, if you ask anything of the Father, he will give it to you *in my name*. Hitherto you have asked nothing in my name; ask, and you will receive, that your joy may be full" (Jn 16:23–24). Such teachings are the revealed foundation of the Church's custom of concluding her prayers *per Christum Dominum nostrum*, a formula we already see frequently in St. Paul, whose letters are full of liturgical language: "I thank my God *through Jesus Christ* for all of you, because your faith is proclaimed in all the world."[2]

Nevertheless, our Lord also taught his disciples to address *him*, the Son and Savior, in prayer: "Whatever you ask in my name, *I* will do it, that the Father may be glorified in the Son; if you ask me anything in my name, I will do it" (Jn 14:13–14).[3] When Jesus says: "You call me Teacher and

---

1 Another example would be Matthew 11:25: "I thank thee, Father, Lord of heaven and earth..."

2 See, e.g., Romans 5, vv. 1, 11, 15, 17, 21, etc.—the Epistle to the Romans is full of the "through Jesus Christ" formula (as well as the related "in Christ Jesus"). Cf. Pius XII, Encyclical Letter *Mediator Dei*, nn. 144–46.

3 The Greek of Jn 14:14 says: *ean ti aitēsēte* me *en tōi onomati mou egō poiēsō*, which the Vulgate accurately renders *si quid petieritis* me *in nomine meo hoc faciam*. Part of the manuscript tradition of the NT lacks the *me* of 14:14, but it is the preferred reading, faithfully reflected both in the Vulgate tradition and in patristic writings. In any event, the phrase "in my name" establishes the point, too, because the thrust of the statement

Lord; and you are right, for so I am" (Jn 13:13), he affirms that his followers are right to turn to *him* as the ultimate authority, the Holy One of Israel. Events, especially miracles of healing, confirmed the truth of these words. "The centurion answered him, 'Lord, I am not worthy to have you come under my roof; but only say the word, and my servant will be healed'" (Mt. 8:8).[4] "The crowd rebuked them, telling them to be silent; but they cried out the more, 'Lord, have mercy on us, Son of David!'" (Mt. 20:31). There are the words of the thief: "Jesus, remember me when you come into your kingdom" (Lk 23:42), and the words of the doubter: "My Lord and my God!" (Jn 20:28).

Again, the spontaneous exclamations of the early Christians are a precious witness that Christ, as true God, was the *addressee* of many prayers, not only a mediator through whom one had access to the Father. "As they were stoning Stephen, he prayed, 'Lord Jesus, receive my spirit'" (Acts 7:59). "To the church of God which is at Corinth, to those sanctified in Christ Jesus, called to be saints together with all those who in every place call on the name of our Lord Jesus Christ, both their Lord and ours: Grace to you and peace from God our Father and the Lord Jesus Christ" (1 Cor 1:2–3). More important than any one verse, however, is the general *tenor* of a number of texts, for example chapter 10 of the Epistle to the Romans, where St. Paul writes:

---

is that the Father will glorify the *Son* by showing the Son's divinity, i.e., his power to save the one praying; it is the Son ("I") who will respond to the prayer. Of course, the Son never responds apart from the Father and the Spirit, but it is important *for us* that we address all three Persons of the Trinity.

4 There are, of course, countless texts in the Gospels in which Jesus is addressed as Lord, *kyrie* in the vocative (*kyrios* in the nominative), which means master, lord, owner, sir—but which can also mean Lord in the proper theological sense, for this usage had already been solidly established in the Septuagint, where the God of Israel is referred to as *kyrios*. In certain passages of the Gospels it is clear that people who address Jesus as *kyrios* are not confessing his divinity but using an honorific title, much as the German title *Herr* means both "Mister" and "Lord." But there are other places where a confession is implied, and one of them is this famous statement of the centurion, whom Jesus praises for his faith in the Master's power to heal, which is a divine attribute.

If you confess with your lips that Jesus is Lord and believe in your heart that God raised him from the dead, you will be saved.... The scripture says, "No one who believes in him will be put to shame." For there is no distinction between Jew and Greek; the same Lord is Lord of all and bestows his riches upon all who call upon him. For, "every one who calls upon the name of the Lord will be saved." (vv. 9, 11–13)

Here, in typical rabbinic fashion, the Apostle to the Gentiles weaves together citations from the Old Testament that are manifestly speaking about the one true God, the God of Israel, and applies them to Jesus Christ. In this way he is not only clearly asserting Christ's divinity, but also urging the Christians who receive his letter to confess this mystery with their lips (a reference to liturgical worship) and to invoke Jesus as God in their prayers.

In the end, both ways of praying are given a succinct endorsement in the solemn words of Jesus that have echoed down the centuries: "I am the way, and the truth, and the life; no one comes to the Father, but by me... He who has seen me has seen the Father" (Jn 14:6, 9). By saying that he is *the way*, he self-effacingly presents himself as Mediator, the Word made flesh, the only way to reach the Father; by saying that he is *truth and life*, consubstantial with the Father, he presents himself as he truly is in the Father's glory—namely, as the Son who, together with the Father and the Holy Spirit, lives and reigns, *one God*, forever and ever. Hence, there can never be any tension, much less contradiction, between praying to the Father and praying to Jesus. For Jesus is Emmanuel, God-with-us, and whoever sees or speaks to him has seen or spoken to the Father.

In regard to ways of praying, it comes as no surprise that traditional liturgies of all rites, Eastern and Western, closely adhere to the witness of the New Testament and the practice of the ancient Church. The classical Roman liturgy—viewed in terms of ethos, ceremonial, spirituality, and the dogmatic theology expressed in the texts—shares much more in common with the Byzantine liturgy than it does with the Novus Ordo Missae.⁵ Perhaps nowhere is this fact more obvious than in regard to the presence, in liturgical texts and ceremonies, of solemn Trinitarian affirmations and their counterpart, a thoroughgoing Christocentrism.

Indeed, there could hardly be a more insistently Christ-confessing liturgy than the Divine Liturgy of St. John Chrysostom. In this liturgy there is a constant hymning both of Christ as the one true God and of the indissoluble unity of the Trinity: "Let us commend ourselves and one another and our whole life to Christ our God"; "For You, O God, are gracious and You love mankind, and to You we render glory, Father, Son, and Holy Spirit, now and ever and forever." Right before the Nicene Creed is recited, the priest sings: "Let us love one another, so that with one mind we may profess"—and the people finish his sentence: "The Father and the Son and the Holy Spirit, the Trinity, one in substance and undivided." Immediately after the consecration the priest sings: "We offer to You Yours of Your own, on behalf of all and for all," to which the people respond: "We praise You, we bless You, we thank You, O Lord, and we pray to You, our God." One of the most beautiful texts in the Divine Liturgy is an ancient hymn that perfectly illustrates the point we are making:

> O only-begotten Son and Word of God, Who, being immortal, deigned for our salvation to become incarnate of the holy Mother of God and ever-virgin Mary, and became man, without change: You were also crucified, O Christ our God, and by death have trampled death, being One of the Holy Trinity, glorified with the Father and the Holy Spirit, save us.

The Byzantine liturgy is overflowing with such texts, boldly confessing the divinity of Christ and the perfect unity of Father, Son, and Spirit.

Now, even if the classical Roman liturgy, with its comparative sobriety and simplicity, is not "overflowing" in the same way as Eastern liturgies tend to be, it too conveys

---

5 See "The Liturgical Reform's Long-Term Effects on Ecumenism," in Kwasniewski, *Resurgent in the Midst of Crisis*, 149–57.

the same theological message, and with many of the same expressions and gestures. It clearly belongs to and derives from the same ancient Christian heritage, where chanting the praises of the divine Word-made-flesh and falling in adoration before the Most Holy Trinity were the pith and purpose of liturgical life.

In marked contrast, the Novus Ordo Missae displays an insistent "Patricentrism" or generic Theocentrism that is characteristic of *no* historically well-established liturgical rite.[6] In its official texts and ceremonial the Novus Ordo exhibits what can only be called a certain Arianizing *appearance* or *tendency*.[7] The presbyter Arius of Alexandria (ca. 256–336), after whom the heresy of Arianism is named, taught that Jesus Christ is not truly and properly divine, but rather, a highly exalted creature and specially favored servant of God—a "son" or "god" by grace, not by nature.

Before discussing this issue, let us lay down some principles:

1. Properly speaking, the Holy Sacrifice of the Mass is offered by Jesus Christ *to the Blessed Trinity*, Father, Son, and Holy Spirit. It is not offered by Christ to the Father "apart from" or in contradistinction to the Son and the Spirit, for the Three are always One in their divinity and never separated, although it is the *Son of God* who offers his human life on the cross, as the Byzantine hymn quoted above so clearly confesses.

2. Our Lord offers the sacrifice of himself in his human nature, which is immolated on the Cross (since the divine nature as such cannot suffer); the sacrifice is infinitely pleasing because the human nature is hypostatically united to the

---

6 See my article "Patricentric Purism and the Elimination of Liturgical Prayer Addressed to Christ," *New Liturgical Movement*, April 12, 2021.

7 There is an abundance of material on the questionable theological tendencies of the members of the Consilium; see, for instance, Roberto de Mattei, "Reflections on the Liturgical Reform" and Dom Charbel Pazat de Lys, O.S.B., "Towards a New Liturgical Movement," both in *Looking Again at the Question of the Liturgy with Cardinal Ratzinger: Proceedings of the July 2001 Fontgombault Liturgical Conference*, ed. Alcuin Reid (Farnborough, UK: St. Michael's Abbey Press, 2003).

Son of God, so that, as the Liturgy of St. John Chrysostom expresses it: "It is You who offer and are offered, You who receive and are Yourself received, O Christ our God."

3. It is also true to say that the sacrifice is offered *to the Father, through the Son, in the Holy Spirit*; and other formulae express other true aspects of the mystery. As Bertrand de Margerie explains: "In conformity to the two equally legitimate patterns of Christian prayer, the pre-Arian and post-Arian, the Mass can be seen as a sacrifice offered to the Father by the Son in the Holy Spirit or as a sacrifice offered to the Father, to the Son, and to the Spirit."[8] The Roman Canon—so ancient that it antedates the Arian controversy itself—is addressed *to* the Father *through* the Son ("Te igitur, clementissime Pater, per Iesum Christum Filium tuum, supplices rogamus, ac petimus"); the oblation is offered to the Father on behalf of the salvation of the world, with Christ as the Mediator between God and man. Pope Pius XII in *Mystici Corporis* 90 says that this is a reasonable way of praying, given the mystery of the redemption and the role in it of Christ as Mediator and High Priest.

4. Jesus Christ is, however, *true God*, the natural (not adopted) Son of God; the Catholic faith is unwavering in its confession of his eternal divinity, against every form of Arianism that has seduced the minds of men. This means that in all his actions and sufferings—no matter how human or creaturely, even those that are incompatible with the divine nature—it is always the second divine Person who is the *subject* of the acts and sufferings. This is what gives them their infinite worth and power for man's salvation.

5. Given the above points, it is clear that if an Arian were in charge of liturgy, he would wish to get rid of, or decentralize, or at least obscure, the confession of Trinitarian equality and majesty (cf. the Preface of the Most Holy Trinity, "Qui cum

---

8 *La Trinité chrétienne dans l'histoire* (Paris: Éditions Beauchesne, 1975), 451. The pre-Arian form is referred to as a "subordinating doxology" while the post-Arian (and anti-Arian) form is referred to as a "coordinating doxology." Both forms were defended by the Church Fathers such as St. Basil the Great, but it was the former in particular whose orthodoxy had to be proved and guarded against subordinationism.

Unigenito Filio tuo"), and by the same token demote Christ to a sub-divine place—as the one, namely, *through whom* the sacrifice of praise is offered to the Father-God. The Arian would understand "*per* Christum" as an implicit denial of the divinity of Christ. While he would be quite mistaken to think that this is the only meaning the formula can have, or even its proper first-level meaning, he would certainly have lent an Arian coloring to the liturgy if he had simultaneously stripped away unambiguous prayers to the Trinity of Persons as well as prayers directed to Jesus Christ as God.

Consider, then, the classical Roman liturgy.

IN REGARD TO THE BLESSED TRINITY

1. A solemn prayer is addressed to the Blessed Trinity both at the conclusion of the Offertory and after the Postcommunion—to give, as it were, the proper theological setting, the first beginning and last end, of the Eucharistic sacrifice: "Suscipe, Sancta Trinitas" (Figure 10) and "Placeat tibi, Sancta Trinitas." These prayers use the *per Christum* conclusion, emphasizing that the sacrifice is offered by Christ in his human nature to the one divine nature, Father, Son, and Holy Spirit.

2. The Preface of the Most Holy Trinity (Figure 11), appointed for all the Sundays after Epiphany and after Pentecost, of which there can be as many as 28, is essentially a summary of the Athanasian Creed, "Quicumque vult," which is itself one of the greatest Trinitarian confessions in the entire Latin tradition.[9]

3. The Gloria expresses, with magnificent beauty, the Catholic confession of the Trinity of Persons in one divine essence. Used in the celebration of every third-class feast (or higher) of a saint or mystery in the life of Christ, the

---

9   The practice of using this Preface for the Sunday Masses after Epiphany and Pentecost was introduced by Pope Clement XIII in 1759; prior to this, the Common Preface was used. Thus, we are looking at a rather "late" development in the history of the Roman liturgy—an excellent example of the rite's *organic* development, which witnesses gradual enhancements and occasional prunings, but not sudden and radical alterations in fundamental structure, content, or ethos.

Figure 10. The priest praying to the Holy Trinity at the end of the Offertory ("Suscipe, Sancta Trinitas..."). Abolished in the Novus Ordo.

Gloria provides the Church militant a way to participate in the heavenly joy of the communion of saints. In practice, given the large number of third-class feasts (and higher), a daily communicant will often hear the Gloria, even several times a week.

4. The "Gloria Patri et Filio et Spiritui Sancto" is used three times—after Psalm 42, after the Introit verse, and after Psalm 25 [at the Lavabo]—counterbalancing the dominant "per Christum." At the principal Sunday Mass, an additional Gloria Patri would be sung after the verse at the Asperges.

5. The sign of the cross—"In nomine Patris, et Filii, et Spiritus Sancti," which mirrors the Gloria Patri—is made by *priest and congregation* at many significant moments: at the very beginning, before Psalm 42; at "Adjutorium nostrum in nomine Domini"; at "Indulgentiam"; at "Cum Sancto Spiritu, in gloria Dei Patris"; at "Et vitam venturi saeculi"; at "Benedictus qui venit in nomine Domini"; and at the final blessing.

6. The act of the priest's blessing this or that item with the sign of the cross is frequent throughout the liturgy, occurring dozens of times. For one who is awake and attentive to symbolism, each act of blessing is a visible witness to the power of the cross and a silent invocation of the Trinity.

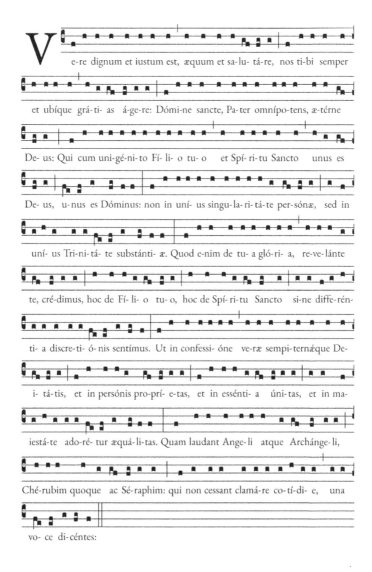

Figure 11. The Preface of the Holy Trinity, sung at least a couple of dozen times each year in the *usus antiquior*. In the Novus Ordo, reduced to once a year.

IN REGARD TO THE DIVINITY OF CHRIST

7. Confessing the true divinity of Jesus, the Church in her ancient liturgy also prays *to* him, most explicitly in:

a) the threefold "Christe eleison" of the Kyrie;

b) the Gloria ("Domine Deus, Rex caelestis, Deus Pater omnipotens. Domine Fili unigenite, Jesu Christe, Domine Deus, Agnus Dei, Filius Patris"; "Tu solus sanctus, tu solus Dominus, tu solus Altissimus, Jesu Christe");

c) the Agnus Dei;

d) the three prayers immediately following the Agnus Dei ("Domine Jesu Christe, qui dixisti Apostolis tuis"; "Domine Jesu Christe, Fili Dei vivi"; "Perceptio Corporis tui, Domine Jesu Christe"). [It is worthy of note that, while the conclusion "per Jesus Christum" is used throughout the liturgy, in these three prayers before communion, a shift occurs, as the priest directly addresses the Lord present upon the altar: "Domine Jesu Christe...qui vivis et regnas Deus" for the first; "Domine Jesu Christe, Fili Dei vivi...qui cum eodem Deo Patre et Spiritu Sancto vivis et regnas Deus" for the second; "Qui vivis et regnas cum Deo Patre in unitate Spiritus Sancti Deus" for the third];

e) the second prayer of ablution ("Corpus tuum, Domine, quod sumpsi").

8. Moreover, there are times when the Church prays expressly *to* Christ in the Collects and other *orationes* of the traditional Roman rite. Some examples, just from the month of October alone:

a) Collect for St. Thérèse (Oct. 3): "O Lord, who hast said: Unless ye become as little children ye shall not enter into the kingdom of heaven: grant us, we beseech Thee..."

b) Postcommunion for St. John Leonardi (Oct. 9): "Comforted by the sacred mysteries of Thy precious Body and Blood, we pray Thee, O Lord..."

c) Collect for St. Francis Borgia (Oct. 10): "O Lord Jesus Christ, who art both the pattern and the reward of true humility..."

d) Collect for St. Margaret Mary Alacoque (Oct. 17): "O Lord Jesus Christ, who didst in a wondrous manner reveal to the blessed virgin Margaret the unsearchable riches of Thy Heart..."

Figure 12. At the conclusion of nearly every Mass: genuflecting at the words "Et Verbum caro factum est..." Abolished in 1964.

e) Postcommunion for St. John Cantius (Oct. 20): "We who have been fed with the delights of Thy precious Body and Blood humbly beg Thy mercy, O Lord..."

9. Finally, nearly every Mass concludes with the Prologue of the Gospel of St. John: "In principio erat Verbum, et Verbum erat apud Deum, et *Deus erat Verbum*...."

In addition, one should attend to the dimension of the ceremonial, because, however justifiably we place an emphasis on liturgical *texts* in order to assess their orthodoxy or their tendencies (as I am doing here), we must not become rationalists who think that texts are the only relevant thing to look at. We are *men*, people of flesh and blood, who perceive and respond not only to words, but also to symbolic gestures, which constitute an even more basic human language that cuts across times and cultures. Thus, in the classical Roman liturgy, the *stipulated* bowing of the head at the mention of the Holy Name of Jesus, the genuflections before the tabernacle (assumed to be in the center, at the high altar, facing eastwards),[10] the bowing at the "Gloria Patri" and the

---

10   I am aware that the placement of the tabernacle at the high altar is a relatively late development in the history of church architecture, but

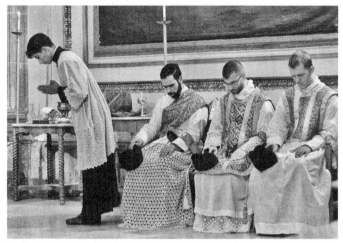

Figure 13. One of many moments in the *usus antiquior* when the clergy remove their birettas and all bow toward the tabernacle at the Name of Jesus.

"Suscipe, sancta Trinitas," the many other bows and genuflections, and so forth—all of these gestures are profoundly theological, conveying in sacred silence a deep Trinitarian and Christocentric meaning; all of them constitute small but true *acts of worship and praise* (see Figure 13).

When such gestures were radically stripped away in the name of simplification and greater "transparency," the moving musicality of the Mass as an ascending hymn of praise to the Trinity was gravely damaged. It became flattened out and socialized, taken over by a wearisome wordiness that has to *explain* everything from start to finish, usually with a goodly dose of ad-libbing. As Pope Benedict XVI has excellently said:

---

unlike the liturgical revolutionaries, I concur with Pope Pius XII's teaching in *Mediator Dei* that the Holy Spirit guides the Church into the fullness of liturgical truth, and that later developments, provided they are in continuity with—one might say, extrapolated from—the Tradition that has come before, are therefore not to be scorned or disapproved of. In contrast, to *remove* the tabernacle from the center once it has become normal is a theological demotion or deprivation that is quite unlike the mere *lack* of this norm in earlier times. See my article "The Removal of Tabernacles and the Desacrificialization of the Mass," *OnePeterFive*, April 8, 2022.

In our form of the liturgy [i.e., the Novus Ordo] there is a tendency that, in my opinion, is false, namely, the complete "inculturation" of the liturgy into the contemporary world. The liturgy is thus supposed to be shortened; and everything that is supposedly unintelligible should be removed from it; it should, basically, be transposed down to an even "flatter" language. But this is a thoroughgoing misunderstanding of the essence of the liturgy and of liturgical celebration. For in the liturgy one doesn't grasp what's going on in a simply rational way, as I understand a lecture, for example, but in a manifold way, with all the senses, and by being drawn into a celebration that isn't invented by some commission but that, as it were, comes to me from the depths of the millennia and, ultimately, of eternity.[11]

Now, while it is impossible *a priori* for a Catholic to maintain that the new Missal as promulgated by Paul VI or John Paul II is actually (that is, formally) Arian or semi-Arian, one may legitimately ask about the private motives and opinions which led to the following changes.

IN REGARD TO THE BLESSED TRINITY

1. *Both* the prayer of offering to the Trinity ("Suscipe, Sancta Trinitas") *and* the prayer of homage to the Trinity ("Placeat tibi, Sancta Trinitas") were abolished.

2. The Preface of the Most Holy Trinity is heard extremely rarely in Novus Ordo liturgies; according to the rubrics it is required only for Trinity Sunday itself. As a result, most Catholics will not be formed in any sustained way by the rich dogmatic teaching of this Preface, which demands to be heard many times before one can begin to grasp what it is saying.

3. The recitation of the Gloria has been severely curtailed to Sundays and major feast days.

4. All iterations of the "Gloria Patri" have been abolished from the Mass.[12]

5. The use of the sign of the cross has been reduced to the start of the liturgy and its conclusion.

---

11   *Salt of the Earth*, trans. Adrian Walker (San Francisco: Ignatius Press, 1997), 175.
12   The Gloria Patri managed to survive in the Liturgy of the Hours.

6. In like manner, the use of the sign of the cross in priestly blessings of objects involved in the liturgy has dwindled to almost nothing.

IN REGARD TO THE DIVINITY OF CHRIST

7. The prayers addressed *to* Christ have been lessened:

a) The "Christe eleison" remains, but reduced to a twofold instead of threefold petition[13] (thus destroying its eloquent 3 × 3 Trinitarian structure).

b) The Gloria, as pointed out, is no longer frequent.

c) The "Agnus Dei" remains,

d) but the prayers following it have been severely deformed. The missal now instructs the priest to *choose* between the second and third preparatory prayers—he is not to say both. Moreover, the Trinitarian conclusions of these latter prayers have been stripped away.

e) The prayers of ablution are abolished, and the rubrics for cleansing the vessels are less detailed and exacting.[14] In many parishes, the sacred vessels are not even cleansed until after Mass; they are left on a tray that is carried out after Mass into the sacristy. Scenarios like this (or worse) are quite common, and show a massive decline in reverence toward the "divine, holy, most pure, immortal, heavenly and life-creating, awesome mysteries of Christ," as the Divine Liturgy of St. John Chrysostom describes the Eucharist.

8. The Novus Ordo missal *systematically* abolished prayers addressed to Jesus Christ. Virtually none of these old Collects, Secrets, or Postcommunions remain. In their place are

---

13 If one is lucky, one might hear a schola sing a threefold Kyrie, since the Ordinaries that require, for musical reasons, a threefold Kyrie remain in the Solesmes books; but singing at that level is rarely heard in Novus Ordo parish settings.

14 This lends strongly, of course, to the Protestant view that Christ comes to be present in the symbolic action of "breaking and sharing the bread and cup"; once the distribution is over, the bread and wine may be treated as ordinary food, since they are no longer serving a sacramental *function*. So, the priest can leave the vessels on the side table and cleanse them afterwards. This happens to be the Byzantine custom, but in that case it is accompanied by many prayers and much reverence, and is *never* done by laymen.

Offspring of Arius in the Holy of Holies

prayers that address "God," "Lord," or "Father" and end with the *per Christum* formula. A notable and welcome exception comes on the occasion of the Solemnity of the Most Holy Body and Blood of Christ, where the Collect and Postcommunion directly address the Second Person of the Blessed Trinity. In this instance, the redactors of the new missal carried over the prayers of the old missal.

9. Last but not least, the customary Last Gospel was dismissed as a medieval accretion, a private pious exercise. As a consequence, the only time a Catholic will hear the sublime Prologue of St. John's Gospel is if he attends the Mass of Christmas Day or the Feast of St. John on December 27th.

More could be said, but the above is sufficient for the purpose of documenting the tendency or appearance I have in mind.[15]

Now, what was it that Pope Pius XII had taught in his great encyclical *Mystici Corporis* of 1943? In no. 90 we read:

> Finally there are those [partisans of the liturgical movement] who assert that our prayers should be directed not to the person of Jesus Christ but rather to God, or to the Eternal Father through Christ, since our Savior as Head of his Mystical Body is only "Mediator of God and men" (1 Tim 2:5). But this certainly is opposed not only to the mind of the Church and to Christian usage but to truth. For, to speak exactly, Christ is Head of the universal Church as he exists at once in both his natures (cf. St. Thomas, *De Veritate*, q. 29, a. 4); moreover he himself has solemnly declared: "If you shall ask me anything in my name, that I will do" (Jn 14:14). For although prayers are very often directed to the Eternal Father through the only-begotten Son, especially in the Eucharistic Sacrifice—in which Christ, at once Priest and Victim, exercises in a special

---

15 There is some consolation to be found in the fact that the postconciliar Liturgy of the Hours, especially in its official Latin text, contains numerous invocations of Jesus and a fair number of prayers addressed to him. One could more successfully exhibit the Church's faith from these books than from the Missal. This in itself shows the magnitude of the problem: however important the Liturgy of the Hours is (and surely it is important in the lives of thousands of religious, not to mention a fair number of lay people), the Mass is the central act of worship of the Mystical Body of Christ, and perhaps not even 1% of the Christian faithful today will be shaped by the Liturgy of the Hours.

manner the office of Mediator—nevertheless not infrequently even in this Sacrifice prayers are addressed to the Divine Redeemer also; for all Christians must clearly know and understand that the man Jesus Christ is also the Son of God and God himself. And thus when the Church militant offers her adoration and prayers to the Immaculate Lamb, the Sacred Victim, her voice seems to re-echo the never-ending chorus of the Church triumphant: "To him that sitteth on the throne and to the Lamb benediction and honor and glory and power for ever and ever" (Rev 5:13).

As happened also with the same Pope's unambiguous directives in *Mediator Dei* (1947) about many other aspects of the liturgy, the teaching contained in the above section seems to have been not only forgotten, but actively opposed, in the actual execution of the "reforms" that the Fathers of the Second Vatican Council demanded—surely, for the most part having Pius XII's understanding in their minds.

Traditionalist authors have, of course, documented the many different ways in which the Roman Rite was deliberately and systematically watered down, as regards, for example, devotion to the Virgin Mary and to the angels and saints, to the Passion of our Lord, to the Real Presence, and so on.[16] My argument here adds one more confirmation that we are looking at not simply a downplaying of this or that incidental aspect, but more disturbingly, *a dechristianization of the liturgy as such*, removing from it what is theologically most distinctive of the Christian faith and most central to our corporate worship.

What was intended to replace this substance? Man himself, modern man, communal man, the worker, the actor, the self-discovering and self-exulting ego—not the Christian humanism of *Gaudium et Spes* but the Enlightenment humanism of an endless catalogue of unbelievers from Descartes and Newton (who professed himself an Arian)[17] to Kant,

---

16 The prominent place of angels in the old rite of Mass and the diminishment of their presence in the new rite is discussed in my article "A Brief Introduction to Angels," *OnePeterFive*, September 8, 2016.
17 See Maurice F. Wiles, *Archetypal Heresy: Arianism through the Centuries* (Oxford: Clarendon Press; New York: Oxford University Press, 1996), especially ch. 4, "The Rise and Fall of British Arianism."

Rousseau, Nietzsche, Derrida, and so on. The anthropological correlative to Arianism is Pelagianism. Just as Jesus, for the Arian, is elevated to divinity through his heroic acts, so we, by *our* heroic acts, elevate ourselves to a position of divinity. So false a view is this that it has led not to Christian victory in a renewed evangelization, but to the banality and sterility of what Robert Barron aptly calls "beige Catholicism."

I would go further and point out that the two heresies most "natural" to fallen man are precisely Arianism and Pelagianism. Leave a Christian community to its own devices and you are likely to end up with some kind of Pelagian and Arian understanding of the faith. And one can see the close link between these two: Pelagius teaches that man (the son of Adam) is really a god, whereas Arius teaches that god (the Son of God) is really a man. In a certain way, if you combine these heresies you end up with Feuerbach. Fallen man is Pelagian man — Promethean, Cartesian, Baconian man. Fallen man is Arian man: the mystery of Christ is too much for us, we try to downplay it, qualify it, let it slip away into a vague spiritualism, or revert to a more primitive Jewish monotheism. The spiritual life of the Church, as expressed supremely in her liturgy, has always fought against these tendencies. The missal of Paul VI removes huge segments of anti-Arian and anti-Pelagian content.[18] Is this not a cause for the deepest concern—indeed, for the deepest doubts about the "reform" and the new missal it launched against unsuspecting believers?

Moreover, is it not true that the more reverence one has toward Christ, true God and true man, Judge of the living and of the dead, the less one will want to tamper with the Mass in which he is not only worshiped but over which he himself presides as High Priest, in which he himself is offered up as victim, and received as our spiritual food? And is it not true that only a person of Pelagian tendencies would think he could or should be "pro-active" with regard to the

---

18 See Anthony Cekada, *Work of Human Hands: A Theological Critique of the Mass of Paul VI* (West Chester, OH: Philothea Press, 2010), especially 219–45.

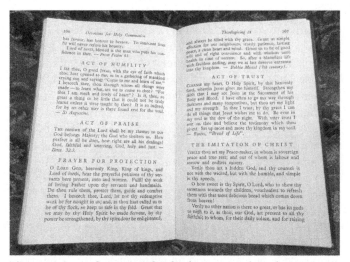

Figure 14. A popular preconciliar book, *Devotions for Holy Communion* (this edition, 1959) shows prayers to Jesus and to the Holy Spirit, and frequent mentions of all three Divine Persons. Perhaps CHW should pick up a copy as part of their future research.

Figure 15. Another popular preconciliar book on devotion to the Holy Spirit, first published in 1939. Unfortunately, since lay Catholics did not know who the "Holy Spirit" was, the book remained largely unread, in spite of going through many editions, apparently because paper was so plentiful around the time of World War II.

liturgy—changing it, reworking it, simplifying here, adding there, as if the responsibility for making it or making it better lay principally with *us*, and not with Christ, the Apostles, and the slow process of time in which the centuries add jewels to a common inheritance jealously guarded? "Jesus Christ is the same yesterday and today and forever. Do not be led away by diverse and strange teachings" (Heb 13:8–9a).

That, as they say, is that. And it is worth noting that a response of the same kind of thoroughness can be made to nearly every paragraph in CHW's five-part series. Faced with the breathtaking balderdash that CHW have served up, one almost feels it would be better to draw a curtain of modesty over their naked corpus, or perhaps a sanitary cover over the corpse; but the *amor veritatis* requires, to some extent at least, the exposure of errors, fallacies, and offenses, however distasteful it may be.

May the Holy Trinity have mercy on rebels against Catholic tradition; may Christ our God deliver us from the hands of His persecutors, especially those in the apostolic college who emulate Judas Iscariot; and may the Holy Spirit forgive the blasphemies against the pattern of divine worship He has inspired across the centuries of faith.

10

Was Liturgical Latin Introduced As—and Because It Was—the Vernacular?

I N SECTION 5 OF THE SYNOPTIC VERSION of their series, CHW make the following claim:

> The Tridentine Mass was itself a reform. Earlier, the Mass came to be celebrated in Latin in the western Church not because it was a sacred language but because it was the vernacular of its day; likewise, earlier still, with Greek. Jesus himself employed Aramaic, the vernacular of his time and place. If he had not, the apostles would have had no clue as to what he was doing at the Last Supper, nor could they then have actively participated in that first Eucharistic liturgy. The same holds true for the faithful today.

Another *Church Life Journal* publication—Angela Franks' "In the Swarm: The Liturgy and Liquid Identity" of January 12, 2023, the transcript, be it noted, of a keynote address for the Society for Catholic Liturgy—echoes this claim. Like CHW, Franks repeats a misconception about church history that has shown a remarkable resilience against all attempts to correct it:

> We need solidity... Let us not, however, dismiss too quickly the balancing reality of liquidity. The history of the development of the liturgy and of sacramental theology bears this out as well. I will not attempt to delve into this history, but let us take one simple example: the changes in the liturgical languages of the Church. *Very early Christian liturgy privileged Greek (although not exclusively), as the language of Scripture and the universal "common" (koine) tongue, but other rites in the vernacular have ancient roots, such as Coptic and Syrian. The standardization of Latin as the Western liturgical language began*

to occur when Latin became the *"common"* tongue. In this and in many other ways, liturgy has developed and changed under the guidance of the Church.¹

The assertion is a familiar one: all historic liturgies were originally conducted in the common language of their time, and whenever that vernacular changed, the language of the liturgy also changed—or, presumably, *should* have changed. The Latinization of the liturgy in the fourth century is therefore to be explained as a transition from a no longer accessible vernacular (*koine* Greek) to a newly ascendant vernacular (Latin).

The trouble with this assertion is that it is, at very least, misleading, and in certain respects simply false. In her classic work *Liturgical Latin: Its Origins and Character*, published by CUA Press in 1957, Christine Mohrmann (1903–88) explained at length, with an abundance of examples, that the Latin of the early Roman liturgy is anything *but* the vernacular Latin of its time. It abounded in archaicisms, Hebraisms, legalisms, odd or intricate syntax, and rhetorical tropes. In this respect it was similar to the unusual Greek of the Septuagint and of early Greek Christian liturgies—which should hardly surprise us, given that the Jews themselves continued to use Hebrew in their worship, which, long before the time of Christ, was a language no longer commonly spoken. Indeed, contrary to CHW's statement, the Son of God would have conducted the Last Supper at least partially in an archaic sacral language that was no longer the common tongue.²

---

1   Emphasis added.
2   "At the time of Christ, the Jews used the language of Old Hebraic for their services, though it was incomprehensible to the people. In the synagogues, only the readings and a few prayers relating to them were written in the mother tongue of Aramaic; the great, established prayer texts were recited in Hebrew. Although Christ adamantly attacked the formalism of the Pharisees in other respects, He never questioned this practice. Insofar as the Passover Meal was primarily celebrated with Hebrew prayers, the Last Supper was also characterized by elements of a sacred language. It is therefore possible that Christ spoke the words of Eucharistic consecration in the Hebrew *lingua sacra*" (Michael Fiedrowicz, *The Traditional Mass: History, Form, and Theology of the Classical Roman Rite* [Brooklyn: Angelico Press, 2020], 153).

The same author defines "the characteristics of a sacred language" as: "(1) a conscious distancing from the words of colloquial language, which

The discussion of language in Michael Fiedrowicz's *The Traditional Mass: History, Form, and Theology of the Classical Roman Rite* is quite illuminating. The entire section (153–78) is well worth reading; I shall quote here only the most immediately pertinent passages.

> Latin translations of the Bible originated in the middle of the second century. But even these developments were not simply a colloquial element within the divine worship. These texts also possessed a sacred stylizing, insofar as the Latin translations bore a strong biblical complexion through a certain literalism, that is, a close following of the scriptural forms of speech, and in this way they acquired a peculiarly foreign style, soon felt to be holy....
>
> An appreciation for the sacred formation of the holy texts was the inheritance of old Roman religiosity. In order to conform to the requirements of a hieratic style, Christian Latinity first had to be perfected to a certain degree and be capable of rising above everyday speech. If the development of a Christian sacred language thoroughly drew on particular elements of style of old Roman traditions, then such an impartial use of Rome's cultural inheritance was conceivable only in the later peacetime of the Church (from 313 on) when the pagan religion no longer presented a serious threat to Christianity; and just as confidently as the Church introduced the spoils of heathen temples into her own basilicas, she made the stylistic forms of ancient prayer texts her own.
>
> *The use of Latin as a sacred language that stylistically tied in with old Roman traditions* would especially have won over to the Christian Faith the influential elite of the empire, who at this time [fourth century] had just begun to discover anew their texts of classical literature. The Church

---

makes the 'complete otherness' of the divine felt; (2) an archaizing or at least conservative tendency to favor antiquated expressions and adhere to certain speech forms from centuries ago, as is well-suited for the worship of an eternal and unchanging God; (3) the use of foreign words that evoke religious associations, as, for example, the Hebrew and Aramaic forms of the words *alleluia, Sabaoth, hosanna, amen, maranatha* in the Greek books of the New Testament; and finally, (4) syntactic and phonetic stylizations (e.g., parallelisms, alliterations, rhymes, and rhythmic sentence endings) that clearly structure the train of thought, are memorable and allow for easy recollection, and strive for tonal beauty" (ibid., 154–55).

had at its disposal a language of prayer whose content was renewed by revelation and at the same time formally bound to the Roman tradition.³

And most to the point:

> The introduction of Latin into the Roman liturgy, then, certainly did not indicate the abandonment of the principle of a sacred language. In that sense, Latinization cannot be understood as an argument for the vernacular, as though with the change of the liturgical language, the Church in Rome were simply accounting for the fact that the majority of the faithful by then were no longer Greek-speaking, but Latin-speaking Christians. The Latin of the liturgy was identical with neither the classical Latin of Cicero nor the colloquial language, Vulgar Latin. It was, at least in the texts of prayers, a highly stylized form of language, which was not readily understandable to the average Roman of the fourth and fifth centuries: "No Roman had ever spoken in the language or style of the Canon or the prayers of the Roman Mass."
>
> It was rather a language that sought to awaken the experience of the sacred and to raise man above the things of this world to God. This rising up to God was accomplished neither by a complete renunciation of language (holy silence, *silentium mysticum*) nor in the form of glossolalia, the gift of tongues (cf. 1 Cor 14:2), which no longer possessed its communicative character; rather, it was accomplished by means of a sacred language that drew from biblical sources as well as from the hieratic idiom of pagan Rome and, not least of all, also made use of ancient rhetoric. As a glance at the historical development demonstrates, the Church did not slip Latin on as a garment that could be replaced with another at any time. Rather, the Roman Church artistically forged for herself her own Latin for her liturgy, and in it she uniquely expressed her identity.⁴

In a recent book—which, incidentally, engages with many of the issues raised by both Dr. Franks in her lecture and by CHW in their series—Dr. Joseph Shaw summarizes and comments on Dr. Mohrmann's research:

---

3 Fiedrowicz, 156–58, emphasis added.
4 Fiedrowicz, 158.

The argument from "expedience" may seem particularly weak today, in light of the stress laid by the reformist party on how the liturgy was translated into Latin to aid the comprehension of the faithful, and how it has been translated into a number of other languages by the churches of the East. This argument, familiar as it is, is misleading. We do not have any records of the reasoning behind the composition of the Latin liturgy, but the kind of Latin used suggests that popular comprehension was not the overriding consideration, in contrast to the importance of appropriating the tradition of solemn and sacred Latin for the use of the Church at a moment when Paganism was no longer a threat....

The Roman Canon would have been at least as incomprehensible to fourth-century prostitutes and bums as Cicero's convoluted orations would have been to their predecessors. In such cases the style, vocabulary, and in general the register is not designed for immediate and universal comprehension. In the case of the Roman Canon, we find archaisms, neologisms, Hebraisms and other foreign loan words, and echoes of the unnatural syntax of sacred and legal language. In any case, from an early date, and quite possibly from the start, it was said silently, by a celebrant hidden from the congregation in the nave by curtains. If verbal comprehension was the object of the Latin liturgy's composition, Pope Damasus (if it was he) and his collaborators went about their task in a most surprising way.[5]

Abbé Claude Barthe develops this point along the same lines (it is useful to show just how many experts on this subject concur, against the facile picture presented by CHW):

The triple invocation has retained the Greek language (*Kyrios, Christos, Kyrios, eleeo*, to have mercy), the language that the Roman liturgy used until about the middle of the third century, in fact until the Roman clergy had assimilated the Latin language sufficiently for them to be able to create a suitable translation of the Greek Bible. The texts, the quotations, and the biblical references are in fact the backbone of the liturgy; and the clergy had now sufficiently digested the Latin of public life, of the orators, the rhetors, the officials, for it to be possible for them to render the liturgy in a Latin of adequate nobility. Nevertheless, no one forgot that Greek had been the first

---

5   Joseph Shaw, *The Liturgy, the Family, and the Crisis of Modernity* (Lincoln, NE: Os Justi Press, 2023), 60; 72.

language of Christian prayer in Rome (more because it was the language of culture and the Bible than because it was the vernacular)....

From the stylistic point of view, the priestly prayers (apart of course from the *Pater noster*) are the best example of the liturgical language that the Church of Rome created when Latin was first used in worship. They are typical of the Late Antique rhetoric in which their clerical composers of the fourth century, and above all, of the fifth and sixth centuries, were trained, adapted to the particular artistic prose of the liturgy, with a rhythm, a vocabulary, and a taste that is sober and solemn. The style found in the great liturgical orations (the prayers, the Preface, the Canon) is that of the *elogium*, the panegyric style (the *celebratio*), intended to produce a speech thanking God in the way that one might thank an emperor or a magistrate, or conversely to thank the magistrate and emperor in the way that one might thank God....

For this purpose liturgical prose makes use of different Roman rhetorical registers—the petition, the supplication, the celebration—and of stylistic devices highly valued by the very literate, including antitheses (earthly goods *vis-à-vis* heavenly goods, for example), parallelism and balance, asyndeton (between nouns or adjectives, for example), assonance (repetition of a sound), hyperbaton (separation of a subject from its verb, of a noun from its qualifier), chiasmus, and wordplay with similar-sounding words, paronomasia, etc. The literary success of this renewal of Latin solemnity and of the Roman *gravitas* is the achievement of a Christian Rome that was determined to surpass the ancients in the honor of Christ. The best examples of this style are the Collects, with their rhythm, their concision, their balanced antitheses, their oratorical flow; as also are the Prefaces; and, with its tone at once solemn and well constructed, the unsurpassable masterpiece of Christian Latinity, a sublime piece of poetry in prose: the Roman Canon. This liturgical Latin of Late Antiquity became a mold imparting its shape to a greater or lesser extent to all the subsequent compositions; much as the basilican plan, reinterpreted by Christian worship, remained visible in all the subsequent architectural variations.[6]

---

6 Claude Barthe, *A Forest of Symbols: The Traditional Mass and Its Meaning*, trans. David J. Critchley (Brooklyn, NY: Angelico Press, 2023), 47; 53–54.

With considerations like these in mind, it becomes clear why we need to be extremely cautious about making claims like "Christian liturgy privileged... the universal 'common' tongue" and "the standardization of Latin as the Western liturgical language began to occur when Latin became the 'common' tongue." Both of these claims are demonstrably false.

As to the first, Christian liturgy, even when first rendered in the language of a certain people or cultural sphere, always exhibited peculiar traits that linguists describe as sacral or hieratic, and which would already have *sounded that way* even to those living at the time it was first used, but much more so to those who come in the generations after, given both the continual development of the vernacular and the tendency toward a strong conservatism of forms on the part of the Church in every one of its historic rites. This, in fact, is the same deep instinct of reverence for tradition that impelled the Israelites—and Christ Himself at the Last Supper with the apostles—to keep at least parts of the liturgy in Hebrew long after Hebrew had ceased to be an everyday language of communication.[7]

---

[7] Let us not forget that a large number of Eastern Christians (whether Catholic or Orthodox) continue to use languages that linguists would categorize as sacral or hieratic: "One has to be careful about claiming that 'use of the vernacular' is characteristic of Eastern rites *in the same way* in which it characterizes the Novus Ordo in the latter's vast number of translations into modern languages. The vernacular *can* be used, as when the Divine Liturgy is offered in English throughout the United States, yet a plurality of older customs will be found too. Greek-speaking churches/patriarchates use Byzantine liturgical Greek. The small Italian-Albanian Church in Calabria and Sicily continues to have most of its liturgy in Greek on Sundays and feasts. Slavic Orthodox churches were long accustomed to the use of Old Church Slavonic; Russians still use it predominantly or exclusively, and while Serbians, Bulgarians, Macedonians, Belarusians, and Ukrainians use much vernacular, Slavonic is still in use. The Romanian Orthodox Church used Church Slavonic/liturgical Greek from the tenth to the seventeenth centuries, when it was replaced by Romanian (which was nevertheless influenced by Church Slavonic, making it quite non-vernacular in feel). The Georgian Orthodox Church uses old literary Georgian as a liturgical language. The Coptic Orthodox use the literary Coptic language, and although its use diminished during long Muslim rule, it is still alive and being reintroduced. The Ethiopian Orthodox use the 'dead language' Ge'ez in their liturgy. The Melkite and Syrian liturgies of the Near East use classical Syrian and Arabic. The

As to the second claim, Latin was spoken for centuries before the Roman liturgy was rendered in Latin; the reason for the delay, therefore, was not that Latin was not a "common tongue" prior to this, but rather, that it still had pagan associations and lacked the resources needed for a distinctively Christian register suitable for divine worship. When Roman society (above all, in its aristocracy) had become more Christianized and an abundant Christian literature was available, the time was ripe for the Latinization of the Roman liturgy. As Fr. Uwe Michael Lang writes:

> The formation of a Latin liturgical idiom was a major contribution to this project of evangelising Roman culture and thus attracting the influential elites of the city and the empire to the Christian faith. It would not be accurate to describe this process simply as the adoption of the vernacular language in the liturgy, if "vernacular" is taken to mean "colloquial." The Latin of the canon, of the collects and prefaces of the Mass transcended the conversational idiom of ordinary people. This highly stylised form of speech, shaped to express complex theological ideas, would not have been easy to follow by the average Roman Christian of late antiquity.[8]

Fr. Lang also explains why the East saw a profusion of languages (including the Coptic and Syrian of which Dr. Franks makes mention):

> The Christian East was in a position to make use of several languages that carried with themselves a certain cultural, social and political weight: in addition to Greek, which retained a strong presence well into the fifth century, Syriac, Coptic Armenian, Georgian and Ethiopic began to be employed in the liturgy. *In the Christian West, vernacular languages were not used in divine worship.* The case of Roman North Africa is instructive: Augustine held Punic in esteem and made sure that the bishop chosen for a Punic-speaking region knew the language needed for his ministry. However, there are no extant documents of a Punic liturgy, whether Catholic or Donatist. *The religious*

Armenians use a classical literary Armenian" (Kwasniewski, *Once and Future Roman Rite*, 282–83).

8 Uwe M. Lang, *The Roman Mass: From Early Christian Origins to Tridentine Reform* (Cambridge: Cambridge University Press, 2023), 109.

prestige of the Roman church and its bishop helped Latin become the only liturgical language of the West. This would prove an important factor in furthering ecclesiastical, cultural and political unity. *Latinitas* became one of the defining characteristics of Western Europe.[9]

So successful was this endeavor that Latin would remain the mother tongue of the Western Church at prayer for the next 1,600 years. The core of the Roman rite continued intact, while growing organically in its calendar, prayer texts, lectionary, rubrical codification, and artistic externals. Truly one and the same Roman rite, as a person is one and the same, though he was once a child and is now a man; yet also the source of an endless profusion of cultural riches on every continent. The traditional liturgy demonstrates the most harmonious interplay of the "solid" and the "liquid" in Western history, in support of a transnational and transcultural unity of religion—an interplay and a unity that have been lost in the demotic babelization and ritual fragmentation caused by the postconciliar reforms.

---

9 Lang, 109–10, emphasis added. Regarding Roman prestige: one can well understand why Charlemagne would have adopted for the Franks the Latin liturgy of Rome.

11
The Dubious Legacy of Leonardo's Last Supper

IN SECTION 4 OF THE SYNOPTIC VERSION of their series, CHW make a case in favor of *versus populum*, that is, having the priest face the people for the Eucharistic liturgy:

> That the priest and the faithful face one another during the Eucharistic canon gives full meaning to what Jesus himself declared and enacted at the Last Supper. The priest, *in persona Christi*, takes the bread and declares to "all of" the faithful that they should "take" and "eat of it, for this is my body, which will be given up for you." Likewise, the priest takes the chalice and again declares that the faithful should "take" and "drink from it, for this is the chalice of my blood, the blood of the new and eternal covenant, which will be poured out for you and for many for the forgiveness of sins." *All of the faithful present* are invited to behold the bread and wine, and are to take, eat, and drink, for in so doing they are incorporated into Jesus' one saving sacrifice offered to his Father.

This is a rather curious argument. In the TLM, the faithful are certainly shown the Body and Blood of Christ, to the extent that these symbols can be seen with the eyes: they are elevated after the consecrations, and the host is held up to the people at the "Ecce, Agnus Dei" prior to the threefold "Domine, non sum dignus." But if what is meant is that the people should somehow behold transubstantiation, that's simply impossible: this change is miraculous, supernatural, and hidden, and not even the priest's eyes can "see" it. All must believe with a faith that—in accord with the very definition of faith (see Heb 11:1)—lacks sight of the truth believed in.

A much more fundamental problem emerges, however, from CHW's manner of describing the Eucharistic liturgy.

They speak as if the Mass is a reenactment of the Last Supper, failing to grasp that it is a re-presentation of Good Friday's sacrifice of Christ on Calvary, of which the Last Supper was a pre-interpretive anticipation. We do not say that we are attending "the Lord's Supper," as Protestants often do; we say rather that we assist at the Holy Sacrifice of the Mass, which is identical to that of the Cross, differing only in manner (unbloody instead of bloody).[1]

That being said, CHW seem to possess a poor grasp even of how the Last Supper itself was conducted; a little study on their part would have shown the impossibility of making the kind of argument they made in defense of *versus populum*. Begging the reader's patience, I will explain the problem by a means of an artistic detour.

In the church where I attend Mass most often, the high altar bears a bas-relief scene just below the *mensa* that reproduces, with a high degree of exactitude, the famous—possibly too famous—*Last Supper* painting by Leonardo da Vinci (Figure 16). Leonardo's *Last Supper* and many others paintings like it—Ghirlandaio's at San Marco and Andrea del Castagno's at the convent of St Apollonia, both in Florence; Giovan Pietro da Cemmo's in the convent of St Augustine in Crema, etc.—were painted for the refectories of religious houses; they were not intended as images for churches, much less for sanctuaries of churches. The open, longitudinal arrangement was designed to place Christ at the center, to make the action at the table clearly visible, and to separate Judas more evidently from the rest of the Apostles. The spiritual lesson of such refectory paintings was manifold: that one should see the figure of Christ in one's religious superior at the head table; that one should decide to be among the good apostles by being a good and obedient religious, and not faithless like Judas; that one should remember how every meal shared with the brethren bears a likeness to this banquet of supreme charity, which explains why the refectory service is a little liturgy in its own right. Because Leonardo's *Last Supper* was

---

[1] On all this, see the dogmatic teaching of the Session 22 of the Council of Trent and any standard manual like Ludwig Ott's.

The Dubious Legacy of Leonardo's Last Supper

Figure 16. Leonardo da Vinci, *The Last Supper* (1495–98), refectory of the Convent of Santa Maria delle Grazie, Milan, Italy.

in a refectory, it was never intended for "public consumption."

I have a hypothesis not so much about the great artist's intentions for his piece as about the deleterious consequences of an overuse of replicas of it in modern churches. If we look now to the altar sculpture of my local church (Figures 17 and 18), we note the person of Christ dominating in the center, looking squarely out at the viewer, with His disciples gathered round. Placed front and center at the altar of a church, this imagery might look somewhat like a priest celebrating Mass *versus populum*.

Michael Fiedrowicz offers a gentle critique of Leonardo:

> Luther had already invoked the Last Supper practice of Jesus for his corresponding demand [that the Eucharist should be celebrated *versus populum*]. A new type of visual representation that began to be implemented during the thirteenth century must have been formative for his notion of the events of that time. This representation is familiar in Leonardo Da Vinci's *Last Supper*: Jesus sitting on the rear side of a table in the middle of the Apostles, turned toward the observer of the scene. If Mass were made to correspond to this artistic presentation, the priest should stand at the altar across from the people and turn his gaze on them. This argument, however, is based on a misapprehension of ancient table manners as they would have been practiced at the Last Supper. There was at that time either a round or a semicircular table at whose open front side the food would be brought, while those partaking of the meal sat or reclined at the rear semicircle of the table. The place of honor was not in the middle, but rather on the right side. The one presiding over a meal never had another partaker across from his place. These original arrangements are shown in the oldest representations of the Last Supper until the Middle Ages. If this finding alone prevents the derivation of celebrating *versus populum* from Jesus' practice at the Last Supper, a look at the historical beginnings of the Eucharistic celebration demonstrates yet more that the primitive Church's congregation in no way repeated the Last Supper as such and did not consider the meal as the ritual original form of the Eucharist.

It is more than a little chilling to read the following words of Martin Luther and to reflect on the current situation of

Figure 17. An *ad orientem* high altar bearing Leonardo's imagery.

Figure 18. Close-up of the same altar.

Roman Catholic worship: "But in the true Mass among genuine Christians, the altar would not have to remain so [*sc.* facing east], and the priest would always turn to the people, as without doubt Christ did at the Lord's Supper. Well, that will be so in good time."[2]

---

2 *Deutsche Messe und Ordnung des Gottesdienstes* of the year 1526, in *Weimarer Ausgabe* 19:80.

Msgr. Nicola Bux makes a similar point as Fiedrowicz:

> Not a few people hold that it was only in late antiquity or the early Middle Ages that the Churches of the East and the West began to prefer administering [communion] directly in the mouth. But did Jesus give communion to the apostles on the hand or asking them to take it with their own hands? Visiting an exhibition of Tintoretto in Rome, I observed some "Last Suppers" in which Jesus gives communion to the apostles in the mouth. One could think that this has to do with an interpretation by the painter after the fact, a little like the posture of Jesus and the apostles at table, in the cenacle of Leonardo, which "updates" in the Western manner the Jewish custom, which was, instead, to be reclining at table. Reflecting further on this, the custom of giving communion to the faithful directly in the mouth can be considered not only as a Jewish tradition, and therefore apostolic, but also as going back to the Lord Jesus. The Jews and the peoples of the East in general had and today still have the custom of taking food with one's hands and placing it directly in the mouth of the lover or the friend. In the West this is done between couples in love and by the mother toward her little one, who is still inexperienced. The text of John is understood in this way: "Jesus then answered him [John]: 'It is he to whom I shall give a morsel of dipped bread.' Then, having dipped a morsel of bread, he gave it to Judas, son of Simon Iscariot. And as soon as he had taken the mouthful Satan entered into him" (13:26–27). But what should be said about the invitation of Jesus: "Take and eat.... Take and drink"? *Take* (in Greek, *labete*; in Latin, *accipite*) also means *receive*. If the mouthful is dipped, it cannot be taken with the hands; rather it is received directly into the mouth. It is true that Jesus consecrated bread and wine separately. But if during the "mystic supper" (as the East calls it) or Last Supper, the two consecrating gestures happened, so it seems, in different phases of the Paschal supper, nevertheless after Pentecost the apostles, aided by Jewish priests who had converted (cf. Acts 6:7), and who were, as we would say, experts in religious worship, united the gestures within the great Eucharistic prayer.[3]

My experience has been that a lot of Catholic church altars—especially the less expensive ones in the United States that were trying to look "traditional," from the late nineteenth

---

3   *No Trifling Matter: On the Inviolability of the Sacraments* (Brooklyn: Angelico Press, 2018), 94–95.

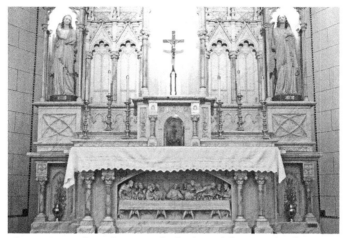

Figure 19. Another *ad orientem* high altar of the same kind.

century up to the middle of the twentieth—feature exactly this image of Leonardo's Last Supper carved into the front, where the priest and people would see it day after day after day.[4] (See Figure 19 for another example of a high altar, Figures 20 and 21 for *versus populum* altars.)

One wonders... Might this repetition of Leonardo's refectory conception have something to do with slowly disposing everyone to reimagine the Mass as an imitation of the Last Supper, and not even as a Jewish meal, but as a banquet fictitiously depicted by Leonardo? Perhaps the near-ubiquity of the *faux*-supper made it easier, when the time came, to justify the dismantling of a high altar that bore upon itself an image seemingly in contradiction with it, while at the same time installing a freestanding table that permitted the "presider" to imitate Leonardo's Christ (and the concelebrating clergy to imitate Leonardo's apostles on either side of Him).

---

4 Note, however, that according to older rubrics, such art should be visible only between the stripping of the altar on Maundy Thursday and the Easter Vigil; for the remaining 362/3 days of the year, it would be masked by the antependium. Alas, antependia tended to go the way of all flesh and are making at best a slow return. See Shawn Tribe, "The Historical, Theological, Liturgical and Artistic Case for Altar Frontals," *Liturgical Arts Journal*, November 16, 2017.

Figure 20. A *versus populum* sanctuary with Leonardo's scene under electric illumination.

Figure 21. Another *versus populum* altar with Leonardo's imagery.

If we look at churches with much older altars, or Liturgical Movement altars, we will see a far greater variety of iconographical images carved into the fronts of altars: the Lamb, especially; wreaths, palms, and other arborial designs; angels; cosmatesque patterns; etc. It seems much more appropriate for an altar to have such symbolic designs or to be dressed in cloth altar frontals in liturgical colors than to bear a by-now overdone Leonardo spin-off. We have here a fine example of how a work of artistic but ahistorical genius can intersect with commercial demand to flood the market with well-intentioned but conceptually harmful kitsch.

One can find images of Christ standing at the other side of the altar, over against the viewer, in Byzantine iconography as well, but this depiction does not suggest *versus populum*

Figure 22. A Byzantine representation of Christ the High Priest blessing the offerings.

as a manner of celebrating. The cross and book are set up for *ad orientem* worship, and, it should hardly be necessary to say, the practice of *versus populum* has never existed in the Eastern liturgical rites. The iconographic style makes it easier to see such an image rather as the expression of a mysterious present reality, the Lord coming into our midst through the liturgy we offer to Him and He offers through us, than of an historical event, a Jewish Passover meal, in Leonardo's reimagined dramatic form.

To sum up: the progressives like to go on and on about how the Last Supper is the original Mass and the model of all the other Masses. That's why (they say) it should be *versus populum* (awkward gasp: they don't even realize this makes no sense in the context of an ancient semicircular table with people reclining at it), and everyone should partake of the chalice, and we should sing a hymn afterwards, etc. Well, there's no doubt the Last Supper was the first Mass. Yet it was a most unusual, "one-off" Mass, because (1) it was a transitional form from Passover to Mass, (2) it was done as an interpretive anticipation of the bloody sacrifice on Good Friday which is the core meaning and reality of every subsequent Mass, (3) the Lord Himself knew, since He is the First Cause, that He would bring about tremendous development in the Christian liturgy over the centuries—this being right, just, gracious, and fitting for His own glory and the benefit of the people. As Archbishop Gänswein said in Heilgenkreuz on March 24, 2023:

> The external freedom [under Constantine] that now gave peace to the Church allowed something to blossom that had lain hidden like a grain of wheat in the catacombs and in the seclusion of the domestic churches. We can see this in the architecture of the churches, in the magnificent mosaics, but above all in sacred music and in the liturgy. Joseph Ratzinger, Pope Benedict, was deeply attached to this beauty of the faith and of the Church. This beauty, however, is not an insubstantial aesthetic surface, but the mirror of the action of the one God. This mirror is unclouded when truth and goodness can flourish unhindered. This unity of the true, the good, and the beautiful finds its highest expression in the liturgy celebrated with love and dignity. This is not merely something incidental, an amusement. It is not an "optional" but an "essential."[5]

So, whether our perspective is theological, aesthetic, or historical, looking to the Last Supper as a template—a "how-to" manual for the Mass—is an absolute non-starter.

That being said, funnily enough the suppertarians don't ever seem to advert to the fact that Our Lord, as the High Priest of the New Covenant, spoke at great length in exhortation and prayer (see the Gospel of John 13:31–17:26, the

---

5 Translation by Pater Edmund Waldstein, O.Cist., "Archbishop Gänswein on Constantine," *Sancrucensis*, March 25, 2023.

"Farewell Discourse" that culminates in the High Priestly Prayer of ch. 17), while the apostles participated by grumbling about the footwashing, whispering over who was the traitor, disputing over who was the greatest among them, swearing to follow Him no matter what (just before they abandoned Him), and then—some of them at least, the ones who boldly occupied the first pews—falling asleep in the Garden of Gethsemane afterwards. If you ask me, this looks like a liturgy in which the High Priest does most of the heavy lifting, and the "congregation" isn't exactly "actively participating" in the best way possible. So, to turn CHW's case on its head, one might envision the Last Supper as an exemplar for the *sacerdotalism* of the traditional rites, but surely it's no exemplar of active participation.

In the end, CHW—who also bring in nuptial imagery in their attempt to justify *versus populum*, saying that "a bridegroom faces his bride"—have misinterpreted the Mass as a romantic tête-à-tête, a candlelight dinner with shared morsels. There has never been any doubt that the Eucharist is divine food and drink for our pilgrimage and that the Mass is a heavenly banquet; but much more fundamentally, the Eucharist is Jesus Christ made really present in our midst, to offer perfect worship to His Father, to renew His redemptive sacrifice in atonement for sin, to pour out graces upon the members of His Mystical Body, and to receive the adoring homage of all who call Him Lord, the High Priest of our confession, the one Mediator between man and God. The trouble with CHW's theology of liturgy is not that it is flat-out false, but that it is too reductive, narrow, earthbound, and anthropocentric; everything seems to be to and from the people, rather than to and from Christ. The TLM is at once Christocentric and Patricentric, expressing the full cosmic and spiritual breadth of divine worship, and drawing us up into it.

12

Games People Play with the Holy Spirit

I RECEIVED A LETTER [PRINTED BELOW] FROM a reader who was trying to make sense of the relationship between the Second Vatican Council, the liturgical reform, and the Holy Spirit. Like the friends mentioned by Newbie Trad, CHW also tightly connect these three things, as if one might place an equal sign between them. My response also thereby serves as a response to some of their fruitier claims. Concerning the Holy Spirit, for example, we read:

> The Holy Spirit was guiding sinful and fallible people—the only kind he had to work with—to undertake this [liturgical] renewal that was desperately needed for the good of the Catholic faithful.... In restoring and promoting the Eucharistic liturgy, the Council is convinced that it is obediently bearing witness to a distinguishing mark of the Holy Spirit's work in the contemporary Church. Not to have borne such testimony would be a defiant denial of the Spirit's activity.... To oppose the Council's intent as expressed in *Sacrosanctum Concilium* is implicitly, if unintentionally, to fault the overarching principle of the entire Council, *aggiornamento*—not the creating of a new Church but the renewing of the one, holy, catholic, and apostolic Church. Such opposition also inherently denies the validity of the liturgical renewal as a genuine work of Holy Spirit in the contemporary Church.... The implementation was not without its weaknesses, missteps, irregularities, and even aberrations. Nevertheless, we are convinced that the Holy Spirit was present and active throughout this implementation process, even in the midst of anomalies that were not of the Spirit. From the outset of the liturgical renewal to the present, the Church was following the lead of the Holy Spirit and bearing witness to the Spirit in its teachings and actions. To deny the good fruit that the liturgical movement has

brought forth during this process would be to deny the Spirit's enduring infallible guidance.

The Council merits their uninhibited laudation, and its critics—or is it the Novus Ordo's critics? or the Holy Spirit's critics?—their severest condemnation:

> Vatican II thus magisterially promulgated a proper and authentic renewal of the Eucharistic liturgy. The Council not only embraced the Spirit-inspired liturgical renewal, but also brought this renewal to its mature and authentic culmination.... Although one can empathize with these concerns, we believe that a return to the Tridentine Mass is liturgically unfortunate and doctrinally unacceptable. As noted earlier, such a return is contrary to the entire Spirit-anointed liturgical renewal that culminated in Vatican II's Constitution on the Sacred Liturgy.... The entire thrust of the Spirit's work of renewing the liturgy, from its origins to Vatican II and beyond, was to ensure that the faithful would participate fully in the sacred liturgy in accord with their baptismal priesthood.... Some [adherents of the TLM] not only reject the liturgical renewal but also Vatican II itself, claiming that the Council "betrayed the Tradition and the 'true Church'".... This impulse [to join the Tridentine movement] is completely contrary to the Council, and to act upon it is to impugn, even if unintentionally, the universal and ecumenical authority of the Council and its reception in the magisterial teaching of every subsequent pope. If bishops and pastors do not reclaim and promote the authentic teaching of Vatican II, the theological and liturgical vacuum will continue to be filled by those who promote the Tridentine liturgy as a way of disparaging the Council.

As I said, equal signs everywhere. It is perhaps worth noting that CHW express here a viewpoint identical to that of Cardinal Roche[1] and Cardinal Cupich.[2] There is certainly

---

1 Writes Cardinal Roche: "All that is taking place [with *TC*] is the regulation of the former liturgy of the 1962 Missal by stopping the promotion of that, because it was clear that the Council, the Bishops of the Council, under the inspiration of the Holy Spirit, were putting forward a new liturgy for the vital life of the Church, for its vitality. And that's really very important. And to resist that is, is something that is really quite serious, too." Deborah Castellano Lubov, "A conversation with future Cardinal Roche, Prefect of Divine Liturgy, Sacraments," *Vatican News*, June 16, 2022.
2 Writes Cardinal Cupich: "My point is simply this: Like St. John Paul II, Pope Francis takes seriously that the restoration of the liturgy

a party line that has developed nicely under Pope Francis. On, then, to the letter and my response.

Dear Dr. Kwasniewski,

Watching *Mass of the Ages* Episode 2 and your interview with Raymond Arroyo brought up some questions I've been struggling with. First, doesn't it seem like the Novus Ordo was close to what the Council Fathers intended? I say this because (a) we know that Bugnini was secretary of the committee that drafted *Sacrosanctum Concilium* and (b) nearly all the bishops after the Council went along with the reforms. My neo-con friends say that *SC* and the new missal are fine—they *should* have resulted in a "smells-and-bells reverent Novus Ordo," but liberals in the Church hijacked the implementation of the Council and of the reform for their own ends and distorted what was good into its opposite. If this is true, then (so my neo-con friends say) there is no need for the TLM; all we need to do is "get the Novus Ordo right." Second, these defenders of the Novus Ordo also assert that, since "the Holy Spirit inspired the Council," the Council was good in all respects, including the reform of the Mass it called for. They contend that if we do not support the Novus Ordo, we are acting against the Holy Spirit. Something doesn't sit well with me in these arguments, but could you help me to put a finger on what's wrong?

Yours in Christ,
Newbie Trad

Dear Newbie Trad,

Thank you for your questions. The first question can be dealt with rather straightforwardly: no, the Novus Ordo is

---

was the result of the movement of the Holy Spirit. It was not about the imposition of an ideology on the church by any one person or group. And so no one should now suggest that Pope Francis (or, for that matter, Cardinal Roche) has any motivation in issuing *Traditionis Custodes* and authorizing the *Rescriptum* other than the desire to remain faithful to the promptings of the Holy Spirit that gave rise to the teachings and reforms of the council.... We should name it [resistance to *TC*] for what it is: resistance to the promptings of the Holy Spirit, and the undermining of genuine fidelity to the See of Peter." "Critics of Pope Francis' Latin Mass restrictions should listen to JPII," *America*, February 27, 2023.

Games People Play with the Holy Spirit

not "close" to what the Council Fathers intended, as can be easily demonstrated in two ways: we can simply compare what *SC* specifies to what actually happened and notice the major discrepancies; and we can look to what well-informed Council Fathers and *periti* said afterwards about those discrepancies. Fortunately, that work of comparison has been done already many times, so all you need to do is a bit of reading up on it. It won't take long and it will be a rewarding exercise.[3] (Further below, I will quote the stunning admission of Joseph Ratzinger in 1976.) In Yves Chiron's biography of Annibale Bugnini, we learn of the advice given by that master of deceit to the committee that drafted *SC* ahead of the Council: We must speak in acceptable generalities and leave a lot of things open-ended, so that we don't risk scaring off the bishops; and then afterwards we may do as we please.[4]

As to why nearly all the bishops went along with the increasingly radical reforms afterwards, in spite of the fact that most of them were singing the praises of tradition prior to the Council and reassuring the faithful that the things they loved would remain in place, the answer may be inferred from looking at how bishops act today and, frankly, at most times in the history of the Church: either as craven hyperpapalists, cowardly bureaucrats, or ambitious careerists (indeed, these three categories are not mutually exclusive). Occasionally, some even become convicted ideologues, like the bishops who gladly hailed Henry VIII as head of their Church, or the ones who gleefully signed off on the Civil Constitution of the Clergy in 1790, or, more recently, the ones who endorsed the Sexual Revolution by opting out of *Humanae Vitae*. In living memory (I hope) is the abject failure of many bishops to reject Pope Francis's false teachings

---

3 On discrepancies between *SC* and the ensuing "reform," see above, p. 22, n11. As for eyewitnesses of the difference between what the Council Fathers asked for and expected and what they got a few years later, see, in addition to Cardinal Stickler's "Recollections of a Vatican II Peritus," Anonymous, "The Old Liturgy and the New Despisers of the Council," *Rorate Caeli*, July 5, 2022, as well as the sources mentioned on p. 66. The sources on this question are very numerous, but that should suffice for starters.
4 For the full quotation and commentary, see my article "*Sacrosanctum Concilium*: The Ultimate Trojan Horse," *Crisis Magazine*, June 21, 2021.

on a host of subjects: sacramental access for the so-called divorced-and-remarried, the "inadmissibility" of the death penalty, God's willing of all religions as he wills the two sexes, and the ecclesial self-contradictions of the Synod on Synodality and the new Constitution for the Roman Curia. Should we be scandalized? Yes. Should we be surprised? I'm afraid the answer is no. There's a reason why, out of innumerable thousands of bishops in Church history, only a small number are found in the *Roman Martyrology*.

Let me plunge into your second and, to my mind, more important question, about the last Council as "inspired by the Holy Spirit." A well-known theologian wrote the following:

> Not every valid council in the history of the Church has been a fruitful one; in the last analysis, many of them have been a waste of time. Despite all the good to be found in the texts it produced, the last word about the historical value of Vatican Council II has yet to be spoken.

Was that a notorious heretic like Hans Küng? No. It was the late Joseph Ratzinger, in *Principles of Catholic Theology*.[5] Another great theologian and church historian cited a Church Father who said, concerning his own time:

> If I must speak the truth, I feel disposed to shun every conference of Bishops; because I never saw a Synod brought to a happy issue, nor remedying, but rather increasing, existing evils. For ever is there rivalry and ambition, and these have the mastery of reason; —do not think me extravagant for saying so; —and a mediator is more likely to be attacked himself, than to succeed in his pacification. Accordingly, I have fallen back upon myself, and consider quiet the only security of life.

That was St. Gregory Nazianzen, quoted by St. John Henry Newman.[6] I quote these passages because I think we need, in general, a mighty dose of realism and theological accuracy when it comes to what can and should be said on behalf of *any* church council—even an ecumenical one.

---

5 Joseph Ratzinger, *Principles of Catholic Theology: Building Stones for a Fundamental Theology* (San Francisco: Ignatius Press, 1987), 378.
6 *Ep.* 55 [Ep. 130], cited in *Arians of the Fourth Century*, www.newman-reader.org/works/arians/chapter5-2.html.

REALISM FROM CHURCH HISTORY

The proponents of Vatican II make outlandish claims for it. "The Holy Spirit *inspired* the Council." Wait a minute; I thought that special inspiration belonged only to the inerrant Word of God in Scripture. "The Holy Spirit *guided* the Council..." Well, then, presumably the same Spirit *inspired* and *guided* the other twenty ecumenical councils as well, from Nicaea to Vatican I (for otherwise you are denying them the status of ecumenical councils!). If so, what sense do you make of this:

> Clerics should not practice callings or business of a secular nature, especially those that are dishonorable. They should not watch mimes, entertainers, and actors. Let them avoid taverns altogether, unless by chance they are obliged by necessity on a journey. They should not play at games of chance or of dice, nor be present at such games. They should have a suitable crown and tonsure, and let them diligently apply themselves to the divine services and other good pursuits. Their outer garments should be closed and neither too short nor too long. Let them not indulge in red or green cloths, long sleeves or shoes with embroidery or pointed toes... All bishops must use in public and in the church outer garments made of linen...
>
> In some provinces a difference in dress distinguishes the Jews or Saracens from the Christians, but in certain others such a confusion has grown up that they cannot be distinguished by any difference. Thus it happens at times that through error Christians have relations with the women of Jews or Saracens, and Jews and Saracens with Christian women. Therefore, that they may not, under pretext of error of this sort, excuse themselves in the future for the excesses of such prohibited intercourse, we decree that such Jews and Saracens of both sexes in every Christian province and at all times shall be marked off in the eyes of the public from other peoples through the character of their dress.... Moreover, during the last three days before Easter and especially on Good Friday, they shall not go forth in public at all...

Those canons are from the Fourth Lateran Ecumenical Council (1215).[7] Lateran IV also hilariously said that the Greeks were more and more keen on ending the schism... during the Latin

---
7 Canons 16 and 68.

occupation of Constantinople, when Greek animosity toward Latins was reaching a boiling point. This cannot fail to remind us of Vatican II's saying that modern man was coming to a greater and greater appreciation of human dignity (*Dignitatis Humanae*, 1). The Holy Spirit does not protect churchmen from making fools of themselves at times; he does prevent their folly from sinking the barque of the Church.

Let's take another example, the Second Council of Constantinople, which was expressly called to undo the scandal and harm caused by a prudential judgment of the Council of Chalcedon. Chalcedon must have been wrong to quash the condemnations of Theodoret, Ibas, and Theodore, because the judgment of Constantinople II was dogmatic while Chalcedon's omission was merely prudential. This example has the added spice that Vigilius, the reigning pope at Constantinople II, violently opposed the move — before giving in and defining the Council's judgment. A historic victory for lay theology, in the person of a not entirely savory Justinian![8]

Fr. John Hunwicke of the blog *Mutual Enrichment* wittily remarks:

> The Council of Vienne had a Spirit of the Council. In that Spirit, the Templars were burned on probably phony charges of Sodomy and their wealth seized. The French government gathered huge sums of money on the understanding that it would lead a crusade... and then just hung on to it all. Does anybody give *that* Council a second thought? When did you last wake up in the night worrying about it? Vatican II is as irrelevant now as the Council of Vienne is. Vatican II was every bit as fully and totally a true, valid Ecumenical Council *cum Petro et sub Petro* as Vienne was... and it is just about as fully and totally irrelevant today.[9]

---

8 It was Justinian who insisted on the condemnation of the Three Chapters. Vigilius had gone so far as to issue a constitution *condemning* that idea, but it was addressed only to Justinian — and he refused to receive it. Good for him! He wasn't operating under the silly idea that you can't ever disagree with a pope. The story is usually told as if Justinian was deeply wicked, but the fact remains that it was *his* doctrine that was solemnly defined.

9 See the blistering nine-minute dress-down of Vatican II by Miguel Ayuso on my YouTube page: www.youtube.com/watch?v=FwO3quaGwwo.

He explains further:

> Vatican II, like so many of its predecessor councils, is obsolete or, at the very least, obsolescent. Yes, there are elements in its texts which are well put and will have continuing value and use. But it did not foresee many of the major problems of our age and, therefore, did not give us guidance for getting through them. Its silly optimisms are no more relevant to our very different, much harsher, age than is the preoccupation of so many medieval councils with "Just-One-More-Crusade." The notion that it was some sort of super-council which displaced and replaced—or even simply relativised—the Councils which preceded it is, in my view, a heresy: because it disregards Councils which did, dogmatically, bind, in favour of a council which did not even claim to bind. Worse even than heresy, it is historical twaddle.[10]

Fr. Zuhlsdorf remarks:

> Regarding General or Ecumenical Councils (all 21 of them), it is possible to be a valid Council but a failed one. Consider Lateran V. Utter failure. Its legislation on ecclesiastical pawn shops went nowhere, which is a darn shame. I'd really appreciate well-regulated ecclesial pawn shops. And—hey!—what ever happened to the "spirit of Lateran V"? Moreover, Lateran I and Lateran II weren't even classified as General or Ecumenical Councils until after the Council of Trent (500 years later).

THE COUNCIL AS A SUPER-DOGMA?

An objector might reply: "Your examples so far are of contingent and changeable affairs. A council is not forever binding in its decrees on such matters. But inasmuch as the councils teach doctrine, we must follow them."

Agreed. If there is doctrinal teaching, it is to be accepted in accord with the rule of faith, in harmony with all that has preceded. But the last council contained just the same kind of temporally contingent and non-binding content as can be

---

10 In another post he gives examples of problems in the history of councils and then observes: "Those whose conciliarist enthusiasms lead them to an exaggerated regard for Vatican II seem blithely, absurdly, unaware of the preposterous historical conclusions to which their views would lead them ... were they but consistent."

found in a Lateran IV or a Vienne. Consider the very title of *Gaudium et Spes*: "Pastoral Constitution on the Church in the Modern World." Or *SC*'s set of recommendations about how to make the liturgy more effective for modern man, based on the assumptions of mid-twentieth-century scholarship— subsequently disproved not only by better scholarship but even more by its lack of effectiveness and the continuing effectiveness of the traditional liturgy (a sore subject to the Vatican II nostalgics). Why don't we take seriously what John XXIII says about why he called a council? *Not* to define dogma or condemn error—as he expressly says in his opening speech—but to achieve the pastoral purpose of "a doctrinal penetration and a formation of consciousness, in faithful and perfect conformity to the authentic doctrine, which, however, should be studied and expounded through the methods of research and through the literary forms of modern thought."

Like earlier Councils, Vatican II has only as much authority as its particular decrees demand by the nature of their statements according to standard theological interpretation, as the explanatory note attached to *Lumen Gentium* clarifies.[11] And since it defined nothing and anathematized nothing, its documents have considerably less inherent weight, all things considered, than those of earlier councils that *did* define dogma and anathematize heresy.

Cardinal Joseph Ratzinger, addressing the bishops of Chile on July 13, 1988, had these strong words to say about those who falsely exalt the last council:

> There are many accounts of it which give the impression that, from Vatican II onward, everything has been changed,

---

[11] "On this occasion the Theological Commission makes reference to its Declaration of March 6, 1964, the text of which we transcribe here: 'Taking conciliar custom into consideration and also the pastoral purpose of the present Council, the sacred Council defines as binding on the Church only those things in matters of faith and morals which it shall openly declare to be binding. The rest of the things which the sacred Council sets forth, inasmuch as they are the teaching of the Church's supreme magisterium, ought to be accepted and embraced by each and every one of Christ's faithful according to the mind of the sacred Council. The mind of the Council becomes known either from the matter treated or from its manner of speaking, in accordance with the norms of theological interpretation.'"

and that what preceded it has no value or, at best, has value only in the light of Vatican II. The Second Vatican Council has not been treated as a part of the entire living Tradition of the Church, but as an end of Tradition, a new start from zero. The truth is that this particular Council defined no dogma at all, and deliberately chose to remain on a modest level, as a merely pastoral council; and yet many treat it as though it had made itself into a sort of "super-dogma" which takes away the importance of all the rest.

This idea is made stronger by things that are now happening. That which previously was considered most holy — the form in which the liturgy was handed down — suddenly appears as the most forbidden of all things, the one thing that can safely be prohibited. It is intolerable to criticize decisions which have been taken since the Council; on the other hand, if men make question of ancient rules, or even of the great truths of the Faith — for instance, the corporal virginity of Mary, the bodily resurrection of Jesus, the immortality of the soul, etc. — nobody complains or only does so with the greatest moderation.[12]

Today, I believe we have moved beyond even the ecclesiological error of treating Vatican II as a "super-dogma" to the more cynical and manipulative notion that the actual statements of the Council are no longer relevant because the poor benighted participants had not yet been enlightened by the "spirit" that the Council uncorked. Massimo Faggioli gave the game away when he complained about conservatives who rely on "propositional" arguments — like, you know, looking at what the documents say — rather than a "dialogical understanding" — which is controlled by the people with the megaphones. The Synodal Way is nothing other than dressing the dictatorship of relativism with episcopal vestments, an institutionalized permanent (r)evolution towards an undefined and undefinable Omega Point. Or rather, the end goal is total secularization, because, if God is "always already" in all things and efficaciously seeking their salvation, the category of the "sacred" — anything distinctive

---

12   For the full text, see "Cardinal Ratzinger Addresses Chilean Bishops," *Corpus Christi Watershed*, November 7, 2019. It is illuminating to read this text again in light of the current agenda of the powers that be.

or separative (traditional, Catholic, Christian, monotheist, religious)—must be overcome, that God may be "all in all" (whatever "God" might mean in this discourse; He, It, seems strangely like a cosmic force).

LITURGICAL MISSTEPS

Ratzinger's mention of the "forbidden (traditional) liturgy" prompts a further question. Have the highest authorities in the Church never made mistakes in the sphere of liturgy? A little homework would undermine that naïve view. Let's consider three examples.

The Quignonez Breviary was a radical *ex nihilo* version of the Divine Office, rationalistically conceived and totally detached from tradition, begun at the instance of Pope Clement VII and issued in 1535 by Paul III—only to be banned by Pius V in 1568.

In 1631, Urban VIII promulgated revised hymn texts for the entire breviary, amounting to a thousand changes in some of the most ancient and noble poetry of Christianity. These changes were rejected *tout court* by the Benedictines, Cistercians, Carthusians, and Dominicans; the revised hymns have earned well-deserved mockery ever since. Ironically, it wasn't until the revision of the hymns after Vatican II that many of the original texts were restored—too little, too late, as the breviary was deconstructed into the Liturgy of the Hours, eviscerated of most of its other traditional features, and hastily put into the vernacular, thus abandoning the entire heritage of Latin poetry.

In the last century, the new Latin ("Bea") psalter was commissioned and promulgated by Pius XII, printed with fanfare in thousands of shiny leather sets—but it met with such a chilly reception that it was quietly scuttled by John XXIII, never to reappear.

It has been said by some defenders of Paul VI's Novus Ordo that Paul III only *allowed* the Quignonez Breviary and Pius XII only *allowed* the Bea Psalter, whereas Paul VI *required* the celebration of the Novus Ordo. Unquestionably it was Montini's *intention* to impose the new missal on all (he left no doubt about that in his various speeches and actions), but the actual promulgation of the new missal was handled strangely—let's say, clumsily bungled—in the Latin version of the constitution *Missale Romanum* of April 3, 1969, in such a way that the Commission of Cardinals convened by John Paul II in 1986 to determine whether or not the previous missal had been abrogated concluded that it had not been, which means that the new missal did not actually replace the old one, but joined it as a second missal.[13]

The foregoing examples are sufficient to show that we should resist runaway inflation of the status of magisterial acts and should keep open the possibility of resistance to what is egregiously contrary to the Church's common good.[14] Fr. John Hunwicke has pointed out:

> If Vatican I and II are anything to go by, conciliar decrees sometimes contain compromises. And, after a council, a dominant fashionable elite in the Church is left at liberty to run with its own side of the compromise and to render the other side dead in the water, a universal irrelevance.
>
> Consider Vatican II on Vernacular in the Mass. I summarise: "(a) Latin is to be preserved. (b) But the vernacular may be extended (c) in the readings and directions and to some prayers and chants (d) and to those parts which pertain to the people, (e) but [*provideatur tamen*] they must still be able to say and sing the parts that pertain to them in Latin. (f) If, in some places and circumstances, an even more radical approach [*profundior aptatio*] is needed, local ecclesiastical authority is to submit proposals to the Holy See" (*SC* 36, 40, and 54).
>
> In less than a decade after the Council, (a) and (e) had become dead letters; and (b), (c), and (d) had been turned into irrelevances because the adroit use of (f), the only de

---

13 Siscoe and Salza in chapter 16 ("The New Mass and Infallibility") of their book *True or False Pope* (Winona, MN: STAS Editions, 2015) demonstrate that the new missal was never juridically *mandated*, and also that vernacular translations of the constitution falsified what the underlying Latin text says. It is precisely this fact that allowed Benedict XVI to claim, in *Summorum Pontificum*, that the old missal had never been abrogated and that its use was always in principle permitted.

14 A point made with considerable force by Thomas Pink in "Papal Authority and the Limits of Official Theology," *The Lamp* online, December 2, 2022.

facto survivor of all this legislation, had stamped the very nearly exclusive use of the Vernacular upon the whole of the Latin Church. "Some places and circumstances" [*variis locis et adiunctis*] had, by the touch of Circe's wand, been turned into the universal general norm.

In other words, we are witnesses to the same *kind* of error that Paul III, Urban VIII, and Pius XII made, albeit on a much greater scope, and the necessary corrective—the future Leo XIV, as it were—has not yet appeared on the scene to rein in the chaos and to restore the lost continuity.

THE HOLY SPIRIT TRICK

We have grown accustomed in recent years, especially since the beginning of Synodultery, to seeing the worst policies defended by a glib appeal to "the Spirit," as if the wolves in sheep's clothing have the Dove in their back pocket ready for quick deployment—a supernatural smartphone downloading apps from heaven. It's rather revealing, isn't it, that they frequently omit "holy" and simply refer to "the Spirit." As Martin Mosebach says, surely there *is* a spirit at work in all this...

Here is a good example of the mentality that attempts to put an equal sign between "Vatican II" and "the Holy Spirit":

> José Rodríguez Carballo mentioned, as an important point of religious life [today], fidelity to Vatican II: "For the consecrated, the Council is a point that cannot be negotiated." And he affirmed that those who locate in the reforms of Vatican II all the ailments of religious life "deny the presence of the Holy Spirit in the Church." He explained that in the Congregation for Consecrated Life, they are "particularly concerned" with this matter: "we are seeing true deviations." Above all because "not a few institutes give not only a pre-conciliar, but even an anticonciliar formation. This is inadmissible, it is to place oneself outside of history."[15]

At Fr. Zuhldorf's blog, a reader left this comment:

---

15 Translation given in "The 'absolutely non-negotiable point' for the Congregation for Religious: 'faithfulness' to (their idea of) Vatican II," *Rorate Caeli*, May 8, 2014.

Just reading [about] the history of the Church and the periods of corruption in the past, is it not clear that while the Holy Spirit is always with the Church, He permits some bad things to go on for a while? Thus, why is the questioning of some parts of the Council necessarily a denial of the presence of the Holy Spirit with the Church?

In other words, we rightly say we believe the Holy Spirit always guides the Church; and yet He allows evils in the Church, sometimes for many centuries. So too, we say we believe the same Spirit guides a Council; and yet He allows imperfections, wranglings, factions, inadequacies, ambiguities, lacunae, etc.

The key point is this. The Holy Spirit never allows the Church to defect in a definitive way from Christ and His Gospel; and similarly, *He never allows a Council to define an error or to anathematize a truth*. It is like papal infallibility: the conditions for its exercise are very precisely laid out by Vatican I.[16] It is not a blanket wrapped around the pope, giving the stamp of the Spirit to everything he says and does.

The guidance of the Church by God prevents total catastrophe and shipwreck, which is what would happen if the faithful were positively *bound* to error or sin; it is not, however, a guidance that prevents erring in "official theology" (as Thomas Pink calls it), meandering, obfuscating, diluting, overemphasizing, underemphasizing, neglecting, or taking on strange partners. As with all evils, these evils are allowed in order that God may bring forth a greater good from them—such as the tremendous explosion of good in the Middle Ages after the *saeculum obscurum*, the Counter-Reformation after the Protestant revolt, or the period right after the French Revolution.

Paul VI in a limited way, John Paul II in a much less limited way, and Benedict XVI in a pretty nearly unlimited way, supported the ongoing use of the traditional Roman Rite, which obviously included its spread (since a living Church is a Church that grows, and one would sin by seeking to suppress supernatural growth). If the TLM should no longer

---

16 See John Joy, *Disputed Questions on Papal Infallibility* (Lincoln, NE: Os Justi Press, 2022).

continue, as your friends argue, then it would be wrong even to allow it as a temporary concession. But if, on the contrary, Pope Benedict was right to say, as a matter of principle, "what earlier generations held as sacred, remains sacred and great for us too, and it cannot be all of a sudden entirely forbidden or even considered harmful"—echoing what he had said years earlier as a cardinal: "the Church, in her entire history, never once abolished or prohibited orthodox liturgical forms, something which would be entirely foreign to the Spirit of the Church"[17]—then it is your friends who are wrong, indeed who *must* be wrong, for otherwise they would be asserting that the form of worship used by the Church for the vast majority of her history, the divine liturgy in which most of our saints participated, was so severely problematic that it now has to be outlawed entirely—and that assertion would be a blasphemy against the Holy Spirit.

Then there is the spiritual side of things, which is by no means negligible. The "reverent Novus Ordo" is an accomplishment of the priest of good taste and a piety—and that it is *his* accomplishment certainly cannot be hidden either from himself or from his grateful beneficiaries.[18] *He* is the one who carries the polymorphous political football of the Novus Ordo past menacing Susans or VGs into the end zone of reverence. "We love Fr. So-and-so's Mass, it's just so *reverent!*," says the relieved layman of this pearl of great price. The priest knows that he is of the 1% or 5% of clergy (or whatever percent; it varies greatly from diocese to diocese) who "do the Novus Ordo as it was intended to be done," although it would be impossible for him to back up that claim, if challenged, with coherent criteria.[19] Doesn't that

---

17 From the address given in Rome in 1998: "Ten Years of the Motu Proprio 'Ecclesia Dei,'" available on the Una Voce America website: https://unavoce.org/resources/card-ratzingers-1998-address-at-anniv/.

18 For more on these points, see my articles: "Men Must Be Changed by Sacred Things, and Not Sacred Things by Men," *OnePeterFive*, September 15, 2021, and "Why the 'Reform of the Reform' Is Doomed," *OnePeterFive*, April 22, 2020.

19 In fact, both Paul VI and Francis have given us reams of evidence (see, e.g., "Revisiting Paul VI's *Apologia* for the New Mass," in Peter Kwasniewski, *The Once and Future Roman Rite: Returning to the Traditional Latin Liturgy after*

prompt him to wonder: "Why do so many of my brother priests *not* say Mass rubrically, edifyingly, devoutly?" These are not healthy subjects of meditation. The old rite, being rigidly determinate and totally focused on the sacred action, more or less avoids this spiritual narcissism completely.

If Vatican II changed Catholic theology so much that the Mass used by the Church for over a thousand years—in some respects over a millennium and a half—is now off limits, then I'm afraid that can only redound to the detriment of the Council, not of the Mass. But of course this view is nonsense. The old Mass is what the bishops at Vatican II celebrated week in and week out, and, as Joseph Ratzinger noted in 1976, most expected it to remain close to what it was:

> The problem of the new Missal lies in its abandonment of a historical process that was always continual, before and after St. Pius V, and in the creation of a completely new book, although it was compiled of old material, the publication of which was accompanied by a prohibition of all that came before it, which, besides, is unheard of in the history of both law and liturgy. And I can say with certainty, based on my knowledge of the conciliar debates and my repeated reading of the speeches made by the Council Fathers, that this [new Missal] does not correspond to the intentions of the Second Vatican Council.[20]

VALID IS ONE THING; WISE, JUST, OR EFFECTIVE IS A DIFFERENT MATTER

Allow me to conclude with the perspicacious comments of a diocesan priest and church historian.

What is meant by "valid" when we are talking about the "validity" of Church councils? If, for example, in saying

---

Seventy Years of Exile [Gastonia, NC: TAN Books, 2022], 109–43) that what a conservative American priest fed on images of TLMs thinks of as a "correct Novus Ordo" is *certainly not* what the pope who first *formally promulgated* the Novus Ordo and the pope who now coerces us to the Novus Ordo had or have in mind. We can already see, for example, that the Ratzinger/Benedict approach to the Novus Ordo—the "hermeneutic of continuity" and the "mutual enrichment"—has been called into question by Team Bergoglio, for whom Sicilian lace is out and African/Amazonian inculturation is in.
20 Quoted in Wolfgang Waldstein, "Zum motuproprio *Summorum Pontificum*," *Una Voce Korrespondenz* 38/3 (2008), 201–14.

that the Council of Constance was valid, you mean that it had lawful ecclesiastical authority, you are saying something which should not be controversial. If, however, in calling the Council of Constance valid, you mean that all of its decisions, including burning Jan Hus at the stake (despite the refusal of the Inquisitor for Germany to indict him for heresy!) must be accepted as right and just, you are saying something incompatible with the intellectual and moral integrity of a Christian.

For myself, in regard to actions by ecclesiastical authority, I use the word "valid" in the narrow sense of lawful. To recognize an action by ecclesiastical authority as lawful should come easily, with the burden of proof being overwhelmingly on the negative position. To question the lawfulness of actions by ecclesiastical authority is dangerous, potentially a flirtation with the sin of schism.

On the other hand, recognizing the lawfulness of an action by ecclesiastical authority certainly does not mean recognizing it as wise, just, or effective. I regard this as an essential distinction. I am obliged, for example, to recognize the Second Vatican Council's decree on the renewal of Religious Life as lawful. I am not obliged, however, to survey the wreckage of multiple religious orders, and the effective disappearance of religious life from many regions of the Church (such as my own), and then pretend that religious life was, in fact, renewed.

Thus, following my distinction, I accept every jot and tittle of the Second Vatican Council as valid and lawful. Those two adjectives do not compel me to add other adjectives, such as wise, just, or effective.

This priest well describes the healthy, balanced, realistic, and sober mentality we ought to cultivate today, not only because it is true to the teachings of our faith, but also because we prize the gift of reason—and we must use our reason to evaluate the causes and effects of the sea-change inaugurated in the Catholic Church by and in the name of the last council, above all with the unprecedentedly vast liturgical reform that followed in its wake.[21]

---

[21] A useful resource for undertaking this evaluation is the anthology *Sixty Years After: Catholic Writers Assess the Legacy of Vatican II*, ed. Peter Kwasniewski (Brooklyn: Angelico Press, 2022).

PART 3
Additional Commentary

13

Church Life Journal *Insults Eastern Liturgies*

ALEXANDER BATTISTA

I HAVE BEEN A READER OF THE *CHURCH LIFE Journal* in the past, and have enjoyed particular articles I have read there, appreciating the journal's tone of "dynamic orthodoxy." When I came across a recent article by Dr. Cavadini, Dr. Healey, and Fr. Weinandy, however, on "Papal Responses to the Emergence of the TLM Movement" (the fourth part of the series), I was taken aback by how grossly inaccurate and insulting the essay was.

Not only were several factual errors made throughout the author's commentary, but as a Catholic who is both a frequenter of the *Usus Antiquior* of the Latin Rite and a descendant of Ukrainian-Greek Catholics of the Byzantine Rite, I found myself flummoxed by how the authors of the essay seem to completely dismiss the good fruit that comes from the "Tridentine Latin Mass." I am equally appalled that the authors paint those who find spiritual solace, and find themselves sanctified by the grace of this ancient rite, as mere "silent spectators." I would like to make a few comments in response to an essay that would have benefitted from more diligent scholarship. I feel compelled to set the record straight on some of the egregious errors and assumptions these authors have made.

First, let me begin by saying I don't begrudge anyone wanting to worship in the "Ordinary Form" according to the Missal of St. Paul VI. As a millennial cradle Catholic, I worship regularly in both the Extraordinary Form and Ordinary Form, as well as the Divine Liturgy of St. John

Chrysostom in the Byzantine Rite. I also enjoy visiting the other Eastern Rites including the Ge'ez Rite, West Syrian Rite, and East Syrian Rite. However, I am typically at a parish run by the FSSP, so most Sundays I participate in the Extraordinary Form of the Mass in the Latin Rite. For someone to say, as the authors of this essay do, that I'm *not participating* in the Mass when I go to the *Usus Antiquior* is a step too far. It is difficult for me to fathom how someone can tell me the Mass I worship at is limited in its ecclesiology and that this ancient Rite was *not* inspired by the Holy Spirit for our sanctification. If this form of the sacred liturgy was uninspired, then Catholics of the Latin Rite were led astray for well over 1,000 years by the Church herself!

I'm astonished at what the authors have written, and especially so because I've held all three in such high esteem. In one breath they affirm how the Holy Spirit worked in "renewing the liturgy," yet tear down the *Usus Antiquior* as being incapable of uniting priest and people to offer the Holy Sacrifice together, and therefore not owing its inspiration to the Holy Spirit. The authors say, "The Church's tradition, of which the liturgy is a constitutive element, is not frozen in time but is a living tradition that develops with the help of the Holy Spirit, in fidelity to the deposit of faith." Do the authors truly believe the Extraordinary Form (the *Usus Antiquior*) is frozen in time?

THE LATIN MASS IS NOT A MUSEUM PIECE

CHW cite an old and irrelevant 1974 document (*Conferentiarum Episcopalium*) that had no way of anticipating that the Extraordinary Form would continue to play an active part in the life of the Church, leading up to the peaceful coexistence of the Ordinary Form and the Extraordinary Form, not to mention other rites and uses like the Anglican Ordinariate Use, the Zaire Use, the Ambrosian Rite, etc. To claim as the authors do that "the Council Fathers" envisioned the "'ordinary form' would become the sole form of the liturgy celebrated in the Roman rite of the Church" is preposterous. Again, the various uses within the Roman Rite show that this view is simply false. In history a certain liturgical pluralism has always been understood to be salutary and beneficial to the life of the Church.

But to further dismiss this notion that the Extraordinary Form is not part of "the living tradition that develops with the help of the Holy Spirit," one need only look to two recent decrees by the Congregation for the Doctrine of the Faith (CDF) in 2020. The first, *Quo magis,* allows several new prefaces to be used during Mass in the Extraordinary Form. As the note for the presentation of the decree says, the decree itself "constitutes the completion of the work previously initiated by the [*Ecclesia Dei*] Pontifical Commission in order to carry out the mandate given by Pope Benedict XVI to add some additional Prefaces to the Missal of the *forma extraordinaria.*" What's more, the note makes clear that

> Four of the newly approved texts, namely the Prefaces *de Angelis, de Sancto Ioanne Baptista, de Martyribus* and *de Nuptiis,* are taken from the Missal of the *forma ordinaria*... From now on, these may be used wherever Mass is celebrated in the *forma extraordinaria.* Two of the seven Prefaces will allow to aptly give more prominence to liturgical celebrations in honor of certain leading figures in God's design, as manifested in the history of Salvation, namely the Angels and St. John the Baptist, which hitherto both lacked a proper Eucharistic Preface in the *Usus Antiquior.*

What we see is not an ossified liturgical rite—only a "museum piece" as other commentators have opined—but instead, organic development and growth in a living liturgical rite of the Church.

The second decree, *Cum sanctissima,* was promulgated "to facilitate the celebration of more recently canonized Saints according to the *forma extraordinaria* of the Roman Rite." 1960 was the last updating of the Roman Martyrology, before the 1962 Missal of Pope St. John XXIII was issued. This means it is now possible to celebrate in the Extraordinary Form the feast days of saints canonized after 1960, often on the dates designated for them on the Ordinary Form's calendar. While these permissions are optional and not obligatory, the note for the presentation of the decree observes:

The new Decree also opens a further possibility for cases in which, whilst following the existing calendar, one wishes at the same time to honor eventual other occurring Saints. Specifically, according to n. 6 of the Decree, an *ad libitum* commemoration of an occurring Saint may be made, if said Saint appears in the *Proprium pro aliquibus locis* or in the future special Supplement.

So not only may saints be commemorated at Mass that were canonized before this decree, but even newer saints like St. Giovanni Battista Scalabrini, who was canonized on October 9th, 2022.

A concrete example of these commemorations being used can be seen in a tweet from a priest of the Institute of Christ the King Sovereign Priest, who decided to celebrate the feast of St. Gianna Beretta Molla, the patroness of the chapel he serves. She was commemorated on her feast day of April 28th with the "common of Holy Women." Even though St. Paul of the Cross is commemorated on this day in the Extraordinary Form's calendar, priests now have the option to instead celebrate Mass in honor of St. Gianna on April 28th if they so wish. In light of these two decrees, it's unclear how the authors of the essay can possibly hold that the *Usus Antiquior* is "frozen in time."

THE HOLY SPIRIT INSPIRED THE ANCIENT ROMAN RITE

But to return to the notion that the Church's Tradition (including the sacred liturgy) "develops with the help of the Holy Spirit," I agree with the authors that this is true. What doesn't make sense, though, is how the authors can seriously imply that the Holy Spirit *did not* help the sacred liturgy develop in a way that would be beneficial and salubrious for the faithful of the Roman Rite in the centuries prior to the Second Vatican Council. How is it that the Holy Spirit could allow a "less adequate ecclesiology," as they put it, and "a rite [which] undermines the doctrine that the ordained priesthood is ordered to the service of the baptismal priesthood of the faithful," to develop and be utilized for over a millennium? To hold such an opinion of the supposed deleterious effects of the *Usus Antiquior* upon the faithful is in direct contradiction of the orthodox teaching of Pope Pius XII. In his 1947 encyclical, *Mediator Dei*, the Holy Father states the following:

> The more recent liturgical rites [e.g., the Tridentine Rite] likewise deserve reverence and respect. *They, too, owe their inspiration to the Holy Spirit, who assists the Church in every age* even to the consummation of the world. They are equally the resources used by the majestic Spouse of Jesus Christ to promote and procure the sanctity of man.[1]

Instead of "the Holy Spirit [assisting] the Church in every age," as Pius XII rightfully observed, the authors would have us believe that the *Usus Antiquior* is a rite that is basically only "position[ing] the faithful as 'silent spectators,'" one that possesses "a more limited and less adequate ecclesiology, one that makes it appear that the Mass is essentially the provenance and activity of the priest," and apparently *not* of the people.

This is simply false.

Again, such an opinion as the three authors seem to hold contradicts not only Pope Pius XII but also the common teaching of the Church that the Holy Spirit guides her in creed and cult from Christ's first coming to His return. This includes the time before the promulgation of the 1969 Roman Missal. How this essay "rise[s] above the controversy that besets many Catholic conversations in the public sphere" is unclear. Unfortunately, it seems only to attack the liturgical life of many Catholics, both living on Earth and among the Church Triumphant, including, but not limited to, great men and women like St. Padre Pio, Sts. Louis and Zelle Martin, St. Jean Baptiste de la Salle, St. Ignatius of Loyola, St. Teresa of Avila, St. Bonaventure, St. Elizabeth of Hungary, St. Francis of Assisi and countless others!

Nobody is saying that the "Tridentine Mass" was in need of no reform around the time of the 1950s. There were abuses that needed to be corrected, as there were in every age. What is erroneous is *even the implication* that the Holy Spirit did not guide the Church and her development of the sacred liturgy during the ages prior to the Second Vatican Council.

---

1   MD 61, emphasis added.

We must also observe lamentably that CHW, by dismissing *Summorum Pontificum* as a merely "pastorally motivated" but unwise decision that "undercut the fundamental principle of the liturgical renewal," misunderstand and misrepresent the Ratzingerian corpus on liturgical theology to such an extent as to call into question the depth of their study of the latter's "new liturgical movement," its origins, aims, and methods. Even a cursory reading of Ratzinger's thought immediately reveals the inaccuracy of this straw man and historically falsifiable claim, which the Pope Emeritus himself preemptively called "just absolutely false!" before Francis made this (false) argument in *Traditionis Custodes*, which CHW sheepishly repeat.

THE TRIDENTINE RITE IS MUCH OLDER THAN TRENT

Also erroneous, bearing in mind the aforementioned list of saints spanning centuries, is the authors' claim that the "Tridentine Mass" has only been around for "400 years" and that "the Tridentine Mass was itself a reform" on a scale similar to the reform enacted by Pope St. Paul VI. First, the *Usus Antiquior* has seen only very slight changes since late antiquity, solidifying in the sixth and seventh centuries to look essentially as the Extraordinary Form of the Mass does today in the twenty-first century. Michael Fiedrowicz observes the following (citing Fortescue's comprehensive 1912 work on the Mass), after laying out the form of the Mass in this time period:

> This structure of the Roman-Latin liturgy of the Mass has seen only slight changes. All further modifications were incorporated into the existing structure in such a way that its most important parts remained undisturbed. Since the time of Pope Gregory the Great (590–604), the text, in particular the Canon, as well as the *Ordo Missae*, survive as a holy tradition that, with the exception of insignificant details, none dared to touch. In this respect, the classical celebration of the Mass can be rightfully referred to as the Rite of St. Gregory.[2]

---

2 Michael Fiedrowicz, *The Traditional Mass: History, Form, and Theology of the Classical Roman Rite* (Brooklyn: Angelico Press, 2020), 12.

But even if some feel squeamish about calling the Extraordinary Form "the Rite of St. Gregory," the Congregation for Divine Worship and the Discipline of the Sacraments basically confirmed what Fiedrowicz lays out above in a decree promulgated in 2003 on the occasion of a new translation of the *General Instruction of the Roman Missal*. In this decree, we find the following:

> In a difficult period when the Catholic faith on the sacrificial nature of the Mass, the ministerial priesthood, and the real and permanent presence of Christ under the Eucharistic species were placed at risk, St. Pius V was especially concerned with preserving the more recent tradition, then unjustly being assailed, introducing only very slight changes into the sacred rite. In fact, the Missal of 1570 differs very little from the very first printed edition of 1474, which in turn faithfully follows the Missal used at the time of Pope Innocent III.[3]

Pope Innocent III reigned from 1198–1216. Even just taking this into consideration, the pedigree of the *Usus Antiquior* is at the very least *double* the length of time indicated by the authors of the essay. Essential continuity between the missal used by Innocent III and that of Pope St. Pius V is clear upon examination, and from St. Pius V down to St. John XXIII we see the same. This is a perod of some 800 years. If one were to look still further back than Innocent III, as do Fiedrowicz, Fortescue, and other scholars of liturgy, the lineage of the Roman missal reaches far back to the time of St. Gregory the Great and into the mists of antiquity.

INSULTING EASTERN CATHOLIC LITURGIES

I could say much more regarding the errors in this essay, but I will leave here a final observation. This essay is an indictment not merely of the *Usus Antiquior* of the Latin Rite, but also of the Divine Liturgy of St. John Chrysostom in the Byzantine Rite, the Holy Qurbono of the West Syrian Rite, and all other traditional rites of the Eastern Churches. *All the "problems" and "deficiencies" the authors point out in the* Usus Antiquior *stare*

---

[3] *General Instruction of the Roman Missal*, Including Adaptations for the Dioceses of the United States of America, no. 7.

them right in the face in liturgies of their very own Eastern Catholic brethren. How can they not be aware of what they're doing and of how insulting their words are to Eastern Catholics?

The authors state that, "Moreover, in the extraordinary form, the faithful are deprived of the incomparably fuller lectionary promulgated after Vatican II. This deficiency is a great loss..." In the Byzantine liturgical year, not to mention that of other Eastern liturgical rites, there is no two- or three-year cycle. It is an annual cycle only. Typically there is but one reading, the Epistle, before the Gospel—just as it is in the Extraordinary Form of the Latin Rite. Would the authors dare to say that the Divine Liturgy of St. John Chrysostom is "deficient" and has "deprived" the faithful because it lacks a larger lectionary? As the Byzantine Catholic Archeparchy of Pittsburgh observes,

> The liturgical year is a system of yearly church celebrations by which the faithful repeatedly relive the salutary mysteries of their salvation. In the liturgical year Our Lord Jesus Christ continues to live with us, to teach us, and to lead us to our heavenly destination.

Each year, Catholics within these particular Churches of the Byzantine Rite relive the same mysteries and read the same Gospel readings, just as all Latin Catholics used to do. Even their Sundays are named after the specific readings, such as "The Sunday of the Man Born Blind," "The Sunday of the Publican and Pharisee," "The Sunday of the Prodigal Son." One cannot simply say that one Lectionary is inferior to the other. Byzantine Catholics, just as Latin Catholics, had a reason for keeping the one-year lectionary, mainly, that it helps the faithful more easily remember, recall, and commemorate the moments of our Lord's life in the Gospels, and other specific moments in the history of salvation throughout the rest of Scripture.

MORE INSULTS AGAINST THE EAST

The authors level another charge against the *Usus Antiquior* that unintentionally indicts the Byzantine Rite as well: "To return to the unreformed rite is to return to a rite that...makes it appear that the Mass is essentially the provenance and activity of the priest. He alone celebrates, at a distance from the onlooking faithful as though the offering were not theirs too." What would the authors say if they walked into a Ukrainian Catholic parish, saw the towering iconostasis separating the clergy from the laity, or the doors in that same iconostasis that only open from the inside by the hand of the deacon or priest? The laity surely look on from a distance as no one except the ordained ministers and male acolytes may even enter into the sanctuary beyond the iconostasis. Since the authors apparently believe that the laity don't offer the Holy Sacrifice along with the priest in the *Usus Antiquior*, isn't the same then also true in the Byzantine Rite? Sometimes, depending on where the laity are sitting or standing, they can't even see the priest celebrant during the Holy Sacrifice because their vision is blocked by the iconostasis! They aren't even "onlookers" at this point, I suppose.

Or what would the authors say if they visited a Syro-Malabar Catholic or Syro-Malankara Catholic parish, or any of the particular Churches that make up the East and West Syrian Rites? At certain times of the liturgy, a curtain is pulled that completely obscures the view of the laity, having a literal barrier between the clergy and lay faithful.[4] Would the authors say that here, too, the offering is no longer the faithful's as well?

I hope that in the future, the Journal and its authors will do more research on liturgical topics before posting such essays again. Their work does great harm by propagating easily dismissed errors, and it serves to drive further wedges not only among Catholics of the Latin Rite, but between them and their Eastern Catholic (and Eastern Orthodox) brethren as well. When we start casting doubt on whether the Holy Spirit was at work in the Sacred Liturgy of years and centuries past, we find ourselves in an untenable position if we then turn around and claim that the Holy Spirit *now, and not then*, is at work in the liturgy—and, *by implication*, is at work *only* in the reformed liturgy of the Latin Rite, since the liturgies of the Eastern Rites (particularly the Byzantine Rite) have remained largely untouched.

---

4 See, for an example on YouTube, "Malayalam Qurbana Part 1 by Catholicos Baselios Mor Cleemis Antiochene Liturgy."

14

The Failures of Reform

FR. SAMUEL KEYES

THEOLOGIANS JOHN CAVADINI, MARY Healy, and Thomas Weinandy have proposed "A Synoptic Look at the Failures and Successes of Post-Vatican II Liturgical Reforms." CHW, with Pope Francis himself, are rightly concerned for the unity of the Church and fidelity to the Second Vatican Council. In what follows I have no intention to dismiss those concerns as unfounded, much less to offer any endorsement to that minority of traditionalists who doubt the authority and validity of the pope, the Council, or the revised *ordo missae*. Rather I believe that the steps taken to address those concerns fail to address the root questions and experiences that stand behind our apparent contemporary impasse.[1] In the end, I am far less sanguine than CHW about the "successes" of reform, and I argue that a true reckoning with its failure requires taking those root questions and experiences seriously.

1

Following an Augustinian hermeneutic of charity, it seems important to treat the authors in the light of their best possible intentions. Even a superficial acknowledgement that "traditionalist" complaints may be valid, in today's ecclesiastical

---

1 The original version of this article was published online at *Covenant*, the blog of the Living Church Foundation, a relatively Catholic-minded Anglican institution. I have modified the content somewhat here, but in that earlier context it was important to explain why these seemingly internecine Catholic arguments ought to matter for others. In short, various Anglican thinkers have observed the fallout from *Traditionis Custodes* with interest, and in some cases they have even compared it with the history of prayer book revision in Anglicanism. Further, as I suggest below, the status of the Roman liturgy, and how the Latin Church governs her liturgical life, has broad ecumenical implications.

environment, can open one up to attack. So I commend CHW especially for (1) an illuminating summary of the historical liturgical movement and its development, (2) repeated acknowledgment of the many ways that the liturgical reforms proposed by the Council in *Sacrosanctum concilium* have not in fact been well implemented, (3) real sympathy with the concerns of traditionalists and critics of the Novus Ordo, and (4) an admirable desire to see a fruitful and united culture of liturgy in the Latin Church.

On this last point, I think the authors seek to echo Pope Francis's pastoral concern, on display in different ways in both *Traditionis custodes* and *Desiderio desideravi*, for a deeper unity in the Church. While I find myself at odds with many of their particular comments about the Tridentine Mass, I agree with this particular call:

> If it is incumbent on those in the Tridentine movement, for the well-being of the Body of Christ, to return to the Church's ordinary liturgical form, it is also incumbent on those who would receive them to work constructively to address their legitimate concerns. Now is the time for them to make their own significant contributions to the present liturgical renewal...

There remains the significant "if" there at the start (an "if" that I largely dispute), but their point is that a ghettoization of the Church into "traditional" and "modern" camps is no real solution, and the obligations fall to both sides. Bishops and pastors who call for traditional Catholics to "return" to the ordinary form will never succeed in that call if they do so by demeaning the rites and traditions that so many of these Catholics find nurturing to the life of salvation. They must be prepared to listen to and accompany (concepts much-celebrated in the Francis pontificate) these faithful, recognizing their concerns as legitimate rather than writing them off as somehow schismatic or old-fashioned. But the faithful in such traditional communities must also be willing to share the treasures they have found, and not hoard them as some kind of exclusive possession for the pure. I have a friend, to give an example, who runs an excellent nonprofit dedicated to teaching Gregorian chant. Certain families refuse to show up when the apostolate's choirs visit ordinary parish churches (i.e., not parishes devoted exclusively to the *usus antiquior*). Perhaps they feel that they are protecting their children from the "taint" of modernism (I suspect the taint will come at them first in other ways!), but in doing so they harden the lines within current ritual cultures of the Church, preventing the riches of the tradition from informing and vivifying the reformed rite. Even if the new rite is somehow beyond repair or renewal, this attitude plays right into the hands of those bishops who see traditional worship as a kind of poison to be avoided at all costs, for it is often just this sort of limited exposure to the tradition that has over the last several decades drawn many people into a greater appreciation of the Catholic faith than they would have otherwise known.

This all-or-nothing attitude among traditionalists faces, rightly I think, strong criticism from CHW. Even if we grant (as CHW do not) that the older rite is intrinsically more reverent or in some other way superior to the new, this admission does not necessitate shunning the Novus Ordo as some kind of theological or ritual poison. As the authors point out, this attitude silences the countless pastors, parishes, and musicians who have and continue to enact beautiful, traditional, orthodox liturgies following the books of Paul VI and John Paul II. Perhaps such liturgies still fall short of the best that the Roman rite can offer, but that could just as easily be said for the actual celebration of the Mass in many places when the *usus antiquior* reigned. Lamenting the abuses present elsewhere—whether the sappy praise-choruses or the improvising entertainer-celebrant with bad homilies—and even lamenting the sloppy way that the reform was implemented by the hierarchy, simply does not require that we write off the entire reformed project as diabolical through and through.

2

The principal weakness in the "Synoptic" essay lies not in its spirit and its hopeful invitations, but in its actual assessment of the liturgical reform's failures and the way that these failures have been criticized. CHW rightly promote a conciliar

The Failures of Reform

hermeneutic of continuity, arguing that the Council, especially in *Sacrosanctum concilium*, had no intention to create an entirely new rite that suppressed an old. Just so. But, astoundingly, it does not occur to the authors to question whether this intention was actually followed by the post-conciliar committee which put together the new Missal. This is not a point I can really argue here, but it is precisely this point that is in dispute. It is hard to overestimate the centrality of this question to the actual experience of liturgical traditionalism. The average person who picks up and compares, say, the Missal of Pius V (1570), the Missal of John XXIII (1962) and the Missal of Paul VI (1970) cannot avoid questioning the claim that the new missal is nothing more than a revision of the old. To be sure, the *ordo* is recognizable in its basic shape, but as Matthew Hazell has shown, a mere 13% of the orations remain fully intact,[2] and, again, as anyone even vaguely familiar with the books will know, the Missal *qua* Missal functions not at all like the Missals between 1570 and 1962, but must of necessity stand as one book among several (especially lectionaries) in the actual celebration of Mass. In this light—which, again, requires no special training or scholarship—claims that the new Missal is nothing more than a light revision of the old come across as a kind of Orwellian newspeak. If the fathers of the Council saw their proposed revision as an appropriate and sensitive updating of the Roman Missal as they knew it, why is it unfaithful to the Council to question whether their desires were actually implemented? CHW and others speak constantly about a fuller implementation of the Council, yet this kind of implementation seems arbitrarily off the table.

Along the same lines, CHW seem to misunderstand or mischaracterize traditionalist concerns in their lengthy defense of the idea of vernacular liturgy. They do not seem to register that this is perhaps the least of concerns among most traditionalists. To be sure, many prefer Latin (as does the Council!).[3] But to imagine that the new Missal, celebrated in its native Latin,

---

2 See especially Matthew Hazell's statistical summary available online: https://bit.ly/3GbClYe.
3 See, e.g., *SC* 36.

would solve all the problems, is quite simply to misunderstand the nature of the critique. Archbishop Lefebvre himself, at least according to hearsay, suggested that he would have preferred the old Mass celebrated in the vernacular to the Novus Ordo in Latin.⁴

According to CHW, the Pauline Missal and its concordant practices (like celebrating Mass *ad populem*) better represent the theology of the Eucharist and, in particular, the priesthood of Christ expressed in the assembly of both clergy and laity. In other words, they assert that it better allows for "full, conscious, active participation" as promoted by *Sacrosanctum concilium*. But, again, this is exactly what is in dispute. They do not truly argue these points; nor, I think, could they, because any assertion to the effect of a rite's intrinsic relation to subjective experience would be so burdened by cultural, sociological, and personal factors as to be entirely beyond demonstration.

Since it is difficult (impossible) to argue about the subjective experience of liturgy, what is left, in objective terms, is the rite itself in its raw form. Joseph Ratzinger (before he was pope) argued in *The Spirit of the Liturgy* that the Council's highest liturgical goal, *participatio actuosa*, was always intended as a *spiritual* reality in which the faithful lift up their hearts and minds (the Catechism's basic definition of prayer!) in union with the central *actio* of the rite. It is by no means straightforwardly apparent that the Novus Ordo somehow makes that *actio* more accessible. I suppose for some people it might. But this is, again, a very experiential question. If anything, in practice, it has made the *actio* more ambiguous. Take, for example, a little handbook published a couple decades ago called *How Not to Say Mass*. In that book, Fr. Dennis Smolarski, in the course of several very useful reminders about rubrics, points out several times how in the new Mass we no longer do what we used to do: "Formerly, we 'offered' bread and wine to God, but now we realize that offering anything other than Christ is theologically inappropriate."⁵ Putting aside whether

---

4 I cannot find any citation for this report, so it may be apocryphal.
5 Dennis C. Smolarski, SJ, *How Not to Say Mass: A Guidebook on Liturgical Principles and the Roman Missal* (Mahwah, NJ: Paulist Press, 2014), 82. This

The Failures of Reform

this is even a correct interpretation of the Missal's texts (it is not), arguably the Missal itself and its rubrics do implicitly open up the possibility of this new theology in the very act of revision from one offertory rite to another entirely new one. How, exactly, are the faithful supposed to actively participate in the action of the rite when all of a sudden the whole meaning of the rite is changed, apparently at the stroke of a papal (or rather bureaucratic) pen? Has the *actio* of the liturgy changed or not? Did the Fathers of the Council desire greater participation in the Mass *as they knew it*, or did they desire a participation in some new and different activity?

In another particular instance, the authors argue quite forcefully for the superiority of celebration *ad populum*. They provide us with the admirable goal of looking together to Christ who becomes present on the altar in our midst. But it never becomes clear exactly why *ad orientem* fails in this regard. For example, referencing the *General Instruction of the Roman Missal*, they note that the altar "is to be positioned such that it can be the focus of both the priest's and the people's singular attention."[6] Was the altar *not* the singular focus of attention in the old rite? The logic of these comments is rather muddy. In the end, it appears that it all comes down to the ability of the faithful to see directly what happens on the altar. But here we fall again into pure subjectivity. Perhaps a show-and-tell approach to liturgy, resonant with a kind of dramatization of the celebrant-priest *in persona Christi*, visibly speaking to the congregation ("given up *for you*" as he gazes around the room in a very sincere tone), appeals to some people. But to others this comes across as phony theatricality. Perhaps in the old rite it is quite possible to *avoid* the central focus of the action, but it would be hard to argue that it is unclear what the action itself *is*.

---

very confident assertion is a bit strange in light of the actual offertory prayers themselves. It is true that the moment in the rite is described as the *praeparatio donorum* (Preparation of the Gifts), yet the liturgy retains an optional Offertory chant (*offertorium*), and the prayers themselves refer to the bread and the wine that "we offer you" (*quem tibi offerimus*).
6   GIRM 299: "Moreover, the altar should occupy a place where it is truly the center toward which the attention of the whole congregation of the faithful naturally turns."

3

When I suggest that the CHW essay falls short in its historical assessment, I mean not that it misunderstands the spirit of liturgical reform as it may have been ideally imagined by the fathers of *Sancrosanctum concilium*, but that it misunderstands and fails to recognize the true devastation resulting from its implementation. I say this not because I am a traditionalist who thinks the Novus Ordo evil or invalid. I am a Novus Ordo priest in almost every sense: I was ordained in the revised rites; I use the revised rites; and my theology is completely indebted to the work of Vatican II (especially *Lumen gentium* and *Unitatis redintegratio*, without which I truly cannot imagine being a Roman Catholic). But it is not sufficient to recognize that the implementation of reform had problems and abuses without a willingness to see the relation of those problems and abuses to the reformed rite itself. Could we make such a clean division, the reform itself would never have been necessary on its own terms. As the authors argue, the pre-conciliar liturgy had certain natural tendencies and associated habits that needed to be addressed. I think even the most ardent devotee of the traditional Mass would appreciate these needs when confronted by the actual celebration of the liturgy in the immediate pre-conciliar era. But if that is so, it is fanciful and irrational to imagine that the post-conciliar liturgy has been somehow magically purified of any negative tendencies. If the Council concluded that, to address problems, the *rite itself* needed to be revised, why are we forbidden from wondering whether there might be some issues with the reformed rite? Those who reject the "rigidity" of adherence to the old rite all too often approach the new rite as if *it* were the true "Mass of the Ages" that will live forever and ever. If we should reject an ideological naïveté about the Mass of 1962, should we not likewise reject an ideological naïveté about 1970?

More importantly, though, the conciliar spirit of reform itself, however admirable and worthwhile its goals, may have been blind to the limitations of its own authority. As Ratzinger laments in *The Spirit of the Liturgy*, the impression arose after the council that "the pope really could do anything in liturgical

The Failures of Reform

matters, especially if he were acting on the mandate of an ecumenical council."[7] But in the end "even the pope can only be a humble servant of its lawful development and abiding integrity and identity."[8] Amidst the ongoing arguments about "the reception of Vatican II," I submit that we are still dealing with the aftermath and reception of Vatican I. The modern papacy seems to swing between various contradictory visions of what popes do and do not have the authority to do. Surely this is not especially reassuring to those considering communion with Rome from the outside.

In another place (the Appendix of the 1987 revision of his book *Eschatology*), Ratzinger notes how the reformed liturgy boldly expurgates almost every single reference to the soul, particularly in its funeral rites. "That such a deeply rooted and central feature of Christian faith and prayer could disappear so quickly," he writes, "must surely arouse astonishment."[9] This breathtaking revision, he suggests, risks making the Catholic theological tradition unintelligible. The need since the 1960s to constantly reinvent theology and liturgy as something "fresh" and "new" robs us of the power of something *given* that stands beyond our own experience in judgment.

This is not the place to fret about questions of authority in liturgical revision. But to say that a pope, with the theoretical backing of a council, *did* revise the liturgy, does not mean that we must say, with CHW, that this is in some simplistic way "the work of the Holy Spirit." That is just bald ultramontanism; backing up the claim with "the pope said it" only makes it worse. Free, therefore, to use our basic rational powers of observation, we might wonder if the radical character of the reformed Missal of Paul VI, apparently un-envisioned by the Council fathers themselves, attempted far too much. In other words, if the Council desired to foster *participatio actuosa*, imposing an entirely new and

---

7 Joseph Ratzinger, *The Spirit of the Liturgy*, trans. John Saward (San Francisco: Ignatius Press, 2000), 165.
8 Ratzinger, *Spirit of the Liturgy*, 166.
9 Joseph Ratzinger, *Eschatology: Death and Eternal Life*, trans. Michael Waldstein, ed. Aidan Nichols, OP, 2nd ed. (Washington, DC: Catholic University of America Press, 2007), 249.

largely unfamiliar rite seems a rather strange way to do it.

Here we find a strange ally in C. S. Lewis, who, considering liturgical experimentation in the Church of England, writes:

> What we laymen fear is that the deepest doctrinal issues should be tacitly settled by what seem to be, or are avowed to be, merely changes in liturgy. A man who is wondering whether the fare set before him is food or poison is not reassured by being told that this course is now restored to its traditional place in the *menu* or that the tureen is of the Sarum pattern. We laymen are ignorant and timid. Our lives are ever in our hands, the avenger of blood is on our heels, and of each of us his soul may this night be required. Can you blame us if the reduction of grave doctrinal issues to merely liturgical issues fills us with something like terror?[10]

Whatever one thinks of the motives of reform, the Pauline Missal is the product of academic and ecclesiastical committee work. This is not in itself some damning claim; Pius V in *Quo primum* makes clear that his Missal is likewise influenced by the work of scholars and historians under his authority. Yet the historical context is rather different. In 1570, that watershed of Roman conformity, the pope, following the Council of Trent, had to confront both the sudden disruption in the Church's unity and the multiplication of liturgical variations thanks to the still-new printing press. Rather than imposing some new thing on the whole Church, Pius imposed a kind of restrained order through a singular and authoritative form of the Roman Rite's Missal and Breviary. Importantly, older custom was explicitly *not* abrogated. One detects in this a strong resonance with the fathers of *Sacrosanctum concilium*.[11] Indeed, as the pope envisions it, certain churches may desire to abandon their own usage for the Roman Missal, but the pope resisted asserting the authority to impose that rite upon

---

10   C. S. Lewis, *God in the Dock* (Grand Rapids, MI: Eerdmans, 1970), Letter 7b, p. 372.

11   SC 4: "Lastly, in faithful obedience to tradition, the sacred Council declares that holy Mother Church holds all lawfully acknowledged rites to be of equal right and dignity; that *she wishes to preserve them in the future and to foster them in every way*. The Council also desires that, *where necessary, the rites be revised carefully in the light of sound tradition*, and that they be given new vigor to meet the circumstances and needs of modern times" (emphasis mine).

them; rather, a unanimous vote of the local ordinary and his local chapter is required.

Yet in 1970 the reform seemed aware of no such limits. While for Pius V, a mere two hundred years of use justified caution, the brave new Missal of 1970 claims to restore this and that ancient custom absolutely and universally, instantly replacing the use of the last four hundred years. It suggests by omission or replacement that certain ritual and ceremonial practices that once were endowed with great meaning are now no longer meaningful. But it does so with the attitude—expressed more often by the authorities than by the texts themselves—that there is "nothing to see here" and everything is just as it was. This kind of centralized, universal change is completely unprecedented in the history of the Church. Who can blame an increasingly educated laity which responds with celebration or lament that the Church has apparently changed her doctrine of the Eucharist? To go around asserting that the doctrine has *not* changed, or that they should not ask such questions, is a kind of spiritual doublethink. What we are dealing with in 2023 is not, I submit, a conflict over whether or not to accept the Council's reforms. We are dealing rather with five decades of liturgical and doctrinal trauma.

4

I have not even mentioned the ongoing crisis over clerical abuse in the Church or the recently reported sense that priests in general do not trust (in general) the bishops.[12] But they relate to the liturgy wars quite directly in that they reveal the overall crisis of trust in the Church. What I describe as liturgical trauma is surely part of this big picture. It is why *Traditionis custodes* had the effect of an explosion happening in an already full hospital waiting room.

CHW believe that Pope Benedict XVI was mistaken in his generous expansion of permissions regarding what in *Summorum Pontificum* he dubbed the "extraordinary form." They believe

---

12 See especially the National Study of Catholic Priests, summarized here: https://catholicproject.catholic.edu/wp-content/uploads/2022/10/Catholic-Project-Final.pdf.

this because they believe, as mentioned above, that the new rite is superior to the old. But let us imagine for a moment that their assertion about that superiority is, at least, questionable; let us imagine that the pope saw the two forms exactly as he says he saw them: not as two competing rites, better and worse, but as two expressions or forms of the same *lex orandi*.[13] Perhaps rather than simply offering a concession to a group of cranky anti-reform-minded faithful, he saw himself as attempting to treat the issue of liturgical trauma at its base—that is, treating not merely the "implementation" of reform, but addressing the rampant distortion of reform as the imposition of some radical new theology. For Benedict, the problem was not so much in those who liked the older form of the Mass; the problem was in those who insisted on reading the new as a radical break, an absolute *either/or* with the old. Allowing the two forms to flourish side by side, he proposed, might at the same time correct the abuses of the new *and* the old, paving the way (perhaps) to a more united Roman liturgical experience in the future.

I am in no position to explain the why and wherefore of Pope Francis's liturgical magisterium or the administrative decisions of his curia. But it does strike me as simply true that the current project of dismantling Pope Benedict's legacy reopens previous wounds that had slowly begun to heal. Perhaps it is true that *Summorum Pontificum* was a temporary patch. In this, I suspect, both those promoting the "spirit of the Council" and those who find that spirit wanting may in some sense agree. The "two forms" model, while it may have promoted a temporary liturgical *pax*, does not ultimately answer the questions that endure about their differences (including

---

13 The *Divine Worship* Missal used in the ordinariates established under Benedict XVI's *Anglicanorum Coetibus* suggests in a few places the mind of the legislator. For example, not one but two Offertory rites are offered, corresponding directly with the classical prayers of the Roman offertory (Form 1, implicitly the more normative form) and with those of the Pauline Missal (Form 2). One may lament the presence of "options" as one problematic aspect of the modern liturgical books, but in this case the side-by-side presence of these rites offers a kind of Benedictine hermeneutic of continuity. In other words, whatever their differences, they cannot and should not be seen as offering two radically different theologies of the offertory. In this sense they present a concrete example of what Pope Benedict seems to have imagined in *Summorum Pontificum* as two "forms" of the same *lex orandi*.

The Failures of Reform

some of the questions proposed by Pope Benedict himself as a private theologian). Pope Francis, like CHW, seems convinced that the problems of the last five decades lie in an incomplete implementation of the Council. Why this incomplete implementation cannot include the Missal itself has always been unclear. As long as this irrational "rigidity" remains, the various calls for and protestations of loyalty "to the Council" will ring hollow and lack moral authority insofar as they ignore the enduring questions from clergy (including popes) and laity alike about the new Missal's ability to represent the depth of a theological and spiritual tradition that started long before 1970 and that nourished the very Council in question.

Finally, the concern with implementation, right as it may be on the surface, still avoids the trauma. It avoids confronting the palpable woundedness of a Church whose voice was, almost overnight, taken away from her and replaced with another. Any true "accompaniment" must acknowledge both the pain and its source.

5

We are no longer in the 1950s. CHW seem to acknowledge this in their recognition of the fact that Latin Mass goers today are often fully Vatican II "compliant" in their full, active, conscious participation. Yet the authors seem stuck in the idea that this is not good enough, that they should somehow remake themselves more in the image of the "participation" of the 1970s—or perhaps the 1970s *as they should have been*. Is not the chief law of the Church the salvation of souls? Does the Church really think that every individual's spirituality needs to look the same?

It is this insistent drive towards liturgical uniformity that most troubles me. As a member of the ordinariate, with our own unique "form" of the Roman Rite (the *Divine Worship* Missal), I have occasionally heard people suggest that there is no point in being different and that we should just "get with the program" and join the "normal" Catholic Church. *Anglicanorum coetibus*, one person confidently told me, was like an entrance ramp to the Catholic highway. We were never meant to *stay* on it. It was, it seems, just a temporary tool to lull me into a sense of familiarity before bringing me to full assimilation. (I never hear anyone making this claim about the "Zaire Use" of the Roman Rite, and I am unaware of any memos from Roman officials demanding that Congolese bishops provide an account of how they will without delay shepherd people into the "unique" *lex orandi* of the Pauline Missal.) CHW seem to think of *Summorum Pontificum* in similar terms. Never mind that this conception reinforces the Protestant Christian's worst caricature of Roman primacy as the forced uniformity of all people under a dictatorial "infallible" pope who takes pleasure in micromanaging people's salvation.

On the one hand, CHW are right to worry. I too doubt that this particular moment of liturgical history is sustainable as it is. The fissures run too deep. But I do not think this excuses the personal and pastoral offensiveness of the attitude, whether from hierarchs or theologians, which writes off entire groups of the faithful as second-class ecclesial citizens. As Benedict wrote in the pastoral letter accompanying *Summorum Pontificum*, "What earlier generations held sacred, remains sacred and great for us too, and it cannot be all of a sudden entirely forbidden or even considered harmful." Organic liturgical development can and should happen, but it should happen within the Church's worship *as it is* rather than as it might be piously imagined to be by a group of experts. Perhaps it is true that our entrance ramps have become too wide, our field hospitals for sinners too stable. But this strikes me as a much more natural development than the dated liturgical committee work of the twentieth century. If, as CHW remind us in the end, "the sacred Eucharistic liturgy here on earth only finds its perfection in the heavenly liturgy," we might be forgiven for thinking that, while we seek that final perfection here on earth, multiple forms and expressions of it will live, grow, and nurture us towards that life that is to come. Perhaps these forms can even help us to recover, over the next several generations, from the doctrinal and liturgical confusions of the twentieth century.

15

Joseph Ratzinger and the New Liturgical Movement

ROLAND MILLARE

UNFORTUNATELY, DIVISION CHARACTER-
izes our present culture and, subsequently, the
Church. Are you a Vatican II Catholic? A traditionalist Catholic? A Novus Ordo Catholic? Identity politics has influenced and shaped our unhealthy discourses about the sacred liturgy.

We now find ourselves locked into a "new" liturgical war when we need the liturgical wisdom of great theologians such as Joseph Ratzinger to guide us back to appreciating the authentic spirit of the liturgical movement, lest we drown ourselves in the present bitter and acrimonious sea that fills up our social media feeds or inboxes.

Joseph Ratzinger, in his autobiographical reflection *Milestones: Memoirs 1927–1977*, argues the need for a "new liturgical movement." The purpose of this movement will be to call to life the "real heritage of the Second Vatican Council." In *Milestones*, Ratzinger calls for a "renewal of liturgical awareness" and a "liturgical reconciliation that again recognizes the unity of the history of the liturgy and that understands Vatican II, not as a breach, but as a stage of development: these things are urgently needed for the life of the Church."

In order to promote liturgical renewal, the early members of the liturgical movement supported the active and intelligent participation of the faithful in the celebration of the sacred liturgy before they called for changes such as celebrating evening Masses, offering the Mass *versus populum*, etc. According to one of its early pioneers, Dom

Lambert Beauduin, the liturgical movement promotes active participation "by means of understanding and following the liturgical rites and texts [of the Mass]."

The first use of the phrase "active participation" (*participatio actuosa*) in a magisterial document comes from Pope St. Pius X's *motu propio* on sacred music, *Tra le sollecitudini*:

> Filled as we are with a most ardent desire to see the true Christian spirit flourish in every respect and be preserved by all the Christian faithful, we deem it necessary to provide before anything else for the sanctity and dignity of the temple, in which the faithful assemble for no other object than that of acquiring this spirit from its foremost and indispensable font, which is the active participation in the divine mysteries and in the public and solemn prayer of the Church.

The fact that the original use of the phrase "active participation" occurs in a magisterial document legislating the widespread restoration of Gregorian chant should disabuse us of the idea that participation should be focused solely on the celebration of the liturgy in the vernacular, the flourishing of liturgical ministries for lay people, liturgy facing the people (*versus populum*), or merely our outward actions and responses within the sacred liturgy.

The real *actio* within the liturgy is *oratio*. In his work *The Spirit of the Liturgy*, Ratzinger argues that participation is not simply our external action during the liturgy, it is our share in God's action whereby each person prays that he "may be transformed into the Logos, conformed to the Logos, and so be made the true Body of Christ." Ratzinger is very clear that external actions are secondary to internal prayer:

> *Doing* really must stop when we come to the heart of the matter: the *oratio*. It must be plainly evident that the *oratio* is the heart of the matter, but that it is important precisely because it provides a space for the *actio* of God.

Oratio assists the worshipping member of the Body of Christ to enter into the self-giving love of Christ.

The manner in which the liturgy is celebrated in the average parish suggests that one should be "doing" something to participate fully in the liturgy. Contrary to this notion that would have us focus on the external at the expense of the internal or the visible over and above the invisible, all of the responses, the singing of hymns, the chanting of the Propers of the Mass, and all liturgical gestures should move us into a transcendent silence lifting us into the celebration of the sacrificial and eschatological nuptial banquet of the Lamb, who was once slain.

The struggle to define and to understand active participation is a fruit of two different conceptions of the liturgy. In one of his interviews with the journalist Peter Seewald, Ratzinger notes that we can view the liturgy as "something living and growing" or "something that has been made." Hence, Ratzinger constantly affirms the view that the liturgy is the "opus Dei" (the "work of God") and not a product of man as symbolized by the false worship of the golden calf in Exodus.

The concern of Ratzinger with the implementation of the reformed post-Vatican II liturgy—more specifically, the Missal of St. Paul VI—is that it has characteristics of something that has been made by a committee of experts and is not the fruit of organic development and growth.

The hermeneutic of reform in continuity remains a foundational theme for Ratzinger/Benedict throughout his thought. It is one of the reasons Ratzinger is critical of referring to the Traditional Latin Mass as the "Tridentine Mass." It is a misnomer insofar as the Missal of St. Pius V (1570) has been revised by Clement VIII (1604), Urban VIII (1634), Leo XIII (1884), Benedict XV (1920), and most recently by St. John XXIII (1962). Hence, we can refer to the TLM as Mass celebrated according to the Missal of St. John XXIII.

In their assessment of Benedict XVI's allowance for the wider celebration of the Missal of St. John XXIII as the "extraordinary form" of the Roman Rite and the Missal of St. Paul VI and St. John Paul II as the "ordinary form" of the Roman Rite, Cavadini, Healy, and Weinandy raise this concern: "By reestablishing the extraordinary form, Benedict unwittingly employed a hermeneutic of discontinuity, as if the revised rite were not in continuity with the old." Benedict's *Summorum Pontificum* and the accompanying letter addressed to the bishops, *Con Grande Fiducia*, articulate a motive of "liturgical reconciliation" intent on preserving the unity between the two forms of the one Roman Rite. In other words, his aim has always been the preservation of the hermeneutic of reform in continuity.

Monsignor Klaus Gamber has been referred to as the "Father of the New Liturgical Movement" by the eminent German theologian Manfred Hauke.[1] Monsignor Gamber argued for allowing the two most recent Roman missals to coexist:

> The traditional *ritus Romanus* [the Missal of St. John XXIII] and the *ritus modernus* [the Missal of St. Paul VI] should both be accepted as legitimate forms of worship. The two rites are to exist as independent rites and must be kept separate and unique in such a way that the traditional Roman rite and the traditionally used *Missale Romanum*, together with all other liturgical texts (*Rituale* and *Pontificale*), be reinstated or be authorized for use in the form in which they existed prior to the Council.

It is not difficult to see how Gamber influenced Benedict XVI's *Summorum Pontificum*. The key distinction between the two is that Benedict maintains the view that there is one rite celebrated in two different forms.

CHW have questioned the rationale and the wisdom of Benedict's *Summorum Pontificum* because, in their view,

> Benedict's accommodation of the Tridentine liturgy, while pastorally motivated, undercut the fundamental principle of the liturgical renewal, for the faithful who now attend that liturgy have little opportunity for active participation.

In light of our discussion above of the authentic meaning of "active participation," I would argue that he did no such thing. One of the key elements necessary to promote active participation is reverential silence, which is often nowhere to be found in the implementation of the reformed liturgy.

One of the fruits of the "mutual enrichment" of allowing the two forms of the Roman Rite to exist is that it may assist the faithful to understand the true nature of "active participation" as envisioned by the liturgical movement. Benedict sought to bring clarity to an active participation that is both interior and exterior within the sacred liturgy. Further, he has tried to recover the notion that worship and

---

1   See http://bit.ly/3M9Yx9d.

participation extend beyond the celebration of the liturgy in the mission of charity toward our neighbor.

Benedict has favored the gift of liturgical pluralism because it can strengthen unity when it is promoted well and given proper pastoral care and accompaniment. I attend a suburban parish that is filled with a diverse body comprised of Nigerians, Hispanics, Latinos, Filipinos, Vietnamese, and Anglos. Mass celebrated according to the Missal of St. John XXIII was offered as one of the main Sunday Masses, and several hundred people attended this Mass regularly. Additionally, there were people who would go back and forth between this Mass and one of the other Masses celebrated according to the Missal of St. Paul VI/John Paul II.

I never encountered any animus toward Vatican II or the "new" Mass. I have and continue to encounter individuals and families in my parish who simply long for reverent liturgy wherein we take beauty and the *ars celebrandi* seriously. I also participated with regularity in Masses celebrated according to *Divine Worship: The Missal* (the liturgy of the Personal Ordinariate for former Anglicans/Episcopalians). I have also had the great fortune of participating in liturgies of the Eastern Churches (Ukrainian, Ruthenian, Syro-Malabar, Maronite, etc.). My participation in liturgical plurality has taught me that we would all benefit from the treasure of rich liturgical and ecclesial diversity.

Benedict, in his pastoral and liturgical wisdom, was not naïve; nor has his vision failed. If anything, the present situation confirms Benedict's wisdom and the veracity of Christopher Ruddy's assessment: "A Church that lives from tradition cannot reject its past without mortally wounding itself."[2]

We need more prayer, fasting, study of the liturgy, liturgical formation, and *dia-logos*. When the history of this period is written, we will come to appreciate that Joseph Ratzinger was the eldest son of the new liturgical movement, and his theology of liturgy may offer us the hermeneutic we need to appreciate the true heritage of the Second Vatican Council on the sacred liturgy.

---

2 Christopher Ruddy, "The Living Branch of the Traditional Latin Mass," *First Things* online, July 26, 2022.

16

Bible by the Pound:
WOULD THE HOLY SPIRIT AGREE THAT MORE BIBLE IS BETTER AT MASS?

FR. PETER MILLER, OSB

NO ONE DOUBTS THAT IF A MAN PRINTED all the Bible readings in the Traditional Rite and did the same for the New Rite and weighed the results, the New Rite would have more pounds of Bible. Very frequently, this technique is thought sufficient to quash all quandaries as to which of the rites is better. More Bible, more better, case closed. But I ask myself, WWTHST (What would the Holy Spirit think)? And as I muse on the facts of history, the scales begin to tip. Before the 1960s, the Holy Spirit never even tried to get more Bible into the Roman Rite. Why the change of mind?

More beguilingly, a close look at the new lectionary shows that more is not always better. Tons of passages have been removed. Right in the middle of readings, certain passages vanish, and important ones too. For instance, "On account of these the wrath of God is coming..." (Col 3:6) or, "Whoever causes one of these little ones who believe in me to sin, it would be better for him if a great millstone were hung round his neck and he were thrown into the sea" (Mk 9:42 and Mt 18:6). Why were these skipped? The reasons are odd, to say the least. The men who created the book thought that certain passages had "no pastoral usefulness[1]" or were "difficult," among other reasons. Declaring a passage "useless" is a bold move, especially when the Holy Spirit (who wrote the Bible) says that *"all* Scripture is inspired by God and is

---

1 See *Lectionarium Feriale*, par. 5, DOL 1836.

useful" (2 Tim 3:16). More and more, my conviction was becoming less and less that the Holy Spirit inspired the new lectionary. In fact, Revelation 22:18–19 calls down curses upon anyone who removes or adds anything written in "this prophecy." Well... the new lectionary's readings of Revelation 22 jumps from verse 17 to verse 20. That's embarrassing.[2]

As I pondered these matters, John Cavadini, Mary Healy, and Fr. Thomas Weinandy wrote over twenty thousand words on the liturgy, arguing for the discontinuation of the old rite and the acceptance of the new rite. Indeed, on two points the authors are abundantly clear: they insist that the Holy Spirit created the New Lectionary, and they insist that those in opposition to the New Lectionary are against the Holy Spirit. Unfortunately, no reasons were offered for why the Holy Spirit started doing something brand new in the 1960s. Moreover, very few reasons were offered for why the new lectionary is better than the old one. Again, while they showed that the new lectionary has "more Scripture" they gave no reason at all why more Scripture would be better. Until the 1960s, the Holy Spirit didn't think that it was better to have more. Again, why the change of mind?

Not believing that anyone who knew the details about the new lectionary would ever defend it, I contacted one of the authors of the CHW articles who was kind and generous enough to discuss the topic with me. We exchanged several friendly emails. While we reached no consensus on the topic, the friendly exchange was instructive for me and I shared my conversation with a friend. He asked if I would write a little summary of the exchange for the benefit of others. In sharing the exchange, I have removed all personal references and pleasantries, and kept only what applies to the lectionary issue. My first email:

---

[2] The differences between the new lectionary and the old one cannot be described accurately simply by noting that the new one skips verses. The old one does too. However, a careful examination reveals beyond doubt that the old one does so for editorial reasons while the new one does so for ideological reasons. Sweeping themes about sin, God's wrath, and His justice are carefully hidden from the listener. Examining all the ways in which this happens is not required for the purpose of this essay.

Dear author,

1 Kings 18–19 is one continuous story of the prophet Elijah conquering the prophets of Baal and ending a drought. The story offers a pithy, dramatic, and unmistakable lesson that God alone should be worshipped and that all other gods are evil, and the worshipers of false gods deserve death.

The Novus Ordo lectionary presents its own edited version of this story from Wednesday to Friday in the Tenth Week of "Ordinary Time" in Year II. The obvious lesson of Scripture has been mutilated and hidden. The edited version is—1 Kings 18:20–39, 41–46 and 1 Kings 19:9a, 11–16, 19–21.

Removed are:
- Elijah's rebuke of Ahab for following Baal (18:18)
- Elijah slaying the prophets of Baal (19:40)
- The mention that Elijah slayed the prophets of Baal (19:1)
- Elijah's jealousy for the True God and his rebuke of Israel for idolatry (19:10)
- The very end and moral of the story, which is that God will destroy by the hand of Elisha all those who bowed to Baal (19:17–18)

This sterilized version of the Bible is, unfortunately, typical of the New Lectionary. Please look at the details of the new lectionary before defending it!

Summary of Reply 1:

I have looked at the details and the new lectionary is not perfect, it can be improved in many ways. However, it is vastly richer and more expansive than the old missal. While the new lectionary tendentiously omits texts regarding sin and judgments, in many cases there are good pastoral reasons to do so. Difficult texts could distract from the focus of the liturgy. A good example is 1 Kings 18:40 and 19:7, which would raise the question whether execution is really the right response to false prophets and would distract from the main points of the story.

Any lectionary will necessarily exclude a large number of texts, as it's impossible to include them all, and when faced with a necessary choice, the difficult ones are reasonably omitted. With that said, I do think it's unfortunate that 1 Kings 19:9b–10 has been omitted.

In any case, it's much better to have the large portion of the story included in the New Lectionary than the small excerpt in the old missal, only 19:3–8.

Bible by the Pound

Several points struck me in this first reply.

1. The new lectionary is described as "vastly richer and more expansive" than the old one, but no explanation is given for what "richer" or "more expansive" means. I wonder, do they mean "more" and "more"? With food, "rich" means one thing and "more" means another thing. Chocolate mousse and liver pâté are rich. But listen to a sentence I pulled off the internet: "Burger King French Fries are the king of big fry sizes." Wow. That means something else. Rich. More. Two different things.

In addition to this, no reason is given for why "rich" and "expansive" are good things when it comes to lectionaries. And if they mean "more," no reason is given why "more" is better either. There is a time for chocolate mousse and liver pâté, but to eat it daily would be sickening. King-size fries may have their place too, but with food, more is not better. With food, "healthy" and "the right amount" is better, because—and this is the main point—food *has a purpose*.

The good is always measured by purpose. While the author's email emphatically proposes the good (e.g., "it's much better..."), it says nothing about purpose. The new lectionary is the king of big-size lectionaries. Okay... but is that a good thing?

2. The only reason I could find for thinking that more would be better (if "rich" and "expansive" really mean "more") is found in that phrase of the last sentence: "of the story." Certainly, if hearing the story were the point of the readings, having more of the story would be better. Stories with missing parts are bad. (I was also struck by several other points to which I will return later.) As this was the only hint implying a purpose for the lectionary—telling the story—I tried to focus on this.

The reference to the "small excerpt" of the story in 1 Kings (in the old missal) is telling. Assuming that the purpose of the reading is to hear the story, I can see why someone would think that small excerpts are not as good as "large portions." At the same time, a little familiarity with the old missal is enough to make this idea a bit silly; only someone entirely unfamiliar with *praying* the old missal would critique it based on the goal of "hearing the story." That would be very similar to someone critiquing the Rosary because it contains only fragments of the story. Well, the Rosary is not for telling stories. It has a different purpose. Let me explain.

The reading of 1 Kings 19:3–8 in the old missal occurs once a year, on Ember Wednesday in Lent. "Ember days" occur four times a year, on the Wednesday, Friday, and Saturday of a given week of each of the four seasons, and have a real connection to the agrarian cycle of planting and harvesting. Although the Ember days went extinct with the Novus Ordo, this was largely due to an oversight rather than a rational choice.[3] Thus, these are penitential days of prayer and fasting that sanctified each season and had some connection with creating food: the planting and harvesting that revolves around seasons.

The Ember days in Lent follow the first Sunday of Lent. Lent is a time of fasting. Perhaps that is obvious, but most people don't fast anymore. Not too long ago, the rule used to be that every Catholic could eat only one meal, on pain of mortal sin, each day in Lent. Now that is gone. But many of those who are praying the old missal are starting to keep the older fast. So, after four days of fasting, the first week of Lent begins. As the faithful begin the penitential season of Lent and start the hard work of uprooting all false gods from their lives, and begin to feel the hunger of having fasted for four days straight (Ash Wednesday through Saturday) what readings will they hear during the following week, the first week of Lent?

On Sunday, they hear about Jesus's forty-day fast and temptation. On Wednesday, they hear about Moses going up to the mountain for forty days (the reading is Exodus 24: 12–18).[4]

---

3 See Matthew Hazell, "Ember days in the Post-Vatican II Liturgical Reforms: An Accidental Elimination?," *Rorate Caeli*, March 10, 2022. It was decided by a large majority of the reformers that the Ember days should remain in the liturgy, but choosing their new dates was delegated to bishops' conferences, and none of the conferences ever got around to assigning dates, so a 1700-year tradition disappeared. (Kind of embarrassing.) And, you don't have to be a liturgical nerd to discover this ancient tradition. Just Google "Ember days" and read the Wikipedia article.

4 Although Moses fasts for forty days during this time, the reading

The extra reading for Wednesday is our 1 Kings 19:3–8 as discussed in the emails (labelled "3 Kings" in the old missal), which briefly describes the forty-day fast of Elijah. Four days later, on Ember Saturday (and again on the Sunday after it), the Gospel recounts Jesus meeting Moses and Elijah during the transfiguration. Thus, all the agony and pain associated with the fasts (and temptations) of these three men are seen on Sunday and Wednesday, and their glory is seen on Saturday. Each year this is presented to the faithful as they begin their fast.

Now, to anyone unfamiliar with these stories, the whole thing will be useless, like someone trying to pray the Rosary without knowing anything at all about the mysteries. But for those who already know these stories, and for those whose belly is beginning to war against their spirit, these readings, like the Rosary, provide an inexhaustible wealth of wisdom, and they provide it at exactly the right time. Moses was enraged at the golden calves, the false gods. Elijah slaughtered the false prophets of Baal, a false god. Both of these men, and Jesus too, fasted for forty days. Christ appeared in dazzling glory on Mount Tabor during the Transfiguration. This glory was shown to Peter, James, and John, who would also see our Lord in agony before His death. (This was a preparatory glory to strengthen them for the Passion.) These same men would be ordained the night before Christ died. The connections between priesthood, fasting, waging war against false gods, ordination, Lent, glory, and countless other details are too numerous and profound to explain here. Indeed, the hidden truths are so profound that a man can hear them each year for the rest of his life, with great profit to his soul.

During Lent, when the faithful try to destroy the false idols in their lives in order to prepare for the death and resurrection of Christ, could there be a better set of readings for

---

from Exodus does not mention it explicitly. One must already know it from Deuteronomy. This is interesting, because it is evidence that the old lectionary presupposes that the faithful already know the story. The lectionary is not there to give the listener all the details, as will become increasingly clear in this essay.

the first week of prayer?[5] The point of the lectionary is not to give us the story. Like the Rosary, which contains about 1% of the Gospel, but nevertheless forms an inexhaustible treasury for prayer, the liturgical year and its accompanying lectionary does the same kind of thing. It presents the right mysteries at the right time in a short, pithy way.

With these things on my mind, I sent my second email:

> It puzzles me why people think that having more Scripture at Mass is better. For instance, your comment at the end of your email that "it's much better to have the large portion of the story..." leaves me wondering, "why would anyone think that?" Is the reason simply that the Council proposed it? (If there were a future council that said "less is better," would this change your position?) Or is it supposed to be self-evident? It would help me to understand my fellow Catholics if I knew why they were thinking this.
>
> For instance, to me it seems much better in this case simply to have the old selection (19:3–8). But this depends upon the point of having readings at Mass at all. If the point were to tell the story or to teach Scripture, then more would be better (although I would not cut things out). But the point of the shorter reading in the old Mass is to encourage us to fast.
>
> Hearing about Elijah's forty-day fast each year, on Ember Wednesday in Lent, is extremely encouraging, and it fosters a whole life-cycle ordered to prayer and worship of God. The purpose of Scripture readings in the Catholic rites (East and West) has never been to teach Scripture or to "tell the story" (as far as I know). As you say, this is not even possible, and many parts of the Bible are dangerous to hear without explanation. The point has always been to take a little gem that forms an integral part of the day's worship of God—as with Ember Wednesday using the short snippet of 1 Kings.
>
> Anyway, I just wonder why people think more Scripture is better.

---

5 I don't know what the other Catholic rites do (the Byzantine, etc.) but perhaps their set of readings for this time is also very fine. The point, however, is that prayer is one kind of thing, and Bible learning or story-hearing is another kind of thing. The liturgical year (with its lectionary) is the first kind of thing, not the second.

Bible by the Pound

A summary of Reply 2:

A full answer to your question would take a long essay. But a brief answer is that God's people need to be fed and nourished by his word continually.

CCC 104—In the sacred books, the Father who is in heaven comes lovingly to meet his children, and talks with them.

Psalm 1:1–3—Blessed is the man... whose delight is in the law of the Lord, and on his law he meditates day and night. He is like a tree planted by streams of water, that yields its fruit in its season, and its leaf does not wither. In all that he does, he prospers.

Jeremiah 15:16—When I found your words, I devoured them; they became my joy and the happiness of my heart, because I bore your name, O Lord, God of hosts.

2 Timothy 3:16–17—All Scripture is inspired by God and is useful for teaching, for refutation, for correction, and for training in righteousness, so that one who belongs to God may be competent, equipped for every good work.

John 8:31–32—Jesus said to the Jews who had believed him, "If you remain in my word, you are truly my disciples, and you will know the truth, and the truth will set you free."

Hebrews 4:12—The word of God is living and active, sharper than any two-edged sword, piercing to the division of soul and spirit, of joints and marrow, and discerning the thoughts and intentions of the heart.

Romans 10:17—Faith comes from hearing, and hearing through the word of Christ.

The pattern of liturgy throughout the whole of salvation history is this: there is a liturgy of the word, then a liturgy of sacrifice and banquet. It is the pattern at the Sinai covenant in Exodus 24, and at the covenant renewal under King Josiah in 2 King 23. And on the road to Emmaus, the risen Jesus revealed himself first by breaking open the Scriptures, then in breaking bread (Lk 24:13–32). And it continues in the early life of the Church (Acts 20:7–11), and to the end of time. The liturgy of the word is not secondary or optional. We cannot know the Jesus we receive in the Eucharist unless we come to know him through his word.

In the case of Elijah, it's unfortunate that 1 Kings 19:3–8 has been dropped. But the point of the reading is not just to encourage us to fast. It is so much richer and deeper than that. We see Elijah being pursued by a wicked king and a murderous, scheming queen—just as John will be in the gospel. We see Elijah being discouraged and downcast, and the Lord encouraging and strengthening him. We see heavenly bread that sustains him on the journey to an encounter with God at Horeb, just as the Eucharist is heavenly bread that sustains us on our journey to God. We see an angel ministering to him in his sorrow, as will happen with Jesus in the Garden. We see forty days, a biblical number of testing. Etc. Etc.

It is not just to provide a little gem, but a rich treasury of the revelation of God that will transform us if we truly listen.

Much in this reply (together with the several points in the first reply that I initially skipped over) is worth noting.

First, the author writes, "the point of the reading is not just to encourage us to fast. It is so much richer and deeper than that." Clearly, the author is thinking about the reading *in the Bible*, not the reading *of the Bible* which is *in the Mass*. I was trying my best to distinguish between reading the Bible simply, and reading the Bible at Mass, and to suggest that the latter has a specific context and purpose.

To my mind, "a little gem" is not opposed to "a rich treasury." In fact, the treasury is so blooming rich that it's pointless to try to learn about it at Mass. Our tools for prayer—Stations of the Cross, Rosary, the Mass—*presuppose* a familiarity with the riches. Study and learning are prerequisites for a flourishing prayer life. Without them, it's useless to try to use prayer as a means for study. The inexhaustible treasury is a source from which the liturgical year draws. The "gems" presented by each yearly cycle of the liturgy are short, dense, and well-placed. By presenting our souls with the right gems at the right times, our minds are guided towards a penetrating view of the treasury that we *already know*. The Bible stories are like the treasure in the chest; the liturgical year is like a fine selection of gems, arranged by the jeweler. The Byzantine, Roman, and Ambrosian jewelers arranged the material differently, but no Catholic rite—except for the new one of Paul VI—tries to give anyone the chest.[6]

---

6 Even so, the new lectionary presents only 13.5% of the Old Testament, and 71.5% of the New Testament (see Felix Just, SJ, https://

While my correspondent provides penetrating insights into the reading of first Kings, my point is that any one of these (and many others) could easily be called to mind by this or that Catholic soul during the beginning of Lent. For a man who knows the stories already, the Holy Spirit could awake in his mind any one of these points as he begins his Lenten journey. Again, the wealth is inexhaustible; the liturgy taps the wealth. It seems to me that this is one of the main purposes of the readings at Mass: to tap the wealth for fitting prayer at fitting times. Here, "king-sized" is not the right measure. Rather, like food, "the right amount, of the right stuff, at the right time" is the right measure. And at times, that might be "miniscule," a word used by CHW to critique the old missal's choice of readings.[7]

Another point stands out. My correspondent called attention to the historical pattern of divine worship as being that of "word" followed by "sacrificial banquet," and gave several examples: the Sinai covenant in Exodus 24; the renewal of the covenant in 2 King 23; the road to Emmaus in Luke 24; the early life of the Church shown in Acts 20.

Interestingly, other examples were omitted: Ezra 6:19–22, and more importantly, the institution of the Passover in Exodus 12. While it's true that my interlocutor's examples show a word-then-sacrifice pattern, it's also true that the

---

catholic-resources.org/Lectionary/Statistics.htm). While this is indeed a much larger amount than is found in the old lectionary, it remains true that the Bible simply cannot be "mastered" at Mass, and even familiarity is difficult, especially in a multi-year cycle. The Byzantine practice of reading nearly the entirety of the New Testament (with the exception of the Apocalypse of St. John) during the liturgical year is a counterexample that nevertheless can be explained in accordance with traditional liturgical principles (especially the primacy of a single-year cycle), but to go into the non-Western rites is beyond the scope of this article.

7 About the liturgy before Vatican II, they write: "Although the lectionary readings were read [from the pulpit or in a missal] in the vernacular, the repertoire of readings was miniscule, especially from the Old Testament (only 1% of which appeared in the lectionary) and from the New Testament epistles, Acts, and Revelation (11%); even Gospel passages were limited (22%). One never obtained a sense of the entire Bible, nor of the individual Gospels. Scripture was foreign territory to most pre-Vatican II Catholics—Protestants knew their Bible, Catholics celebrated their Mass."

omitted examples do *not*, and furthermore, if we look at the author's examples carefully, the details seem to reveal a *purpose* for the "word" part. If we focus on the purpose, we begin to see that the biblical examples themselves actually support the idea of a "miniscule" repertoire instead of a "large portion"-style lectionary.

The road to Emmaus is not a discourse to those who already believe, but to those who *don't yet believe*. Jesus was instructing them *so that they might believe* in the Resurrection. Does it make sense that He would re-instruct them at every single Mass, covering all the Scriptures each time? Or does it make more sense that after this initial instruction, he might call to mind this or that passage at the appropriate time of year—a passage already covered in this initial instruction? This passage from Luke has more do to with new converts than with a "type" of a normal Mass. And for almost two thousand years, the Holy Spirit did not use this verse as a template for making Christian liturgies.

Again, the passage from Acts is not just a typical Mass. Paul was about to depart for another place, leaving his new converts behind. The night before his departure, he talked so long that a guy fell out of a window. Furthermore, the sequence of events was not just "word then sacrifice" but "word then sacrifice then more word." That is, even after he "broke bread," he still talked "till daybreak." This also seems more like instructing new converts than a type of the Mass. After the consecration and communion, there is not another set of readings (the Last Gospel plays a different role in the traditional Mass, where it is a final moment of meditative thanksgiving for what has just transpired).

I have mentioned one purpose for the lectionary: to tap the treasure already known, at the right time of year. But the author's next examples, the Sinai covenant in Exodus 24 and the renewal of the covenant in 2 Kings 23, might reveal another purpose of the lectionary.[8] In Exodus 24,

---

8 Exodus 24 does not seem to be a Passover sacrifice but a sacrifice in order to ratify a covenant. It takes place in the third month (cf. Ex. 19) after the departure from the red sea, while the Passover takes place in

the "word" part consisted of moral commands (laws) to a stubborn people inclined to sin. These people had already murmured in Exodus 17 (a reaction God abominated) and Exodus 19–23 consists in receiving various laws from God. Directly after this, in Exodus 24, Moses reads the laws to the people before offering sacrifices, and the people's response is "we will do it." This is not "hearing the story," but rather hearing commands about what to do and not to do. It is moral exhortation. How much they needed it is shown by the fact that soon after the sacrifice, in Exodus 32, the people were already worshiping the golden calf.

In 2 Kings we see something similar. For a long time, the people had worshipped false gods. Josiah destroyed the false gods and killed their priests. He reads the law to the people in verse 2, did a lot of other things in verses 3–20, and then orders the Passover to be kept in verse 21. How much time passes between verse 2 and verse 21 is not clear. The parallel passage in Chronicles 33–34 also mentions "reading the law" and offering the Passover, but again, the intervening time is not clear. It may have been weeks. It is not obvious that either of these examples establishes a clear "word-then-sacrifice" type for worship.

What *is* clear is that the purpose of the "word" part is not to tell a story, but to exhort a stubborn and sinful people to keep God's law. This same purpose is found (very much) in the old missal. When I (as a priest who celebrates the traditional Mass) had to start preaching each week, I was repeatedly struck by how often this missal has St. Paul telling people to stop fornicating and indulging in other vices, often of the flesh. Priests who start to hear confessions soon realize how necessary this is. Nevertheless, it harmonizes with my experience of life. Keeping God's law is not easy, and people (myself included) are generally stubborn and inclined to sin. Most Catholics don't even go to Mass, and the ones that do are mostly playing with mortal sin. Repetitive exhortation

---

the first month. However, while the Passover seems to be *the* type of the Mass, perhaps these lesser sacrifices have implications for the Mass as well. (The renewal in 2 Kings is a Passover sacrifice.)

to virtue is most necessary. It would be nice if most men were good and we could just tell them stories. But reality is reality, and ==most men need a wholesome fear of hell and repetitive exhortations to avoid sin and strive for virtue.== The exhortations are not just for beginners either, because even the most spiritual of men need to uproot and destroy the spiritual analogues of physical sin. St. John of the Cross speaks, for instance, of spiritual fornication and spiritual gluttony. The old missal presents—almost constantly—exhortations to virtue and threats against sin, and these are beneficial to *all* souls, not just those toying with mortal sin.

The scriptural depictions of liturgy that my interlocutor *omitted* are also instructive. In Ezra 6, the Passover is mentioned without mention of a "word" part. Is the "word" part not even required for the Passover? Regarding the true Passover sacrifice (the Mass), St. Caesarius seems to think so. He writes:

> The Mass does not take place when the holy Scriptures are read in the church, but when the gifts are offered and the Body and Blood of the Lord are consecrated. For you can just as well read the lessons at home, whether they are taken from a prophet, from the apostle, or from the Gospel, or you can listen to other people reading them; but you can hear and watch the consecration of the Body and Blood of Christ only in the house of God. That is why anyone who wants to participate in the entire Mass and benefit his soul thereby must stay in the church, in a humble posture and with a contrite heart, until the moment when the Lord's Prayer is said and the blessing is given to the people. (Sermon 73)

He does not say, of course, that reading the Bible is useless or unimportant, but simply that it is not essential. That is, the Mass can exist without it.

In Exodus 12, the Passover sacrificed is established. There is no explicit mention of a "word" part, but two intriguing verses stand out. In verse fourteen, the Lord says, "This day shall be for you a memorial day...." In verse twenty-six, the Lord says, "When your children say to you, 'What do you mean by this service?' you shall say, 'It is the sacrifice

Bible by the Pound

of the Lord's Passover, for he passed over the houses of the people of Israel in Egypt, when he struck the Egyptians but spared our houses.'" Perhaps from this last verse came the ritualistic tradition whereby the eldest Jewish son would ask the father about the meaning of the meal. The father would answer.

We can learn from this tradition. The ritualized question and answer is not for the sake of "hearing the story." Indeed, unless the son were a complete idiot, he would already know the story well enough from past years, and no question-answer ritual would be required year after year. But the purpose of the ritual is something else. This day is not a learning day, or a "hearing a large portion of the story" day, but rather, "This day shall be for you a *memorial* day...." When sacrificing the unblemished Lamb, a specific salvific act of God (slaying the firstborn of Egypt and delivering the Israelites from slavery) is fittingly called to mind. The question-answer is not for learning, but for calling to mind fitting mysteries in order to worship God more perfectly. Once again, the old missal, the true heir and continuation of the worship of Israel, does the same kind of thing.

Simply looking at the readings in the old missal as they actually exist, and also looking at these considerations of the "word-then-sacrifice" descriptions found throughout Scripture, it seems to me that the primary purposes of the lectionary in the Roman Mass[9] are: 1. Providing fitting material for

---

[9] The old Mass is deservedly called the "Roman Mass," for it was developed in Rome from about 300 to 800 and then further developed in other parts of the Roman empire from about 800 to 1200. Around 1200, it was received back into Rome, perfected in Rome, and from that time forward, it was substantially stable until the 1960s. At that time, a new missal was created which lacked many of the characteristics of the centuries-old Roman one, yet the new one was also called (by fiat of authority) "Roman." This is comparable to an emperor of China outlawing lo mein and eggrolls and legislating spaghetti and burritos instead, and then demanding that we call these latter things "Chinese food." We might oblige, but we would know all along that they were being called "Chinese" because of positive law, not because they were developed and perfected in China. The word "Chinese" would take on two different meanings. And, really, everybody would still know that the one dish was Italian and the other Mexican.

the day's worth within the context of a cyclical liturgical year, and 2. Exhorting stubborn and sinful people to keep God's law, in order that they might offer a worthy sacrifice.[10] *Neither* of these goals requires "more Scripture." *Neither* is about "hearing the story." And the very texts offered by our author's email, combined with the omitted ones, seem to support this idea.

When I presented these ideas to my correspondent, the substantial part of the reply was something like this:

> I encourage you to read what the Church herself teaches about Scripture and about the liturgy of the word, for instance the Vatican II documents *Dei Verbum* and *Sacrosanctum Concilium*; the *Catechism*, especially 101–8 and 132–41; *General Instruction of the Roman Missal*, 55–60; and Pope Benedict XVI, *Verbum Domini*, especially 56–57. As you will see, the liturgy of the word is not a learning exercise, nor is it a mere moral exhortation. Rather, it is hearing Christ himself, the Lord and divine Bridegroom, speak through his word. It is hearing God our Father speak to us, his children, opening up to us the mystery of redemption and salvation and offering us spiritual nourishment.

To my mind, this is opaque. When Christ tells the woman caught in adultery, "go and sin no more," is she supposed to meditate on the profound truth that the words she hears are

---

[10] There is another purpose of the lectionary that I did not present to my interlocutor and is beyond the scope of this essay, but is worth mentioning. Four elements are important in any sacrifice: the person who is offering, the thing offered, the people for whom it is offered, and the person to whom it is offered. In the ancient sacrifices, both pagan and true, the thing offered consisted in food. More than anything else, this was to call to mind man's dependance on God, without Whom he would not exist. But God's word is true food: "Man does not live on bread alone, but on every word that comes forth from the mouth of God" (Cf. Deut 8:2–3 and Matt 4:4). Both Ezekiel and St. John were told by God to eat the scroll and then to prophesy (cf. Ezek 2–3 and Rev 10). During the high liturgical sacrifice, the word is chanted with elaborate ritual as part of "what" is offered in the sacrifice. This accounts for the words of the bishop when he ordains the Subdeacon and the Deacon, who read the epistle and Gospel. He commands them to read *"pro vivis atque defunctis,"* that is, "on behalf of (or for the benefit of) the living and the dead." The dead do not hear the readings, but they benefit from the offering.

the words of the person speaking to her? Or is she supposed to stop adulterating so that she can worship God in Spirit and in Truth?[11] Once again, moral exhortation. And even if the "liturgy of the word" is "hearing God our Father speak to us, his children," still, He is saying *something*. It seems to me that this "something" is the important thing. God spoke to a lot of people, and it didn't do them any good.

When I looked at the suggested sources from the GIRM, CCC, Pope Benedict, and Vatican II, I found that they repeated the same kind of thing. For instance, Pope Benedict writes, "The proclamation of God's word at the celebration entails an acknowledgment that Christ himself is present, that he speaks to us, and that he wishes to be heard" (*Verbum Domini*). But what would Christ think if, after commanding "go and sin no more," He heard the woman say, "Your proclamation entails my acknowledgment that you are present, that you are speaking to me, and that you desire to be heard" (!)? Jesus does not speak to be present. In fact, He told Pilate that He became man (present to us) in order to speak: to bear witness to the truth. Again, He even tells his disciples that it is better for them that He depart, because the Holy Spirit will come and call to mind the words of Christ. The point of speaking is the words spoken, not the making present of the speaker. Enough of this.

A glance at the list of Scripture quotations in the author's second email will bring this essay to an end.

Psalm 1:1–3—These verses speak about meditating on God's law "day and night," and not simply at Mass. For this to be an argument for an expanded lectionary, we would have to have Mass "day and night." However, if a man lives this constant meditation, and attends the old Roman Mass, he will find a delightful and profound lectionary that helps him pray the liturgical year and offer a worthy sacrifice. This psalm encourages us to do what we should do in order to benefit from liturgical prayer. It does not propose what should be done at liturgical prayer.

---

11 I'm mixing up two stories of the Gospel, but it doesn't matter. The point is found in both.

Jeremiah 15:16—Imagining Jeremiah "devouring" the new lectionary is like imagining a Shakespeare enthusiast "devouring" the Cliffs Notes. The new lectionary was edited to avoid "difficult" and "useless" passages.

2 Timothy 3:16-17—This verse states that "all" Scripture is useful. The new lectionary is constructed on the basis that some passages are not useful. There are some passages, so its creators claim, that "have no pastoral usefulness."

John 8:31-32—Again, the "truth that sets us free" is oftentimes softened and hidden by the new lectionary. And this same critique applies to the next verse, Hebrews 4:12. It speaks of God's word as "sharper than any two-edged sword" and yet the new lectionary in many ways dulls the sword. In the old rite, the readings are often short and to the point. A sharp dagger, which is short, is much more effective than a wooden sword, which is long. Again, "more" is not the same thing as "sharp."

Romans 10:17—The fact that faith comes from hearing is an argument for why *unbelievers* should be *taught* the Scriptures, not an argument for why those who already know them should read (or be read) more Scripture before offering the sacrifice of the Mass.

In the end, it seems to me that Christians should be instructed in their faith either as children, or when they are converting, or both, and that all Christians should make the study of Scripture a part of their lives as disciples of Christ. As *learning* the mysteries of the Rosary is necessary prior to *praying* them, so learning the Bible is necessary prior to assisting at Mass as fruitfully as possible. And just as the "miniscule" announcement of each mystery prior to praying each decade is a little gem which directs our mind to God in a fitting way, the miniscule biblical repertoire of the old Mass is the same kind of gem. Let us not forget that even medieval peasants, illiterate, had a broad exposure to the characters and stories of the Bible through the popular mystery plays, stained-glass windows, and homilies of which we have many records.

In the old law, ritual purity was required before offering an acceptable sacrifice. In the new law, moral purity is required.

While the sacrifice of the Mass could be offered without any readings at all (as when a priest in a concentration camp clandestinely offers it), nevertheless the sharp word of God is read to the faithful in order to help them achieve moral purity and to provide fitting thoughts to accompany the sacrifice. The Mass does not consist of two separate things: "word" and "sacrifice." Rather, the Mass *is* a sacrifice, and the word part is entirely ordered to offering this sacrifice well.

Giving percentages of the miniscule repertoire of Scripture covered at Mass does not prove that the Mass is defective any more than it would prove that the Rosary is defective. Rather, it proves that the ones who are giving the percentages as decisive arguments misunderstand the context and purpose of Scripture at Mass.

With this said, I want to thank my correspondent for being generous with time and talent. I have learned a lot from the CHW article series and from my email exchanges, and have been able to correct certain errors which I previously overlooked in my own way of thinking. Although we disagree about the Mass, I benefit from the friendship that binds together the followers of Christ, even amidst their disagreements.

17

The One Thread by Which the Council Hangs

DOM ALCUIN REID, OSB

"DON'T TOUCH THAT! IF YOU DO, EVERY-thing will collapse!" The warning is clear enough. Any sensible person would rapidly desist, lest their one seemingly minor act bring everything crashing down, undoing the work of many days, weeks, years or even decades.

I am not sure whether these were the exact words used by a number of bishops at the beginning of the pontificate of Pope Benedict XVI, but, whatever words they chose, these bishops forcefully conveyed to him their opinion that he could not under any circumstances permit a wider use of the older liturgical rites without perilously detracting from the authority of the Second Vatican Council. "Don't do it," they insisted, "or the Council will seem to have been reversed and will lose its authority."

Of course, Benedict XVI did "do it" with his motu proprio *Summorum Pontificum* (July 7, 2007) — having first spent a cheerful morning or two telephoning many of the bishops who had previously shouted at him, in order personally to 'explain' that they had little or nothing to worry about. The world did not come to an end. The Church did not implode, and the Second Vatican Council's true authority was not undermined.

At least, not in the minds of those who understand the Second Vatican Council to be a valid Ecumenical Council of the Catholic Church which occupied itself with pastoral aims — principally how the Church could more effectively preach the Gospel in the modern age — and who know that it defined no dogmas and decreed no anathemas, but outlined policies which were judged to be expedient at the time and which were to be interpreted in a hermeneutic of continuity with the Church's Tradition, including the dogmatic definitions of the other twenty Ecumenical Councils of the Church.

But in the minds of those for whom the Second Vatican Council did in fact define a dogma—indeed, a super-dogma—Pope Benedict's actions most certainly risked undermining the Council and bringing its entire edifice crashing down in ruins. The dogma it supposedly defined?—that "Vatican II changed all of that, radically, irreversibly," where "that" stands for any previous liturgical, doctrinal, moral, or pastoral teaching or practice that is deemed inapplicable (read "inconvenient") to contemporary man.

This super-dogma has been applied to every area of the life of the Church in subsequent decades, from catechetics to cathedral choirs, from seminaries to Catholic schools, from missionary territories to the minefield of morality in the modern world, from relations with non-Catholics and non-Christians to its dealing with increasingly secular states, etc. But nowhere is this super-dogma more clearly visible, indeed nowhere is it more tangible, than in the liturgical rites promulgated by the pope in the decade or so following the Council's close in 1965. The "new Mass" is just that; it is not the old one. The old one is gone—and forbidden in the minds of those for whom "Vatican II changed all of that, radically, irreversibly." And their emotional and psychological attachment to this super-dogma runs very deep indeed.

If you doubt this for one minute, take a young priest, have him catechise his people on the patristic, spiritual, and pastoral value of celebrating the (new, vernacular) Mass *ad orientem*—with the priest and congregation facing together towards the [liturgical] East—and have him announce the date on which he shall commence the practice. Then borrow his telephone. The chancery or even the bishop will call promptly enough to forbid him. You see, "Vatican II changed all of that," even if in 2016 Pope Francis's own choice as Prefect of the Congregation of Divine Worship had the temerity to explain that, in fact, it did not. (He, too, got a telephone call.)

THE GRIP OF THE SUPER-DOGMA

When we recognise this super-dogma for what it actually is—a lie upon which generations of clergy and laity have built their ecclesiastical careers (by no means am I referring to "simple layfolk" who just want to love and serve God and get to heaven)—we can begin to understand the manic severity that is meted out to those who refuse to subscribe to it and, indeed, we can begin to comprehend the extreme lengths to which its devotees will go in propping up and jealously defending everything that they have built upon this foundation, most especially the reformed liturgy. For the new liturgy is the touchstone of Vatican II. It is the single thread by which (in the minds of many) the Council (of their own conception) hangs.

This explains the grave concerns expressed by ecclesiastical authorities about whether or not those who wish to celebrate the unreformed liturgical rites "accept Vatican II." What, in fact, is there to accept? The prudential judgements of the Council in respect of pastoral policy? One may be a faithful Catholic and have different opinions about their value, particularly with some sixty years of hindsight, surely?

Of course, authorities are more specific in their demand: one must accept the legitimacy of the liturgical reform of Vatican II. Here we get to the crux of the matter. Every Catholic must indeed accept the *validity* of the liturgical rites duly promulgated by the pope (and which do not contravene the divinely instituted elements of the rites—no pope or council can substitute bread and wine at Mass with cookies and cola). But with greatest respect to the authorities—who repeat this demand often—*that is as far as it goes*. That the liturgical and historical travesty known as "Eucharistic Prayer II" validly confects the Eucharist is undoubtedly true. But whether it *should* be (or ever have been) placed in any Roman missal, or for that matter, in any liturgical book, is very much open to legitimate debate. Even Protestant scholars recoil from the embarrassing way in which it came into its present form and use. And this, very worryingly, is quite possibly the Eucharistic Prayer that practicing Catholics most often encounter at Mass.

You see, if you don't "accept" this reform—or worse still, if you question it, or habitually avoid it by frequenting or celebrating the unreformed liturgical rites—you are classed as a "Vatican-II denier." And in the contemporary Catholic Church which boasts of its mercy, inclusivity, accompaniment, its listening and its openness to diversity, there is little if any place for you—regardless of the fact that you have never once denied the reality of the Second Vatican Council or that it was a legitimate Ecumenical Council of the Catholic Church and you accept each and every one of its solemn doctrinal definitions (all *none* of them). Once labelled a "Vatican-II denier," a "traditionalist," or whatever, you are *beyond the fringes*—because you have dared to touch that one thread on which, many hold, the Second Vatican Council hangs.

CAVADINI, HEALY, AND WEINANDY

In an article in which I have been requested to respond to "A Synoptic Look at the Failures and Successes of Post-Vatican II Liturgical Reforms" by John Cavadini, Mary Healy, and Thomas Weinandy (originally published as a series of five articles, gathered into one on December 1, 2022), I have taken a long time getting to the authors' writing itself. However, I make no apology for the length of the introduction above. Once the issues and realities outlined there are understood, one can begin to assess what they write. I hasten to add that I do not accuse them personally of holding all of the positions I have highlighted. But with their series they have wandered—somewhat recklessly I would say, even with the best of intentions—into the minefield at the heart of the "liturgy wars" that have been reignited by the new Prefect of the now "Dicastery" of Divine Worship, his cronies, and those whom they have been able to influence.

There are many, many things that could be said in respect of their more than 20,000-word foray and, if they are to be taken at their word (and there is seemingly no reason to doubt them), they are sincerely trying to grapple with the problem of the liturgy of the Roman rite that has once again reared its ugly head, and quite violently, since Pope Francis's motu proprio *Traditionis Custodes* (July 16, 2021), exacerbated by Archbishop (now Cardinal) Roche's responses to questions over the motu proprio (December 18, 2021), and underlined by the pope's apostolic letter on liturgical formation *Desiderio Desideravi* (June 29, 2022).

The gist of all of these documents—one might reasonably say that it is their raw political aim—is the reassertion of the reformed liturgical books published after the Council as the sole form of worship in the Latin Rite of the Catholic Church, brusquely rescinding the freedoms established by Pope Benedict XVI for the use of the older liturgical rites. These documents don't *quite* go as far as to set a date for everyone to be voluntarily enclosed in a liturgical straitjacket (perhaps yet another document is on the way? If so, it will only further harm and divide the Church) but their gist is that Eucharistic Prayer II and all the rest are here to stay and that everyone *shall* like them, no matter what.

Cavadini, Healy, and Weinandy are honest in seeing that this poses quite a problem when there is at least one generation of Catholics, young and growing in number, for whom the reformed liturgical rites are practically unknown. They have discovered or even have grown up with the *usus antiquior*—the older liturgical rites—and they are now raising their own children accordingly, having been assured by popes and prelates across the world—even by the likes of the then Archbishop Roche[1]—that this was perfectly acceptable and did not in any way damage the communion of the Church; indeed, that it enriched it as an expression of that legitimate plurality that is part of the One Church of Christ. These generations, who have produced numerous vocations to the priesthood and religious life and whose young people have formed faithful and fruitful marriages, see no need for the reformed rites. They will have nothing to do with a Stalinist liturgical re-education ordered from on high to ensure that everyone *really does* like Eucharistic Prayer II.

---

1 See his October 14, 2015 interview: "Connect 5: Archbishop Arthur Roche on the Liturgy Wars," *Salt and Light Media*.

THE GENIE IS OUT OF THE BOTTLE

Here we arrive at the first major problem with Cavadini, Healy, and Weinandy's series of articles. The fact is that the liturgical genie is out of the bottle, and attempts to get it back inside are futile. Their articles may be cathartic to write and satisfying (for some) to read, and by publishing them they may be happy to be supporting the draconian measures ordered by Rome, but they will convince no one. Indeed, they will fuel (and they have fuelled) more trenchant exchanges across the increasingly deeply drawn partisan lines of the liturgy wars.

Certainly, bishops can close down Masses celebrated in the older form and forbid access to the Sacraments. They can bully and threaten fiscally dependant clergy into submission and hiding, but they cannot *convince* them. The generation of Catholics born and formed during the pontificates of St John Paul II and Benedict XVI are not going to rush to establish an International Society of St Paul VI to promote his liturgical rites any time soon, even if some are forced to celebrate them. Why? Because *the intellectual and pastoral argument about the theological, liturgical, and most especially the pastoral superiority of the reformed liturgical rites has long since been lost.* And here we run into the gaping holes in Cavadini, Healy, and Weinandy's series.

Intellectually, because it is a well-established fact that the new rites promulgated by Paul VI after the Council were not the modest, organic development of the heretofore Roman rite for which the Council called (see *SC* 23) but were a radically new product of the body entrusted by Paul VI to implement the Council's liturgical Constitution (the *Consilium*). Both proponents and opponents of the new rites accept this reality. The *Consilium* intentionally went beyond the Constitution—with, in the case of many of its members, the best of intentions, and certainly, in the end, with the backing of papal authority. As anyone who studies the Council itself will rapidly learn, the Council did not intend the liturgy to be entirely in the vernacular; it mandated no new Eucharistic Prayers; it insisted that Gregorian chant should have pride of place; it never said a word about the priest turning toward the people; etc., etc.

All of this is to say that *it is intellectually false to assert that to question or reject the reformed liturgy is in some way to "undermine Vatican II,"* as our three authors, and others, would have us believe. (Note the fear here that the super-dogma will be denied.) The reformed liturgy is a set of prudential judgments made *after and not at* the Council by enthusiasts and experts in the hope of producing rites that would be pastorally effective in the modern era. The Council's liturgical Constitution was viewed by the *Consilium* as a starting point, not as a set of terms of reference. Fact. One can question the judgements made liturgically and historically without in any way denying that the Council was legitimate as a Council and, indeed, that it rightly took up questions of liturgical reform. Fact. (There was a time when Eucharistic Prayer II was not. Fact.)

PASTORAL JUDGEMENTS AND RE-EVALUATIONS

One can also question the judgements made by the *Consilium* and Paul VI *pastorally*, and it is here that we find the next gaping hole in this series of articles. Pastorally, as repeated statistical studies from various countries demonstrate, the reformed liturgy has simply not delivered the ecclesial renewal promised. Promised? Yes: the assumption that guided ("motivated"? "sold"?) the introduction of the new rites was that *if* the liturgy were simplified, modernised, made more contemporary, *then* people would participate in it more fruitfully and a new springtime in the life of the Church would be ushered in. Alas, the opposite has proved to be true.

That is not to say that there are not many good, committed people who find in the modern rites the source and summit of their Christian life and who receive many graces therefrom (but, of course, the same is true of those who frequent the *usus antiquior*), nor is it to deny that the dramatic decline in liturgical practice in Western Catholicism is due to many and varied factors. But it *is* to say, very clearly, that the modern liturgical rites have not *of themselves* proved to be part of the solution; of themselves they have not retained, let alone attracted, people to the practice of the Faith. *Today* we may, then, legitimately raise questions about their pastoral utility and about the wisdom of following the assumptions and policies of sixty years ago that led to their production.

In this light it is interesting, and very welcome, that our authors are open to considering a reform of the liturgical reform. They are, perhaps, unaware that in recent decades merely to broach this possibility was utterly forbidden in the Congregation (now Dicastery) of Divine Worship, even under Benedict XVI. According to the partisans who controlled its corridors, the new liturgical books are "irreformable"—even if the Sovereign Pontiff (at the time) thought otherwise. That Cavadini, Healy, and Weinandy are open to considering such questions and to making an honest appraisal of the weaknesses of the liturgical reform is to their credit, though it will probably not gain them any new friends in the Roman Curia at present.

For the Curia currently follows the party line found in a late summer 2017 speech by the Holy Father in which he affirmed "with certainty and with magisterial authority that the liturgical reform is irreversible" (August 24, 2017). This is a curious use of "magisterial authority," not only because a speech is an unusual and very low-ranking form of pontifical utterance for the serious exercise of magisterial authority, but also because unless it means the liturgical reform *in all its specifics*, it can mean nothing at all. Hence Eucharistic Prayer II (and all its friends) are irreversible; they could never be changed or abolished. Ultimately, this seems to be a somewhat cheap use of the term "magisterium" that only serves to undermine the value of the currency.

The problem with such a papal claim is that modern and ancient liturgical history prove exactly the opposite. If *Summorum Pontificum* (2007) can be abolished by *Traditionis Custodes* (2021) and if the Breviary of Cardinal Quignonez published under Paul III in 1535 could be repudiated several popes later in 1558, the Missal of Paul VI could—legitimately, in whole or in part—be abolished or reformed, most particularly in an era when a pernicious political papal positivism seems to be the main criterion in play. Suddenly abolishing the new missal would be a draconian act and would be pastorally insensitive and harmful (as is *Traditionis Custodes*), but it could be done. (There may yet be a time when Eucharistic Prayer II is not.)

PNEUMATOLOGICAL ENTHUSIASMS

But for the partisans of the Mass of Paul VI, this is unthinkable—even academically. And to protect themselves from even its discussion, the authors we are considering assert, quite incredibly, that opposition to the reformed liturgy "inherently denies the validity of the liturgical renewal as a genuine work of the Holy Spirit in the contemporary Church," and that a return to the older rites "is contrary to the entire Spirit-anointed liturgical renewal that culminated in Vatican II's Constitution on the Sacred Liturgy." Put simply, their argument is that to critique or to reject the reformed liturgical rites is tantamount to blasphemy against the Holy Spirit, because the new rites are the direct result of His activity in the Church.

To put it politely, our authors are suffering from a little too much enthusiasm here, for they are practically making *the liturgical reforms themselves* a matter of faith, of Divine Revelation, to be believed in by all the faithful. But the reforms are not. They are the product of prudential judgements of men, submitted to a pope who promulgated them. Certainly, these men did (we hope) fervently invoke God the Holy Spirit to assist them in their work—and in this life we shall never know to what extent He did so assist them. (Could God the Holy Spirit really have been personally responsible for all the errors that resulted in Eucharistic Prayer II?)

It is therefore not the sin of blasphemy to question the liturgical reform any more that it is blasphemy to assert that the College of Cardinals is perfectly capable of invoking the Holy Spirit at the beginning of a conclave and then of electing a truly bad pope, as any history of the papacy more than clearly demonstrates. That a man is the pope and acts with the requisite authority is a matter which can be legally verified. That a man is the choice of God the Holy Spirit is something that one may personally hold, but it is not something that may be asserted as a truth of the Faith. This applies *mutatis mutandis* in respect of liturgical reforms. Indeed, scholarship increasingly shows that there were many other influences at work in the liturgical reform following the Council—just as there are in papal elections. Personally, I am no fan of the maligning of the reform through *ad hominem* attacks on the reformers themselves: the new rites should be critiqued on liturgical grounds and in the light of the principles of *Sacrosanctum Concilium*—and there is more than enough material here to show their defects!

PARADOXES IN PARTICIPATION

Cavadini, Healy, and Weinandy rightly underline the centrality to the liturgical reform of *participatio actuosa* (of real, conscious, fruitful participation) in the Sacred Liturgy. This had been the desire of popes and of the twentieth-century Liturgical Movement for decades prior, and the prominence given it by the Council is unquestionably apposite. It's not a doctrine of the Faith, but it is a pastoral orientation/policy which is, arguably, fundamental for the good of every baptised person.

But our authors get bogged down in a quagmire of activity rather than actuality, emphasising the many things people *do* in the modern rites, almost as if this activity is an end in itself—an assumption that has proved to be the quicksand that has swallowed up any possibility of liturgical participation in many souls. How many children who have been made thus to "participate" in Masses in their schools or parishes no longer practice the Faith, having never in fact been introduced to Christ, the principal actor in the Sacred Liturgy? For if we are not formed in "the spirit and power of the liturgy," all this activity is futile, as the Council itself stated bluntly in the same article (*SC* 14) that calls for *participatio actuosa*.

They really should re-read (and study the *Acta* and the contemporary commentaries on the Constitution) article

36 (which they quote): "To *promote* active participation, the people should be encouraged to take part by means of acclamations, responses, psalms, antiphons, hymns, as well as by actions, gestures and bodily attitudes..." (emphasis added). This is one of the most misunderstood articles of the Constitution: *participatio actuosa* can certainly be *promoted* or fostered by the activities mentioned, but it itself is something else, something deeper—something of the mind, heart, and soul that is accessible even if it is not one's turn to read or serve or perform any other ordinary or extraordinary ministry at Mass; indeed, even if one never has or could. The fact is that liturgical activity has been increased, whilst we still await the Council's desire for full, conscious, actual participation by all.

Interestingly, Cavadini, Healy, and Weinandy note, correctly, that those who attend celebrations of the *usus antiquior* today do so with a "Vatican II mindset"; i.e., they expect to *participate* in the older rites. Of course, when you arrive for Sunday Mass in the *usus antiquior* you don't run the risk of being press-ganged into doing the second reading, taking up the Offertory procession, or filling in for the extraordinary minister who has called in sick. You may well have a public ministerial function, but more often your ministerial function will be to exercise the priesthood conferred by your baptism in co-offering the Sacrifice of Christ re-enacted on the altar by His ministerial priest, through a full, conscious, and actual participation in the liturgical rites that doesn't involve that much external activity. Indeed, the relatively unbusy ambience of even solemn celebrations of the *usus antiquior* is highly conducive to *participatio actuosa*, which is something essentially internal, indeed contemplative.

This is of the uttermost importance. For if, as our authors rightly assert, this participation was what the Council desired above all, and if, as they implicitly acknowledge, it can be (as indeed it is) found in contemporary celebrations of the *usus antiquior,* then the ritual liturgical reforms that followed the Council *are not of themselves necessary* to achieve the aim of the Council itself.

This belies their spurious assertion that "for the Council Fathers, what is now termed the 'ordinary form' would become the sole form of the liturgy celebrated in the Roman rite of the Church." Firstly, the Council Fathers did not and could not foresee the "ordinary form" as it was promulgated six (very charged) years after they voted on the Constitution on the Sacred Liturgy; secondly, a number of them reacted with disappointment when it appeared; thirdly, and most importantly, if *participatio actuosa* could be achieved without all the fuss, as it were, they would have been utterly content.

To be fair, the formation in the expectation of participation with which younger generations arrive at celebrations of the *usus antiquior* is indeed a fruit of decades of that very expectation, inaugurated by the Council. But the fact that the Council's most fervent desire can and is being realised some sixty years later in celebrations of the unreformed rites is more than telling. One might even speculate that this could be something of "what the Spirit is saying to the churches" (Rev 3:22) in respect of liturgical issues in our day. This, in the present author's opinion, is a reality which our authors and the authorities they seek to serve have yet to comprehend, let alone respect. It is crucial that, in all humility and without delay, they attribute it the respect it commands.

WHAT THREATENS COMMUNION?

There are many other observations one could make about Cavadini, Healy, and Weinandy's articles, including the paucity of their liturgical history and the lack of a range of sources in their footnotes. Their constant reference to "the eucharistic liturgy" is annoying and narrow—the Council sought to broaden people's understanding of the Sacred Liturgy beyond the Mass alone—and their blithe assumption that "immediately prior to Vatican Council II" the norm was "inadequate theological understanding and deficient liturgical practice" is simply insulting: the same charge could, in fact, be made of most worshipers today, perhaps with even more grounds.

But I would be remiss if I did not acknowledge the "dishonourable mention" accorded to myself in the last of their articles.² They attribute the reasoned stance taken by our monastery in celebrating much-needed ordinations, long since overdue, last year outside the normal channels³ to "the desire to celebrate the pre-conciliar rite" and of thereby establishing our monastery as a "church apart from the Church." Ecclesiology 101 please, dear professors! Not even the Society of St Pius X are accorded such a status—the Holy See has for decades regarded their situation as a disciplinary matter *within* the Catholic Church. And our (clearly argued, conscientious) disobedience to canonical norms did not involve episcopal consecrations. Rather, it involved our decision to accept a life-line when it was offered instead of accepting the involuntary euthanasia being forced upon us because of pressure on our bishop from the Holy See—as subsequent events have clearly demonstrated.

Ours was also, apparently, "an act of disunity, ripping apart the communion of the Church in order to celebrate the pre-conciliar rite." No, it was an act of conscientious disobedience in order to survive and live our vocation in an integrity hitherto approved by the Church and which was under grave threat of extinction through no fault of our own. Perseverance in one's vocation is what is owed to Almighty God, and it is not a fault or an ecclesiastical crime.

Cavadini, Healy, and Weinandy's overreaction here is illustrative: "Don't touch that! If you do, everything will collapse!," they are shouting. Are they afraid that others shall follow suit? If the draconian implementation of *Traditionis Custodes* continues, or if even further measures are enacted against the *usus antiquior* and those who celebrate it, some may well follow suit. And it will be *these* measures and those who enforce them—not those persevering in fidelity to their vocation and their ministry—who will be ripping apart the communion of the Church in order to impose a uniformity that is simply not necessary in order to be a member of the Catholic Church that Our Lord Jesus Christ founded.

---

2   I accepted the task of writing a response to the series before the final installment had been published.
3   Details published in the "Statement–Communiqué" of May 14, 2022 (www.monasterebrignoles.org/news/statement-communique).

The One Thread by Which the Council Hangs

CONCLUSION

It is only a matter of time before the one thread by which the Council as understood by many ("Vatican II changed all of that, radically, irreversibly") snaps, and the whole edifice built upon this false premise—including its supposedly untouchable and purportedly divinely-inspired liturgical reforms—comes crashing down. One could be tempted to say that the sooner this happens, the better for all concerned. But such a crash will traumatise, if not even scandalise, many for whom this false assumption is indeed a super-dogma. Falsehood must be refuted, as St Paul insists (cf. 1 Tim 1:3; 2 Tim 4:2–5), but those entrapped in its snares must be rescued, not lost. (There may even be valid pastoral reasons to permit the occasional use of Eucharistic Prayer II.)

Pope Benedict XVI attempted such a rescue. He sought to lead the Church along the path of interpreting the Council according to a hermeneutic of reform-in-continuity, not one of rupture, and, in seeking a greater reconciliation within the Church and a greater reconciliation of the Church with her own tradition, he decreed that the older liturgical rites were free to live and breathe and influence the life of the Church in our times. He imposed nothing. He forbade nothing (not even Eucharistic Prayer II). He permitted much and gently left the rest to God the Holy Spirit.

Unfortunately Pope Benedict's inclusive policies have been reversed with a cold severity that has profoundly scandalised people, particularly in its demand that all must now bow down before the new liturgical rites, which have been set up—let it be said clearly—as nothing less than an idol. So-called "traditionalists" have often been charged with idolising the older liturgical rites, but their attachment to them doesn't even approach the rigid exclusivity with which *Traditionis Custodes*, Cardinal Roche's *Dubia* responses, or *Desiderio Desideravi* are replete.

The thread from which all of this hangs is old, thin, and worn. It will break soon enough. In the meantime, as regards "what earlier generations held as sacred [and which] remains sacred and great for us too, and ... cannot be all of a sudden entirely forbidden or even considered harmful,"[4] let ours be the mind of St Peter and the apostles who stated before the High Priest's Council: "we must obey God rather than men" (Acts 5:29). Those in ecclesiastical authority and those who, including our three authors, are enthusiastically promoting their repressive policies, might like to read further in that chapter of the Acts of the Apostles and ponder the advice of Gamaliel: "Keep away from these men and let them alone; for if this plan or this undertaking is of men, it will fail; but if it is of God, you will not be able to overthrow them. You might even be found opposing God!"

---

4   Benedict XVI, *Con Grande Fiducia*, July 7, 2007.

18

The Art of Missing the Point

JOSEPH SHAW

IT WOULD TRY THE PATIENCE OF READERS, and more than exhaust the time I have available, to comment on the whole series of five articles published in *Church Life Journal* by John Cavadini, Mary Healy, and Thomas Weinandy. Instead I will focus on just two points in the concluding article of the series: "The Way Forward from the Theological Concerns with the TLM Movement."

Throughout this article they keep repeating two fundamental misunderstandings of the movement for the Traditional Mass, misunderstandings which make their analysis and recommendations beside the point. It is a principle of academic discussion that before criticising a position one must first be able to summarise it in a way which would be acceptable to those who put it forward. In this, CHW have, I am afraid, completely failed.

The first misunderstanding is in the motivation of the movement. It is all the more remarkable in that they express their own understanding as their reading of a passage from Peter Kwasniewski which says something entirely different. Dr. Kwasniewski, as CHW quotes him, says this:

> If at all possible, we should avoid participating in a form of prayer that deprives the Lord of the reverence that is due to Him. The *Novus Ordo* systematically does this by having removed hundreds of ways in which the Church showed her profound reverence for the Word of God and the holy mysteries of Christ.

CHW comment:

> Such critiques presume that the reformed rite must be an occasion of significant irreverence; there is little appreciation

of the many celebrations of the reformed liturgy with profound reverence, feeding the souls of countless members of the faithful in parishes throughout the world.

CHW want the argument to be about celebrants and perhaps the congregation lacking a spirit of reverence. But this is not what Dr. Kwasniewski is talking about. He refers to the *Novus Ordo*'s authors having "removed hundreds of ways in which the Church showed her profound reverence." An obvious example would be the removal of the genuflection by the celebrant before each of the elevations. The personal reverence of the celebrant is another issue altogether.

Nor does Kwasniewski deny that people can be spiritually fed by the *Novus Ordo*. Like me and nearly all adult members of the Traditional Movement, he was fed by it himself for many years before discovering the Traditional Mass. What he felt, on making this discovery, is what he says in this passage: that there are things in the texts and rubrics of the Traditional Mass which express more clearly the reverence due to God than are to be found in the *Novus Ordo*.

I think this is extremely hard to deny, and perhaps that is why CHW don't want to engage with this argument. Traditionalists could supply them with a mountain of examples, and also point to the published words of liturgists in no way committed to the Traditional Mass who have made similar arguments on particular points. Cardinal Ratzinger—as he then was—thought that the silent Canon was preferable, more reverent, more conducive to prayer, than the Canon proclaimed aloud. He and Cardinal Sarah have said the same thing about worship *ad orientem* being preferable to worship *versus populum*. Non-traditionalist liturgists have published critiques of the reformed Lectionary, the reformed Offertory Prayers, the *Novus Ordo* Sign of Peace, the reformed manner of receiving Holy Communion, and many other things. What is more, the Holy See itself has accepted some of these criticisms, such as those about the way the Collects were edited. In the 2008 edition of the reformed Missal a whole lot of words and phrases which had been cut out of them by the *Consilium* were actually restored.

The Art of Missing the Point

Are CHW going to attack all these people for rejecting Vatican II? For failing to maintain communion with the Church? For lacking a proper respect for ecclesial authority? For failing to read the signs of the times? I very much doubt it. It is only when these arguments are made by Traditionalists that they are wrong. But this is ridiculous. There can't be one law for us and another for everyone else.

The second misunderstanding is about how Traditional Catholics define themselves. CHW claim it is by reference to the Rite they attend: for trads, they say, "'Church' is now defined by which Eucharistic rite one attends."

This is easily disposed of. Among Traditional Catholics, there is absolutely no sense that the ancient Roman Rite is the only "true" or adequate or reverent liturgical form. If this seems surprising, consider the attitude of Traditional Catholics towards the ancient Dominican Rite, the ancient Ambrosian Rite, or the Eastern Rites.

I can imagine CHW protesting: Oh this is not what we meant! No, indeed: you didn't think your statement through, did you? Trads are not fixated on the Roman Rite. The other rites are not so easy for most of us to attend, but we think they are great, and express in a beautiful way the universality and genuine pluralism of the Catholic Church. Typically trads regret the loss of liturgical diversity following the Council of Trent, and lament the 'Latinisation' of Eastern Rites both before and after Vatican II; again, it is among Trads that you will find enthusiasts for the revival of the Sarum Rite and the regional Rites of France.

Given that CHW's statement as written is totally false, can we say what *is* the defining feature of Traditional Catholics? It is what it says on the tin: we are concerned with *tradition*—the passing on down the generations of a living patrimony of prayer, as opposed to the artificial manufacture of liturgy by committee (to paraphrase Cardinal Ratzinger).

This may make CHW a little uncomfortable, but it should be obvious that the rupture in this process of handing on, which Ratzinger referred to and which is undeniable by anyone with any knowledge of the matter coupled with intellectual honesty, is a *problem*. It is a problem, perhaps, with no easy solution. But it is right for Catholics to see it as a problem, because reverence for tradition is part of what it means to be Catholic.

Let CHW come out and deny that, if they can.

Postscript. In 2020 I wrote a response to an article by Professor Healy in the *Homiletic & Pastoral Review*.[1] In the comments below the article there is a response by a "Fr Tom W." Between this and Healy's article, it is clear that they have learnt nothing and forgotten nothing in the last two years.

---

[1] Joseph Shaw, "The *Novus Ordo* at 50: Loss or Gain? A Reply to Prof. Mary Healy," *Homiletic & Pastoral Review*, February 10, 2020.

EPILOGUE
New Liturgical Anathemas for the Post-Conciliar Rite

GREGORY DIPIPPO

ON THE FIRST SUNDAY OF LENT, THE BYZantine Rite appoints the liturgical proclamation of the Synodikon of Orthodoxy, a decree of the Seventh Ecumenical Council that anathematizes the iconoclasts and various other heretics.[1] Since the post-Conciliar Rite adopted into itself so many oriental customs wholly extraneous to the Roman Rite, well might one wonder why this custom was not among them.

Wonder no longer. With a decree issued on Tuesday,[2] the Sacred Congregation for Rites has finally closed this gap, promulgating a set of liturgical anathemas that admirably reflect the most exciting new developments in ecclesiology and liturgical theology. NLM is very honored to be the medium by which the Sacred Congregation has chosen to divulge these, while we wait for the official Latin text of the decree, which will be titled *Ludens feci*, to be officially published in the *Acta Sanctae Sedis*.

The very first encyclical letter of the current pontificate warned the Church against the temptation to self-referentiality,[3] and as more recent events have shown us, the best possible way to combat this temptation is for the

---

[1] See Gregory DiPippo, "The Sunday of Orthodoxy," *New Liturgical Movement*, February 24, 2023.
[2] See "*Rescriptum ex Audientia*—From Yesterday's Audience of Francis with Card. Roche regarding details of implementation of *Traditionis Custodes*," *Rorate Caeli*, February 21, 2023.
[3] See Fr. Thomas Berg, "*Evangelii Gaudium*: exhorting a self-referential Church," *Catholic News Agency*, December 5, 2013.

Church to spend four years talking to itself about itself. This will explain the fact that these anathemas are all, as it were, inward-looking, a part of the necessary process of self-reflection by which the Church will shake itself free of that temptation. In the finest tradition of the post-Conciliar liturgy, these anathemas may be adapted to local realities, but never, of course, to local ideas, and indeed, the careful reader will immediately note that it is only ideas that are anathematized, and not realities. Of course, we cannot but admit that we were very surprised to see where some of these ideas that are now being anathematized come from, but such is the way of the god of surprises.

It is foreseen that the text will be re-written continually, year by year, as the process of liturgical inculturation initiated by the Council continues to bear ever more mature fruits which even the Council itself never envisioned.[4]

RUBRICS FOR THE PROCLAMATION

1. Following the Byzantine tradition, these anathemas may be proclaimed on the first Sunday of Lent, but also on any other Sunday of Lent, or a Sunday of another season, or on any other day. The authority to determine another appropriate day for their proclamation rests with the local bishops' conferences, which, however, are strictly forbidden from making any such determination without the approval of the Sacred Congregation for Rites, to be requested in writing.

2. As in the Byzantine tradition, the ordinary minister of the anathemas is the deacon, but if there is no deacon, they may be proclaimed by a lay person, who, for this occasion only, may also wear a dalmatic if one is available.[5] Whether worn by a deacon or a lay person, the color of the dalmatic may be violet, since the traditional day for their proclamation

---

[4] "Cardinal Grech: Synodal process is mature fruit of Vatican II," *Vatican News*, October 5, 2022.
[5] The authority to determine the use of a cope rather than a dalmatic for their proclamation rests with the local bishops' conferences, which, however, are strictly forbidden from making any such determination without the approval of the Sacred Congregation for Rites, to be requested in writing.

New Liturgical Anathemas for the Post-Conciliar Rite

is the first Sunday of Lent, in which the liturgical color is violet, in order to symbolize in a more profound and meaningful way that the season is Lent. However, it may also be white, to symbolize the purity of intention with which the Church proclaims them; red, to symbolize the fervor with which She proclaims them; or green, to symbolize the flourishing of the Faith that comes from proclaiming them. The authority to determine the liturgical color for the proclamation of the anathemas rests with the local bishops' conferences, which, however, are strictly forbidden from making any such determination without the approval of the Sacred Congregation for Rites, to be requested in writing.

3. The anathemas are to be proclaimed from the same pulpit from which the Scriptural readings, general intercessions, sermons, and announcements are proclaimed. But they may also be proclaimed during a procession, after the Mass, before the Mass, or in a separate "service of the Word" to be held apart from the Eucharistic celebration, if local pastoral realities determine this to be useful. The authority to determine another appropriate occasion for their proclamation rests with the local bishops' conferences, which, however, are strictly forbidden from making any such determination without the approval of the Sacred Congregation for Rites, to be requested in writing.

4. In keeping with the Byzantine tradition, the response of the people to the anathemas may be "Anathema, anathema, anathema." However, other responses more appropriate to local pastoral realities may be used instead, such as a verse from Scripture. A brief period of meditation may also follow the proclamation of each anathema, in place of a vocal response. The authority to determine another appropriate response rests with the local bishops' conferences, which, however, are strictly forbidden from making any such determination without the approval of the Sacred Congregation for Rites, to be requested in writing.

THE ANATHEMAS

1. If anyone shall say that the bishops of the Catholic Church "have the sacred right and the duty before the Lord to make laws for their subjects, to pass judgment on them and to moderate everything pertaining to the ordering of worship and the apostolate,"[6] let him be anathema.

2. If anyone shall say that the bishops of the Catholic Church are "(not) to be regarded as vicars of the Roman Pontiffs, for they exercise an authority that is proper to them, and are quite correctly called 'prelates,' heads of the people whom they govern,"[7] let him be anathema.

3. If anyone shall say that it is "up to the bishop, as moderator, promoter, and guardian of the liturgical life of the Church of which he is the principle of unity, to regulate the liturgical celebrations, to authorize in his churches, as local Ordinaries, the use of the *Missale Romanum* of 1962, applying the norms of the motu proprio *Traditionis custodes*, and to determine case by case the reality of the groups which celebrate with this *Missale Romanum*,"[8] let him be anathema.

4. If anyone shall say that authority over the liturgy in a diocese resides with the local bishops rather than with the Roman Curia, let him be anathema.[9]

5. If anyone shall say that "there must be no innovations (made to the liturgy) unless the good of the Church genuinely and certainly requires them; and care must be taken that any new forms adopted should in some way grow organically from forms already existing,"[10] let him be anathema.

6. If anyone shall say that "the use of the Latin language is to be preserved in the Latin rites" or that "Gregorian chant,

---

6 Second Vatican Ecumenical Council, Dogmatic Constitution on the Church *Lumen Gentium*, 27.
7 Ibid.
8 Pope Francis, Letter to the Bishops of the Whole World Accompanying *Traditionis Custodes*.
9 See Ed Condon, "Does Roche's rescript dispense with Vatican II?," *The Pillar*, February 22, 2023.
10 Second Vatican Ecumenical Council, Constitution on the Sacred Liturgy *Sacrosanctum Concilium*, 23.

being especially suited to the Roman liturgy, should have the chief place in liturgical services,"[11] let him be anathema.

7. If anyone shall say that "holy Mother Church holds all lawfully acknowledged rites to be of equal right and dignity" or "that she wishes to preserve them in the future and to foster them in every way,"[12] let him be anathema.

8. If anyone shall say that "What earlier generations held as sacred, remains sacred and great for us too, and it cannot be all of a sudden entirely forbidden or even considered harmful,"[13] let him be anathema.

9. If anyone shall say that the Holy See should "guarantee respect for the rightful aspirations of all those Catholic faithful who feel attached to some previous liturgical and disciplinary forms of the Latin tradition,"[14] let him be anathema.

10. If anyone shall broaden his tent to include those who love the traditional Roman Rite, show them mercy, accompany them, dialogue with them, or listen to them,[15] let him be anathema.

---

11   Ibid., 36.1; 116.
12   Ibid., 4.
13   Pope Benedict XVI, Letter to the Bishops *Con Grande Fiducia* Accompanying *Summorum Pontificum*.
14   Pope John Paul II, Apostolic Letter *Ecclesia Dei Adflicta*, 5c.
15   See Phil Lawler, "Understanding the Vatican crusade against tradition," *Catholic Culture*, February 23, 2023.

ACKNOWLEDGMENTS

CHAPTERS 1 THROUGH 5 AND 15 WERE PUBlished at *Crisis Magazine*; chapters 6 and 18 at *Rorate Caeli*; chapters 12, 13, and 17 at *OnePeterFive*; chapters 8, 10, and 11 and the Epilogue at *New Liturgical Movement*; chapter 14 at *Covenant* of the Living Church Foundation.

Chapter 9 reproduces chapter 6 from Peter Kwasniewski's *Resurgent in the Midst of Crisis: Sacred Liturgy, the Traditional Latin Mass, and Renewal in the Church* (Kettering, OH: Angelico Press, 2014), and chapter 7 reproduces part of chapter 2 from Peter Kwasniewski's *Reclaiming Our Roman Catholic Birthright: The Genius and Timeliness of the Traditional Latin Mass* (Brooklyn, NY: Angelico Press, 2020).

Chapter 16 appears here for the first time.

My thanks to John Riess of Angelico Press, Eric Sammons of *Crisis Magazine*, Timothy Flanders of *OnePeterFive*, and Gregory DiPippo of *New Liturgical Movement* for kindly granting republication rights, and to Janet Smith for her help in many ways. I also very much appreciate the advice received from friends and former students. God reward you.—*PAK*

SELECT BIBLIOGRAPHY

Anonymous. *Saint Edmund Campion Missal for the Traditional Latin Mass.* Third edition. Manchester, NH: Sophia Institute Press, 2022.

Barthe, Claude. *A Forest of Symbols: The Traditional Mass and Its Meaning.* Translated by David J. Critchley. Brooklyn, NY: Angelico Press, 2023.

Baur, Dom Benedict. *Light of the World: Daily Meditations on the Traditional Mass.* Manchester, NH: Benedictus Books, 2022 [original edition 1952].

Bergman, Lisa. *Treasure and Tradition: The Ultimate Guide to the Latin Mass.* Homer Glen, IL: St. Augustine Academy Press, 2014.

Bullivant, Stephen. *Mass Exodus: Catholic Disaffiliation in Britain and America since Vatican II.* Oxford: Oxford University Press, 2019.

Chiron, Yves. *Annibale Bugnini, Reformer of the Liturgy.* Translated by John Pepino. Brooklyn, NY: Angelico Press, 2018.

———. *Paul VI: The Divided Pope.* Translated by James Walther. Brooklyn, NY: Angelico Press, 2022.

Davies, Michael. *Cranmer's Godly Order: The Destruction of Catholicism through Liturgical Change.* Fort Collins, CO: Roman Catholic Books, 1995.

———. *Pope Paul's New Mass.* Kansas City, MO: Angelus Press, 2009.

Dekert, Tomasz. "Tradition, the Pope, and Liturgical Reform: A Problematization of Tradition in the Catholic Church and Catholic–Orthodox Rapprochement." *Nova et Vetera* (English ed.) 20.1 (2022): 101–31.

de Mattei, Roberto. *Apologia for Tradition. A Defense of Tradition Grounded in the Historical Context of the Faith.* Translated by Michael J. Miller. Kansas City, MO: Angelus Press, 2019.

———. *Love for the Papacy and Filial Resistance to the Pope in the History of the Church.* Brooklyn, NY: Angelico Press, 2019.

———. *Saint Pius V.* Translated by Giuseppe Pellegrino. Manchester, NH: Sophia Institute Press, 2021.

———. *The Second Vatican Council: An Unwritten Story.* Translated by Patrick T. Brannan, Michael J. Miller, and Kenneth D.

Whitehead. Edited by Michael J. Miller. Fitzwilliam, NH: Loreto Publications, 2012.

Dulac, Raymond. *In Defence of the Roman Mass*. Translated by Peadar Walsh. N.p.: Te Deum Press, 2020.

Fiedrowicz, Michael. *The Traditional Mass: History, Form, and Theology of the Classical Roman Rite*. Translated by Rose Pfeifer. Brooklyn, NY: Angelico Press, 2020.

Gamber, Klaus. *The Reform of the Roman Liturgy: Its Problems and Background*. Translated by Klaus D. Grimm. San Juan Capistrano, CA: Una Voce Press and Harrison, NY: The Foundation for Catholic Reform, 1993.

Gihr, Nicholas. *The Holy Sacrifice of the Mass Dogmatically, Liturgically, and Ascetically Explained*. St. Louis: B. Herder, 1949.

Guéranger, Dom Prosper. *The Traditional Latin Mass Explained*. Translated by Dom Laurence Shepherd. Brooklyn, NY: Angelico Press, 2017.

Houghton, Bryan. *Judith's Marriage*. Originally published by Credo House, 1987; repr. Brooklyn, NY: Angelico Press, 2020.

———. *Mitre and Crook*. Originally published by Arlington House Books, 1979; repr. Brooklyn, NY: Angelico Press, 2019.

———. *Unwanted Priest: The Autobiography of a Latin Mass Exile*. Brooklyn, NY: Angelico Press, 2022.

Kwasniewski, Peter A. *Holy Bread of Eternal Life: Restoring Eucharistic Reverence in an Age of Impiety*. Manchester, NH: Sophia Institute Press, 2020.

———, ed. *From Benedict's Peace to Francis's War: Catholics Respond to the Motu Proprio* Traditionis Custodes *on the Latin Mass*. Brooklyn, NY: Angelico Press, 2021.

———, ed. *John Henry Newman on Worship, Reverence, and Ritual: A Selection of Texts*. N.p.: Os Justi Press, 2019.

———. *Ministers of Christ: Recovering the Roles of Clergy and Laity in an Age of Confusion*. Manchester, NH: Crisis Publications, 2021.

———. *Noble Beauty, Transcendent Holiness: Why the Modern Age Needs the Mass of Ages*. Kettering, OH: Angelico Press, 2017.

———. *The Once and Future Roman Rite: Returning to the Traditional Latin Liturgy after Seventy Years of Exile*. Gastonia, NC: TAN Books, 2022.

———. *Resurgent in the Midst of Crisis: Sacred Liturgy, the Traditional Latin Mass, and Renewal in the Church*. Kettering, OH: Angelico Press, 2014.

———. *Reclaiming Our Roman Catholic Birthright: The Genius and

Timeliness of the Traditional Latin Mass. Brooklyn, NY: Angelico Press, 2020.

———. *The Road from Hyperpapalism to Catholicism: Rethinking the Papacy in a Time of Ecclesial Disintegration*. 2 volumes. Arouca Press, 2022.

———. *True Obedience in the Church: A Guide to Discernment in Challenging Times*. Manchester, NH: Sophia Institute Press, 2021.

Lang, Uwe Michael. *The Roman Mass: From Early Christian Origins to Tridentine Reform*. Cambridge, UK: Cambridge University Press, 2022.

———. *Signs of the Holy One: Liturgy, Ritual, and Expression of the Sacred*. San Francisco: Ignatius Press, 2015.

———. *Turning Towards the Lord: Orientation in Liturgical Prayer*. San Francisco: Ignatius Press, 2004.

———. *The Voice of the Church at Prayer: Reflections on Liturgy and Language*. San Francisco: Ignatius Press, 2012.

Lefebvre, Dom Gaspar. *Catholic Liturgy: Its Fundamental Principles*. Translated by a Benedictine of Stanbrook. Revised and enlarged. Kansas City, MO: Romanitas Press, 2022 [original edition 1924].

Leonard of Port Maurice, St. *The Hidden Treasure: Holy Mass*. Charlotte, NC: TAN Books, 2012.

Meloni, Julia. *The St. Gallen Mafia: Exposing the Secret Reform Group within the Church*. Gastonia, NC: TAN Books, 2021.

Michel, Dom Virgil. *The Liturgy of the Church According to the Roman Rite*. Foreword by Dom Alcuin Reid. Waterloo, ON: Arouca Press, 2022 [original edition 1937].

Mohrmann, Christine. *Liturgical Latin: Its Origins and Character*. Washington, DC: Catholic University of America Press, 1957. [Reprint available from Lulu.]

Mosebach, Martin. *The Heresy of Formlessness: The Roman Liturgy and Its Enemy*. Revised and expanded edition. Translated by Graham Harrison. Brooklyn, NY: Angelico Press, 2018.

Muggeridge, Anne Roche. *The Desolate City: Revolution in the Catholic Church*. Revised and expanded. New York: HarperCollins, 1990.

Normandin, Yves. *Pastor Out in the Cold. The Story of Fr. Normandin's Fight for the Latin Mass in Canada*. St. Marys, KS: Angelus Press, 2021.

Pristas, Lauren. *The Collects of the Roman Missals: A Comparative Study of the Sundays in Proper Seasons Before and After the Second*

Vatican Council. London/New York: Bloomsbury T&T Clark, 2013.

Ratzinger, Cardinal Joseph. *The Spirit of the Liturgy*. Translated by John Saward. Commemorative edition, with Romano Guardini's work of the same name. San Francisco: Ignatius Press, 2018.

———. *Theology of the Liturgy: The Sacramental Foundation of Christian Existence. Collected Works of Joseph Ratzinger*, volume 11. Edited by Michael J. Miller. San Francisco: Ignatius Press, 2014.

Reid, Alcuin, ed. *A Bitter Trial: Evelyn Waugh and John Carmel Cardinal Heenan on the Liturgical Changes*. San Francisco: Ignatius Press, 2011.

———. *The Organic Development of the Liturgy. The Principles of Liturgical Reform and Their Relation to the Twentieth-Century Liturgical Movement Prior to the Second Vatican Council*. Second edition. San Francisco: Ignatius Press, 2005.

———. ed. *T&T Clark Companion to Liturgy*. London/New York: Bloomsbury T&T Clark, 2016.

Rivoire, Réginald-Marie. *Does 'Traditionis Custodes' Pass the Juridical Rationality Test?* Translated by William Barker. Lincoln, NE: Os Justi Press, 2022.

Schneider, Athanasius. *The Catholic Mass: Steps to Restore the Centrality of God in the Liturgy*. Manchester, NH: Sophia Institute Press, 2022.

———, with Diane Montagna. *Christus Vincit. Christ's Triumph Over the Darkness of the Age*. Brooklyn, NY: Angelico Press, 2019.

———, with Paweł Lisicki. *The Springtime That Never Came*. Translated by Justyna Krukowska. Manchester, NH: Sophia Institute Press, 2021.

Shaw, Joseph, ed. *The Case for Liturgical Restoration*. Brooklyn, NY: Angelico Press, 2019.

———. *The Liturgy, the Family, and the Crisis of Modernity*. Lincoln, NE: Os Justi Press, 2023.

Spataro, Roberto. *In Praise of the Tridentine Mass and of Latin, Language of the Church*. Translated by Zachary Thomas. Brooklyn, NY: Angelico Press, 2019.

von Cochem, Martin. *The Incredible Catholic Mass*. Originally published in English as *Cochem's Explanation of the Holy Sacrifice of the Mass*. Charlotte, NC: TAN Books, 2012.

CONTRIBUTORS

ALEXANDER BATTISTA is a Catholic writer in the United States.

GREGORY DIPIPPO, a native of Providence, Rhode Island, has studied Latin, Greek, Church Slavonic, classics, and patristics. He has been a regular contributor to the *New Liturgical Movement* website since 2009 and editor since 2013. His writings cover a wide variety of topics, but his first specialty was the study of the reforms of the Roman liturgy before the Second Vatican Council. DiPippo lived in Rome for almost thirty years. He is on the faculty of the Veterum Sapientia Institute.

FR. SAMUEL KEYES was raised Baptist in Mississippi and became an Episcopalian as a young adult. He served as an ordained minister in the Anglican tradition from 2011–2019, working at parishes in Massachusetts, Alabama, and a boarding school in Maryland. Receiving into the Roman Catholic Church in 2019 through the Ordinariate of the Chair of St. Peter, he was ordained to the Catholic priesthood in June of 2021.

PETER KWASNIEWSKI (B. A. in Liberal Arts, Thomas Aquinas College; M. A. and Ph.D. in Philosophy, Catholic University of America) taught at the International Theological Institute in Austria before helping to establish Wyoming Catholic College, where he taught theology, philosophy, music, and art history and directed the choir and schola. Today he is a full-time author and speaker on topics concerning Catholic Tradition and continues to compose sacred choral music. He has written or edited many books, including most recently *The Once and Future Roman Rite: Returning to the Traditional Latin Liturgy after Seventy Years of Exile* (TAN, 2022). His work has been translated into at least nineteen languages.

ROLAND MILLARE, STD is the Vice President of Curriculum and the Director of Clergy Initiatives for the St. John Paul II Foundation (Houston, TX). He is the author of the book *A Living Sacrifice: Liturgy and Eschatology in Joseph Ratzinger* (Emmaus Academic, 2022).

PETER MILLER, OSB, is the founder of the Monks of Mary, Mother of the Word, in the Diocese of Spokane.

ALCUIN REID, OSB, is the founding Prior of the Monastère Saint-Benoît in Brignoles, France, and a liturgical scholar of international renown—author of *The Organic Development of the Liturgy: The Principles of Liturgical Reform and Their Relation to the Twentieth-Century Liturgical Movement Prior to the Second Vatican Council* (Ignatius Press, 2005), which bears a Foreword by Joseph Ratzinger, and the editor of the *T&T Clark Companion to Liturgy* (Bloomsbury, 2015), among many other collections of scholarly papers.

JOSEPH SHAW, a doctor in philosophy, was a member of Oxford University's Philosophy Faculty for eighteen years, during which time he taught moral philosophy, Aristotle, Aquinas, and the philosophy of religion. He is Chairman of the Latin Mass Society of England and Wales and President of the International Una Voce Federation (FIUV).

JANET E. SMITH, Ph.D., is retired from Sacred Heart Major Seminary in Detroit, where she held the Father Michael J. McGivney Chair of Life Ethics. She is the author of, among other works, *Humanae Vitae: A Generation Later* and *A Right to Privacy* and edited *Why Humanae Vitae is Right: A Reader* and *Why Humanae Vitae is Still Right*. Dr. Smith served three terms as a consulter to the Pontifical Council on the Family and also served for eight years as a member of the Anglican-Roman Catholic International Commission III. She has received three honorary doctorates and several other awards for scholarship and service. In her retirement she is helping victims of the priestly sexual abuse crisis and writing on the glories of the Traditional Mass.

Made in the USA
Monee, IL
20 June 2023

36436791R00152